DANIEL BOUD

Andrew P Street is the author of *The Short and Excruciatingly Embarrassing Reign of Captain Abbott* and *The Curious Story of Malcolm Turnbull, the Incredible Shrinking Man in the Top Hat*. But before he ventured into political commentary he was a music journalist. He's been published internationally in *NME*, *Rolling Stone*, *Time Out*, *GQ*, the *Guardian*, and Virgin's *Voyeur* in-flight magazine. Locally he's appeared in pretty much every masthead with a freelance budget, from the *Sydney Morning Herald* to *Elle*, the *Big Issue* and *Australian Guitar*. He also played in an Adelaide band (or two), The Undecided and Career Girls.

Other books by Andrew P Street

The Short and Excruciatingly Embarrassing
Reign of Captain Abbott

The Curious Story of Malcolm Turnbull,
the Incredible Shrinking Man in the Top Hat

THE LONG AND WINDING WAY TO THE TOP

FIFTY (OR SO) SONGS THAT MADE AUSTRALIA

ANDREW P STREET

ALLEN&UNWIN
SYDNEY • MELBOURNE • AUCKLAND • LONDON

First published in 2017

Copyright © Andrew P Street 2017

All rights reserved. No part of this book may be reproduced or transmitted in any form or by any means, electronic or mechanical, including photocopying, recording or by any information storage and retrieval system, without prior permission in writing from the publisher. The Australian *Copyright Act 1968* (the Act) allows a maximum of one chapter or 10 per cent of this book, whichever is the greater, to be photocopied by any educational institution for its educational purposes provided that the educational institution (or body that administers it) has given a remuneration notice to the Copyright Agency (Australia) under the Act.

Allen & Unwin
83 Alexander Street
Crows Nest NSW 2065
Australia
Phone: (61 2) 8425 0100
Email: info@allenandunwin.com
Web: www.allenandunwin.com

Cataloguing-in-Publication details are available
from the National Library of Australia
www.trove.nla.gov.au

ISBN 978 1 76029 372 7

Set in 13/17 pt Adobe Caslon by Midland Typesetters, Australia
Printed and bound in Australia by Griffin Press

10 9 8 7 6 5 4 3 2 1

The paper in this book is FSC® certified. FSC® promotes environmentally responsible, socially beneficial and economically viable management of the world's forests.

To James P Street.
May all your adventures have
a glorious soundtrack.

To listen to many of the songs mentioned in this book
go to Andrew's Spotify play list at
https://open.spotify.com/user/andrewpstreetplaylist/
56vkN9RusgrLMc8Tl56JT0

or watch
www.youtube.com/watch?v=ZF9rS90U3-U&list=
PLykiZAB2RssAOtBx4cqdVaZ7oJKrKqgwY

Contents

Count In			1
1	1958	The Wild One *(Johnny O'Keefe and The Dee Jays)*	5
2	1963	He's My Blonde-Headed, Stompie Wompie, Real Gone Surfer Boy *(Little Pattie and The Statesmen)*	11
3	1963	Royal Telephone *(Jimmy Little)*	17
4	1965	The Carnival is Over *(The Seekers)*	23
5	1966	Friday On My Mind *(The Easybeats)*	29
6	1969	The Real Thing *(Russell Morris)*	35
7	1970	Turn Up Your Radio *(The Masters Apprentices)*	41
8	1971	I Am Woman *(Helen Reddy)*	47
9	1971	Eagle Rock *(Daddy Cool)*	53
10	1974	You Just Like Me Cos I'm Good in Bed *(Skyhooks)*	59

11	1975	It's a Long Way to the Top (If You Wanna Rock'n'Roll) *(AC/DC)*	65
12	1976	(I'm) Stranded *(The Saints)*	71
13	1978	Khe Sanh *(Cold Chisel)*	77
14	1979	Shivers *(The Boys Next Door)*	83
15	1980	Shaddap You Face *(Joe Dolce)*	89
16	1981	Down Under *(Men at Work)*	95
17	1982	True Blue *(John Williamson)*	101
18	1982	Great Southern Land *(Icehouse)*	107
19	1983	Cattle and Cane *(The Go-Betweens)*	113
20	1983	I was Only Nineteen *(Redgum)*	119
21	1984	Throw Your Arms Around Me *(Hunters & Collectors)*	125
22	1985	What You Need *(INXS)*	131
23	1985	Blackfella/Whitefella *(Warumpi Band)*	137
24	1985	Working Class Man *(Jimmy Barnes)*	143
25	1985	Man Overboard *(Do-Ré-Mi)*	149
26	1986	Wide Open Road *(The Triffids)*	155
27	1986	Don't Dream It's Over *(Crowded House)*	161
28	1986	You're the Voice *(John Farnham)*	167
29	1987	I Should Be So Lucky *(Kylie Minogue)*	175
30	1987	Beds Are Burning *(Midnight Oil)*	181
31	1988	Under the Milky Way *(The Church)*	189
32	1990	I Touch Myself *(Divinyls)*	195

CONTENTS

33	1990–91	Took the Children Away/From Little Things Big Things Grow/Treaty *(Archie Roach/Paul Kelly and Kev Carmody/Yothu Yindi)*	201
34	1991	The Horses *(Daryl Braithwaite)*	213
35	1993	Sweetness and Light *(Itch-E and Scratch-E)*	219
36	1994	Berlin Chair *(You Am I)*	225
37	1994	Tomorrow *(Silverchair)*	231
38	1995	(He'll Never Be An) Ol' Man River *(TISM)*	237
39	1995	Where the Wild Roses Grow *(Nick Cave and the Bad Seeds featuring Kylie Minogue)*	245
40	1998	These Days *(Powderfinger)*	253
41	2000	Frontier Psychiatrist *(The Avalanches)*	259
42	2002	Get Free *(The Vines)*	265
43	2003	Angels Brought Me Here *(Guy Sebastian)*	273
44	2003	The Nosebleed Section *(Hilltop Hoods)*	279
45	2004	Breathe Me *(Sia)*	285
46	2005	Shark Fin Blues *(The Drones)*	291
47	2007	My People *(The Presets)*	297
48	2015–16	Blue Neighbourhood trilogy *(Troye Sivan)*	303

| 49 | 2016 | Never Be Like You *(Flume featuring Kai)* | 311 |
| 50 | 2016 | January 26 *(A.B. Original featuring Dan Sultan)* | 317 |

| Fade Out | 323 |
| Acknowledgements | 325 |

Count In

In which your humble author explains the thing you're holding in your hands

You know what? Music is great. (You almost certainly agree if you've picked this book up—that, or you're spoiling for a weirdly one-sided fight for some reason.)

Music gives us so much. It lifts us when we feel down. It soothes our ravaged soul in times of crisis. It covers our squelchy sex noises and gives us a thing to play loudly in our bedrooms after we tell our parents that they don't understand us.

And it illustrates the journey of our nation.

At least, that's the premise of this book, which is the definitive and final statement determining once and for all exactly which are the most important songs ever to be made in our nation's history and yes, I'm joking.

This is an attempt to tell a story—certainly not *the* story—of Australian culture, signposted by fifty-ish songs which mark important points along the way. Which seemed like a nice, easy, fun sort of idea right up until the point I started making a list of what songs would obviously need to go in such a book, got to 476 and went, 'Oh, this might be a lot harder than I thought.'

And that's a testament to just how much killer music our nation has produced since the first primeval guitarist crawled out of the oceans and engaged in a mating display by putting its foot atop a prototype stage monitor and doing a bitchin' power chord.[1]

There's another reason to write this now. At this particular point in Australian history there seems to be no shortage of blowhards determined to define what is and what isn't an Australian Value and, when patriotism is being weaponised into nationalism for short-term political advantage and long-term cultural damage, it's a really good time to be reminded that there are plenty of things about which Australians can be enthusiastically excited and legitimately proud.

Australia consistently punches above its weight in the creative arts, especially music, which is a little something worth remembering next time you hear that a newly gentrified suburb is shutting its live rooms or the ABC is having its funding cut or community radio stations are being squeezed out for commercial radio licences. As you'll see in these pages, our enviable creative legacy is a result of our live scene and our

---

1 I'm pretty sure this is in Darwin's *On the Origin of Species*. It's, um, somewhere near the end.

access to the airwaves, and those things need to be aggressively protected if there's to be any hope of a sequel to this book in sixty years' time.

Many of these songs could sustain entire books of their own, and by necessity this is going to be a race at breakneck speed through several decades of magnificent songsmithery. So maybe think of this as a compilation album: some well-loved hits, a few unfamiliar tracks and at least three absolute stinkers that hopefully inspire you to do some exploration of your own.[2]

The songs in this book have been chosen on the grounds that they either changed the national conversation in a significant way or they illustrate something about Australia at the time in which they appeared. That's especially true of some of the later ones, where their cultural impact is less a matter of historical record than an educated guess.

And while you've already probably looked at the contents and gone, 'Hey, why isn't [awesome song] there?', take some comfort in the fact that a lot of songs get referenced in the course of the book even if they don't get to be the focus of a whole chapter. There's a lot of songs in here, is what I'm saying.

There were a couple of ground rules: one song per artist, with as much of a spread of genres as possible, and a genuine attempt not to get bogged down in Australia's ridiculously fertile 1976–1990 era. As you'll see, none of these rules ended up working especially well. Sorry, country music lovers and fans of Australia's underrepresented dance music community. I had the noblest of intentions, honest.

---

2   See if you can spot them all!

The songs also err towards the popular, principally because a song needs to have a certain amount of cut-through in order to be in any way influential. This certainly isn't *The Fifty-Odd Most Underrated Songs in Australian Musical History*, although I could write that book in a heartbeat and it would have all the Fauves songs I couldn't find a good enough reason to include here.[3]

Hopefully there'll be a few moments of 'Oh, I had no idea about that!' in here that make you listen to some familiar songs in a new light.

And every arbitrary list needs an arbitrary starting point, so let's choose the birth of Australian rock'n'roll with a little number called . . .

---

3 Spoiler: Starting with 'Everybody's Getting a Three Piece Together'. Incidentally, #1 on that underrated list would be 'Au Revoir Sex Kitten' by the Plums. Goddamn, how was that not a global smash?

1

1958

The Wild One

Johnny O'Keefe and The Dee Jays

In which Australia learns, finally, to get its kicks

In the 1950s Australia had a difficult choice to make. Would we continue to gratefully accept the cultural cast-offs and scraps from an increasingly contemptuous Britain, or would we use our post-war prosperity and newly forged Anzac spirit to finally stand up and gratefully accept the cultural cast-offs and scraps from the genuinely indifferent United States?

This was an important decision, because those were literally the only two options on offer. Australia was deep in the aesthetic and intellectual naptime that was the era of Robert Menzies, so seditious notions like 'independence' or 'being a republic' were, um, still about as far away as they'd continue to be for the subsequent eight decades and counting. Thus, as with so many of our significant leaps forward, we turned to a huckster from overseas to identify how to fleece some rubes and make a tidy profit.

Rock'n'roll came to Australia as part of the larger obsession with all things American—drive-ins, speedways, fast food—and the arrival of television (first in Sydney, in 1956, before being rolled out nationally), where many of the most popular personalities were American—or, at least, American-sounding. Seeing bucks to be made, the savvier concert promoters started adding US artists to their rosters. One of the first to do so was Lee Gordon, who had come to Sydney from the US in 1953 and founded the agency The Big Show the following year. He was not a rock'n'roll promoter right out of the gate—early tours included Ella Fitzgerald, Abbott and Costello, Stan Freberg, Frankie Laine—but, apart from successful tours by Louis Armstrong and His All Stars and Johnnie Ray, his efforts ranged from middling successes to complete flops. An attempt to interest Australia in the hot new American trend of roller derby also tanked.

Then, in 1957, he toured a rock'n'roll package headlined by Bill Haley and the Comets. The band was riding high with 'Rock Around the Clock', a song whose insidious message of rebellion was well on its way to destroying western civili-sation thanks to its inclusion in the otherwise nondescript film *Blackboard Jungle*. The tour was a major success, not least for an aspiring young singer (and occasional Johnnie Ray impersonator) named Johnny O'Keefe.

O'Keefe had been playing on the local club circuit for a few years, but hearing Haley in 1955 changed his life. He and

US-born sax player Dave Owen decided that they too were going to rock around whatever clocks they could find and hastily recruited other players to form the Dee Jays, which eventually consisted of O'Keefe, Owen, bassist Keith Williams, Johnny 'Catfish' Purser on drums, second saxophonist Johnny Greenan and guitarist Lou Casch.[1] When Haley toured, O'Keefe charmed him sufficiently for the American star to give him a song—'(You Hit the Wrong Note) Billy Goat', which was to be his debut single—and for Gordon to take notice.

In October 1957, Gordon put together his second rock'n'roll package tour, this time with Little Richard, Gene Vincent and Eddie Cochran, but Vincent and his band were held up in Hawaii. Gordon approached O'Keefe to fill in for two shows. O'Keefe agreed, on the condition that the Dee Jays could perform some of their own material. Gordon consented, since he had no real alternative, and so Johnny O'Keefe and the Dee Jays took the stage before a packed crowd at the Crown Theatre in Woolloomooloo . . . and were promptly booed and pelted with vegetables.

The next moment became the stuff of legend: O'Keefe took the mic and declared, 'You may boo me, and you may throw things at me. But you all pay your money to see me— because you love me!' And, bizarrely, his ballsiness worked. JO'K became a beloved star, consolidated by the release of the EP *Shakin' at the Stadium* in March 1958, with the lead single 'The Wild One'.

---

1 While Australia in the fifties was generally unrelentingly white, it's worth noting that Lou Casch was born in Western Sumatra and was known to his mum as Lodewyk Nanlohy.

Legend has it that the song is based on a gig that O'Keefe and the Dee Jays had played in Newtown the previous year. Apparently the venue was holding an Italian wedding reception downstairs while the band were playing at a dance upstairs. This very poor bit of venue management allegedly led to fisticuffs between the band's audience and the wedding attendees, which developed into a full-scale riot, requiring intervention by the police and the navy shore patrol.

While the story—related by Casch several decades later—is a good one, it's unlikely to be true. A cursory look through the newspapers of the time fails to mention any such riot (and surely riots requiring military involvement weren't so commonplace at the time as to go unreported by the press), and the song itself is entirely about dancing and impressing girls rather than fighting angry wedding guests in the inner west. Though maybe they had to leave out a verse for space.[2]

Issues of origin aside, there are still some pretty solid question marks over the authorship. Officially the song is credited to Johnny O'Keefe, Tony Withers, Johnny Greenan and Dave Owens. It's generally accepted that Withers—a radio DJ—was only given a credit as a financial incentive to spin the record on the air. In fact, it's even debatable whether or not O'Keefe himself actually contributed to the songwriting or if it was the work of Owens and Greenan alone.

The EP was a hit, mainly in Sydney, and now the man known as 'the Wild One' had a reputation to uphold. In 1959 O'Keefe and the Dee Jays became the house band for the

---

2 Presumably that verse would go something like: 'I'm gonna raise some hell-a / Spillin' trays of mortadella / Gonna bust a reception / With a naval intervention / I'm a wild one . . .'

ABC TV program *Six O'Clock Rock*, with O'Keefe becoming the host of the show after a mere six episodes. At the same time the band were the group of choice for the emerging rocker movement (with the chaps known in Australia as 'bodgies' and the dames as 'widgies'), with their regular residencies notorious for violent audiences—as Johnny Rebb and the Rebels learned to their venue-fleeing cost after replacing O'Keefe and company at the bi-weekly Leichhardt Dance.

O'Keefe's drinking was also getting heavier, which helped to destroy the US tour that had been planned to break him internationally. Chagrined and broke, he returned to Australia in 1960 and resumed *Six O'Clock Rock* duties while touring madly. In June that year he had a major car accident when he drove his Plymouth Belvedere into a gravel truck north of Kempsey while driving between Sydney and the Gold Coast. O'Keefe, Greenan and Greenan's wife Janice were all badly injured. O'Keefe was airlifted to Sydney, where multiple operations were required to repair his face and hands. Those close to him claimed that he was no longer the same man after the accident.

His record sales started to decline in 1963, after the death of Lee Gordon, although he remained a popular television host and personality. Perhaps ironically, as a pioneer of Australian rock'n'roll, he didn't much care for the modern music (notably refusing to allow the long-haired Missing Links to appear on his Channel 7 show, *Sing, Sing, Sing*), and his own material became increasingly middle-of-the-road. The death of Elvis Presley in 1977 hit the depressed and increasingly marginalised O'Keefe hard, and on 6 October 1978 he died of what was ruled to have been an accidental overdose of barbiturates.

O'Keefe never lived to see his legacy recognised as 'The Wild One' became a touchstone for Australian rock'n'roll. The song has also become part of Australia's musical DNA for the last few generations via the ABC's venerable music video program *Rage*, which uses part of the twelve-inch version of Iggy Pop's 1986 cover, renamed 'Real Wild Child (Wild One)'[3] as its theme song, with archival clips of O'Keefe belting it out on stage incorporated into the opening visuals that have remained unchanged for two decades.[4] Iggy also re-covered the song as a single with Jet in 2008—the same year that the Living End played it at the ARIA Awards, hailing it as the song that created the template for rock in Australia.

That seems like a good enough reason to use the single as Year Zero for this book too—although anyone expecting rock'n'roll to suddenly stride in and start making Australia exciting should probably lower their expectations for a bit. First, there was some stomping to do.

---

3   This seems as good a place as any to talk about how many names the song has, before someone writes in and complains that the song is actually called 'Wild One' (without the 'The'). It's also been called 'Real Wild Child', without the parenthetical '(Wild One)' of Pop's version, on its initial release outside of Australia. Basically, anything will do as long as 'Wild' is in the title, it would appear.

4   Or possibly more than two decades by the time you read this: *Rage* first screened on 17 April 1987, which was also a good couple of years after the term 'rage' was part of the hip vernacular of the young people.

2

1963

He's My Blonde-Headed, Stompie Wompie, Real Gone Surfer Boy

Little Pattie and The Statesmen

In which a Sydney teenager takes the nation on a stompin' safari

Despite the groundbreaking work of O'Keefe and his fellow pioneers, the birth of a distinctively Australian form of pop music was far from recognised at the time. Indeed, this newfangled rock'n'roll nonsense was clearly not an art form but a fad—the fidget spinner of its day[1]—and thus needed to be pumped out as quickly as possible, ideally having been hastily welded to another passing trend for maximum profiteering. In 1963 such a trend was ripe for the exploiting: the dance onomatopoeically known as the stomp.

---

1 At the time of writing—August 2017—fidget spinners were still a thing. For all I know they've been replaced by the inevitable yo-yo resurgence by now.

It's hard to explain why the stomp was so enormously popular, beyond the fact that it was easy to learn and had no complicated steps. One merely, um, stomped. The dance had emerged from US surfing culture—named, it would appear, for the 'surf stomp' dances held in California by legendary guitar twangsman Dick Dale in 1960. Surfers in not-entirely-reliable beach footwear needed to be able to get down at the post-surfing carnival dances in a manner that was suitably energetic but avoided running the risk of a tragic thong blowout.[2]

US surf culture found a welcome home in Australia, especially in the beachside suburbs of Sydney, and stomping became the dance of choice for the city's surfies. Indeed, so popular was the dance that the stomp was outlawed in many dance halls on the grounds that it might raze the building to the ground.

'See, there's quite a number of halls in municipalities that have been standing for many years,' Sydney City Council's Alderman Frank Moran explained to the ABC at the height of Sydney's outbreak of virulent stomp fever in 1963, 'and I do think the foundation would be considerably weak and if you have an excessive load on them, well, they could render the whole building unsafe.'[3]

---

2   This is 'thong' in the Australian footwear vernacular, not the American term for underwear in which a 'tragic thong blowout' would presumably involve serious gastric distress.

3   You may mock the idea that stomping could level buildings, but Frank Moran's fears proved to be justified. After all, in 1962 Japan's beloved tourist spot Atami Castle had been stomped to splinters in *King Kong vs Godzilla*, and a mere two years later the entire city of Nagoya was stomped completely flat in *Godzilla vs Mothra*. And can it be mere coincidence that Alderman Moran passed away in 2003, and only a year later Godzilla crushed the Sydney Opera House underfoot and stomped hundreds in Darling Harbour during his battles with his US doppelgänger (renamed Zilla) in 2004's powerful *Godzilla: Final Wars*?

HE'S MY BLONDE-HEADED, STOMPIE WOMPIE, REAL GONE SURFER BOY 13

Despite the urgent threat of stomping-related destruction, entrepreneurs were more concerned to address the urgent issue of how to use this hot new dance as a way to separate teenagers from their money.

Youth dance crazes had already proved wildly profitable for those able to exploit them before trends moved on, as the twist had amply demonstrated in the preceding few years, and had even managed to spearhead a few new ones with songs which handily explained the mechanics of the dance in the lyrics, such as 1962's 'The Loco-Motion'. Clearly the time had come for some songs that told the youth all about stomping and the stomping-related arts. All it needed was a spokestomper.

Sydney teenager Patricia Amphlett had been a hit singing on TV variety shows such as *Opportunity Knocks* and *Saturday Date* when she appeared in 1962 at the tender age of thirteen. The fresh-faced blonde-headed kid was also a recognised part of the local surf scene, as her band—the Statesmen—had a weekly gig at Bronte Surf Club, where she was discovered by singer/songwriter Justin McCarthy, known professionally as Jay Justin. The fact that Amphlett's schoolyard nickname was 'Little Pattie' was a pleasing coincidence, since the singer of 'The Loco-Motion', Eva Boyd, had been credited on the recording as 'Little Eva'. The stars were clearly aligning.[4] Justin helped secure Pattie a deal with EMI and with record producer Joe Halford co-wrote both sides of what was to be her debut single, 'He's My Blonde-Headed, Stompie

---

4 The nickname was allegedly bestowed in recognition of the fact that she was very short—147 centimetres, or just over four foot eight—and that her social circle contained two taller Patties. Whether or not they were also given distinguishing prefixes remains a mystery, but let's assume they were called 'Ultra Pattie' and 'P-Medium'.

Wompie, Real Gone Surfer Boy', and its flip side, 'Stompin' at Maroubra'—a single whose comprehensively generous levels of stompery has yet to be equalled in Australia or abroad.

The single was a mighty local hit, only held off the top of the Sydney charts by 'I Want to Hold Your Hand', by some English band from Liverpool, and managed a top 20 placing nationally. (It also led to an explosion of stomp-related songs, including 1964's 'Let's Stomp Australia Way' by Tony Brady, written by the Bee Gees,[5] who wisely declined to record it themselves.)

The song itself is notable mainly for its stop-start verses and innovative development of the adjective 'stompie wompie', as well as Pattie's infectiously enthusiastic 'yeah yeah yeah yeah'. Mysteriously, the backing singers seem to have confused the singer with someone else, since they were exhorting a 'little Sandy' to get going and get moving, and the guitar break has a conversation between 'Sandy' and Johnny which, frankly, sounds like Johnny's indifference doesn't end with not having bothered to learn Pattie's name. ('Ah, Johnny,' she sighs during the spoken-word break over the guitar solo that pads out the 103 seconds of the song. 'Ah,' a distracted sounding Johnny replies, 'it's . . . great.')

At least Johnny had her name right by the time of the follow-up, 'We're Gonna Have a Party Tonight', which contains a similarly scintillating exchange between the pair after Pattie meets Johnny on the corner (spoiler: it turns out that they're looking forward to the titular party). He appears again in

---

5 It's worth clarifying that the claim that the stomp was 'getting around in Adelaide town / Stomp is here to stay' proved both premature and optimistic.

HE'S MY BLONDE-HEADED, STOMPIE WOMPIE, REAL GONE SURFER BOY 15

'Drag Race Johnny', suggesting that Justin and Halford were at least as interested in this mysterious 'Johnny' fellow as they were in their artist, not least because he unexpectedly vanishes in the song and Pattie laments that she doesn't think he's coming back, thereby bringing a disquieting conclusion to Little Pattie's haunting Johnny Trilogy.

And if Little Pattie didn't quite have the sophistication of European contemporaries like France Gall or Sandie Shaw, her audible youth gave songs like 'Surfin' Time Again' an energetic innocence. She became the youngest performer to sing for the troops in Vietnam in 1966, and was evacuated out mid-appearance as the Battle of Long Tan began a scant few kilometres from the camp at which she was performing. She was also one of the vocalists on the 'It's Time' advertisement for the 1972 election campaign that made Gough Whitlam the first Labor prime minister in twenty-three years. But eventually even she tired of the world of pop, first embracing country music (and her birth name) before retiring from performance in the eighties and becoming a fierce figure in the union movement and the vocal coach to a new generation of young pop singers, including the briefly beloved teenage sensation Nikki Webster.

In 2009 Little Pattie was inducted into the ARIA Hall of Fame by her cousin Chrissy Amphlett,[6] with Lisa Mitchell performing an inappropriately languid arrangement of Little Pattie's signature tune in tribute, in which she didn't even engage Johnny in conversation over the guitar break.

---

6   . . . who turns up again in chapter 32, because this entire book fits together like an artfully constructed jigsaw puzzle.

Tragically, the number of Australian stomp-themed singles released since the sixties has dropped sharply. Sydney swamp revivalists the Snowdroppers courageously attempted to spearhead a stompnaissance in 2009 with their single 'Do the Stomp', but Australia clearly felt it was still too soon. Whether we shall ever truly be able to innocently stomp again as a nation remains an open question. Perhaps this book can start that long-overdue conversation.

3

1963

Royal Telephone

Jimmy Little

*In which Australia's first Aboriginal superstar shows
exactly how Australia likes their non-white people:
neat, religious and unthreatening*

It's necessary to backtrack a little at this juncture to point out that there was a flourishing music industry in Australia before rock'n'roll raised its shaggy head. This is important because a) it provides important context for what is to come, and b) will hopefully pre-empt furious letters demanding to know why Slim Dusty didn't make the cut.[1]

Before rock'n'roll infected our innocent and impression-able youth, Australian music was country music. That's where

---

1 Honestly, I could write another two perfectly strong versions of this book with all the songs I left out, and then a fourth one with all the Models and Humming-birds and Falling Joys songs I wanted to include but couldn't justify, damn it.

the superstars were—people like Dusty, Smoky Dawson, Reg Lindsay and Chad Morgan. Australia wasn't nearly as urban as it was to become, with country regions still being well populated by people who required entertaining, and this had led to a heathy regional touring and gigging scene.

However, some of the greatest country music was coming from Aboriginal communities, where it had become infused with the gospel and devotional music of Christian missions where so many children had been (and continued to be) forcibly relocated. In the US this blending of country and gospel led to rhythm and blues before morphing into rock'n'roll, but in Australia the music of the subjugated underclass developed in different ways.[2]

Jimmy Little Senior had been part of the Wallanga Gumleaf Orchestra, which merged with the vaudeville troupe based at Cummeragunja Reserve on the NSW side of the Murray, near what's now the town of Barmah in Victoria. It was there he met his future wife Frances, who was a singer and yodeller, and the pair became prominent members of the vaudeville circuit in the towns and settlements along the river. They had seven children, of whom Jimmy Junior was the first, but life on the reserve was not an entirely happy one. Neglect and financial mismanagement by the NSW Aborigines Protection Board meant living conditions were poor, and the authorities had little interest in making things better for the inhabitants. After several people died from starvation on

2   This chapter can't possibly do justice to the extraordinary history of Aboriginal country music. Get your hands on Clinton Walker's definitive work *Buried Country* and prepare to have your mind blown. Honestly, the story of Vic Simms is a book in itself.

what was a successful and profitable farm the community had had enough; this led to the great Cummeragunja walk-off of 1939, with families leaving the reserve in defiance of the white managers and crossing the river to Victoria, settling in rural towns like Mooroopna and Shepparton.[3] The Littles, however, moved east to Wallaga Lake, where Jimmy Senior's family originated. It was there, in 1945, that Frances died of tetanus infection from a mussel shell.

After this tragedy the Littles moved north to Nowra, closer to the bright lights of Sydney. With both parents being performers it was no surprise that Jimmy took up the family trade, learning guitar and developing a smoothly pleasant singing voice at age fourteen. As he told Clinton Walker, 'I realised if I can—I didn't think commercially, then, but I'm using these words now—if I can capitalise commercially on a homegrown ability, I could take what I felt was a gift and expand it through an audience, and that audience would be my extended family.'

His talent made him a rising star and Little was a born crowd-pleaser from the very first, tailoring his material to appeal to whoever was listening. And if that sounds obsequious, it's worth adding that this was entirely the point of popular music at the time. As he told Benjamin Law in a 2011 interview for *Frankie*, 'Before the 1960s, there was no teenage music. It was just kindergarten primary-school music, and adult music. There was no teenage music until a thing

---

3   This was to be significant decades later, when another proud Yorta Yorta man from Shepparton became a prominent celebrity as well as a prime mover in another musical genre beloved by Aboriginal performers. It's a while off; you can pace yourself.

called rock'n'roll appeared on the horizon, and we were at the right age to be a part of that boom.'

That's largely true, except that Little was never rock'n'roll and that boom was the sound of careers exploding—including his own. Indeed, it was the rise of bands like the Beatles that knocked Little and his contemporaries off the charts and ushered in a new wave of local beat combos. In 1964 he beat the likes of Little Pattie and Billy Thorpe to be named Pop Star of the Year by *Everybody* magazine. By 1965 he was considered old news.

And Little had been an honest-to-god star, thanks to a single that roared to #2 on the Sydney charts in 1963: a saccharine little affair called 'Royal Telephone'. This was significant for a range of reasons, none of which could be summed up as 'because it's such a kick-arse song'.

The plodding gospel number had been a US hit for Burl Ives in 1961, and Little's version uses an almost identical arrangement (although, as a Baptist, Little's version wisely chooses to leave out the verse about 'Pentecostal fire'). Little's honeyed vocal is far more appealing than Ives' twinkly and avuncular gee-shucks delivery, but it's not a song that leaves the performer especially much with which to work. The lyrics incorporate as many phone/prayer metaphors as possible before the song collapses under its own premise, sounding both clunky and corny to modern ears.[4]

It was a mighty smash, though—and part of the appeal was pure timing. Home telephone use was becoming widespread

---

4   The song remained in Little's live set throughout his life, and he'd give it more of a country swing which made it a bit less ghastly—but still, there's only so much one can do with it.

in the early sixties, although the technology was still in its infancy. Indeed, the network was struggling to keep up with the slow roll out of the coaxial cable that allowed hundreds of multiple calls per exchange: the upgrade only began in 1964, initially between Sydney, Melbourne and Canberra.[5] Another convenient coincidence was the launch of Dial-A-Prayer by the Seventh-day Adventists, ensuring that the connection between religion and telecommunications was foremost in the public imagination.

But more importantly, it showed what Australian audiences wanted from black performers. Little was by no means the only Aboriginal artist working at the time—though he was perhaps the most polished, having been raised by parents who were professional entertainers—but the combination of his inoffensive music, his neat and tidy presentation and his polite religiosity made him the sort of Aboriginal star who didn't make anyone think too uncomfortably hard about certain genocidal elements of the national history or the policies still removing children from their families as late as the mid–1970s.[6]

That said, Little's politeness should not be confused with docility. He was never deferential, running his own career with care and trusting in his instincts as an entertainer, and subtly raising Aboriginal issues in the mainstream consciousness even while making records your nan would enthusiastically spin. Significantly, he was also the first Aboriginal artist to record a song by an Aboriginal songwriter, cutting 'Give the Coloured Boy a Chance'—a song written by Jimmy Little Senior—in 1959.

---

5   Draw your own NBN comparison here.
6   That shiver of horror you just got down your spine? That's your conscience rightfully going '. . . the HELL?'

However, 'Royal Telephone' also marked the apex of Little's time as a high-charting star. Fashions were changing and Little's next single, 'One Road' (written by emerging Bee Gees star Barry Gibb), attempted to split the difference between the emerging pop sound and 'Royal Telephone'—in fact, it had supposedly been written as a love song before Gibb was instructed to religion up the lyrics to appeal to 'Royal Telephone' fans.

Even as his chart position fell, Little remained a potent live draw for another decade and a half before moving into full-time acting, though he returned to music in the nineties, becoming the Australian equivalent of Johnny Cash with albums of classic songs reinterpreted in his immediately recognisable voice.[7]

In 2010 he retired from performing. The following year his beloved wife Marjorie died and less than a year later—on 2 April 2012—he also passed away. The fact that Little was an Indigenous artist who succeeded commercially and culturally in a country that proudly subscribed to a policy explicitly called 'White Australia' set an important precedent for some of the most exciting music to come—as you shall see.

---

7 If you've not heard it, please note that 1999's *Messenger* is a freakin' masterpiece. With Karma County's Brendan Gallagher overseeing the project, the album consists exclusively of Australian songs. Little's jazzy version of the Church's 'Under the Milky Way' is arguably the definitive one.

4

1965

The Carnival is Over

The Seekers

*In which Australia's first international success story
comes from the most unlikely pop stars the nation
could possibly create*

I'm about to make a claim that might give some readers pause, but here goes: the Seekers were our Beatles.

Yes, the Easybeats were cooler, had the closest thing we ever got to a Lennon/McCartney partnership in Vanda and Young, and made records that didn't sound like soundtracks for a wholesome church group frolic, but the facts speak for themselves: the Seekers were higher selling, more popular internationally, and even got in early with the whole unexpected-break-up thing.

The numbers are astonishing. At one point their biggest seller, 'The Carnival is Over', was selling more than 90,000 copies a day in the UK, for a total of 1.41 million copies.[1] They were worldwide-million-sellers at a time when Australia barely registered in the global consciousness. They gave Paul Simon his first hit and saved his stillborn musical career.[2] They were the first artists to put Aussie music on the international map.

Even so, it's hard to get away from the fact that the Seekers were so uncool that they never even became cool by virtue of not ever trying to be cool. They posed for photos in sensible knitwear; they kept their hair short and tidy, as though concerned that they might have to go in to work the next day; and they sang close-harmony folk songs that would shock and horrify absolutely no-one's parents. For freak's sake, their debut single was a cover of 'Waltzing Matilda'. As a representation of Australia under Robert Menzies, they were perfect: sexless, unthreatening and snowy white.

Even their split was undramatic: singer Judith Durham told the rest of the band—double bassist Athol Guy and guitarists Keith Potger and Bruce Woodley—that she was quitting for a solo career and they, well, agreed. Even then she gave them six months' notice, lest it be too great a shock.

So drama-free was their ascent to stardom and convivial split that the writers of *Georgy Girl*, the Seekers' jukebox musical, were initially hindered by the fact there was no story worth telling. In the end librettist Patrick Edgeworth created

---

1 According to the Official Charts Company in 2012 'The Carnival is Over' was the thirty-sixth highest-selling single in Britain of all time, beaten by the Beatles' 'I Feel Fine' but edging out Coolio's 'Gangsta's Paradise'. Given the way sales have declined in the years since, that result is unlikely to change. Sorry, Coolio.

2 They covered his 'Someday One Day' after meeting him in London, where he was licking his wounds after the comprehensive failure of Simon & Garfunkel's debut album *Wednesday Morning, 3AM* to light up the charts.

THE CARNIVAL IS OVER 25

a Durham-focused Cinderella story cribbing elements from the story of the song in lieu of anything remotely controversial.

But if 'Georgy Girl' is arguably their best-known song, 'The Carnival is Over' was the one that made them superstars. It was a #1 hit in Australia, Ireland and Britain and very nearly in the United States, stalling at #2 on the *Billboard* charts. And, like almost all of the Seekers' material, they didn't actually write it. The music came from a Russian folk melody, while British singer Tom Springfield wrote the lyrics.[3] Tom, the brother of Dusty, was pursuing a rather less immediately successful solo career after the demise of their band, the Springfields, when his path crossed with the newly arrived quartet. He soon became their main songwriter, giving them the hits 'I'll Never Find Another You', 'A World of Our Own' and, with lyricist Jim Dale, 'Georgy Girl'.

But the stately pace and close harmonies of 'The Carnival is Over' conceals the song's excitingly vicious past. The tune's origins are unknown, beyond that it was sung in the Volga region perhaps as early as the fifteenth century, but the poet and cultural ethnographer Dmitry Sadovnikov wrote new lyrics for it in 1883 that told the tale of Cossack commander and folk hero Stepan Razin, the leader of a peasant uprising against the tsar in 1670. In Sadovnikov's version, the lyrics tell of Razin returning from another successful military campaign with a captured Persian princess, whom he promptly murders by throwing her into the freezing depths of the Volga River. The reasons for his sudden enthusiasm for princess-drowning

---

3 More importantly, though, Tom's real name was Dionysius P.A. O'Brien, which is inarguably the greatest name in the entire history of everything.

vary between different versions of the song, but most seem to indicate Razin did so to prove his manliness after his soldiers accused him of going all soft and non-murdery after enjoying a night of passion.[4]

It's not entirely clear how Springfield would have become aware of what was, after all, a pretty geographically specific Russian folk song most popular in the 1890s, but a decent guess would be via another archivist of folk music traditions: the US singer Pete Seeger, who recorded an English language cover of it in 1953. Springfield wisely chose to leave out the whole murdering-a-prisoner-of-war plot line and instead told a more generic tale of a love torn apart by, um, a literal carnival being literally over. This presumably means that the narrator is a carnie, which makes it even weirder. After all, what sort of true love can be torn asunder by the relentless responsibility of manning the Tilt-a-Whirl?[5]

Whatever the interpretation, the song clearly resonated with audiences and traditionally was used to close Seekers gigs— and became so closely associated with finales that it became the default song to close pretty much every single Australian event, from agricultural shows to sporting carnivals to official

---

4   Um . . . leaving aside the 'murder by drowning' bit, a night of passion between a military leader and a captured prisoner is, at the very least, unlikely to have been entirely consensual. Bizarrely, 'The Carnival is Over' still regularly comes up in online lists of Songs For Weddings, proving that the internet is basically one giant prank.

5   Actually, there's one other odd thing in the lyrics, specifically that the song claims that the joys of love are fleeting 'for Pierrot and Columbine'. These are two stock characters from the commedia dell'arte—Pierrot the sad clown, Columbine (or Columbina) a servant girl who is also Pierrot's faithless wife. So presumably there's some adulterous business going on in there with Harlequin that's ended this particular carnival. See, Mum? That Bachelor of Arts degree is *still* paying off.

functions. Predictably, the Seekers were to perform it at the end of the closing ceremony of the 2000 Olympics in Sydney on 1 October, but Durham broke her hip and the band was forced to pull out. Appropriately, they did end up performing the song at the Paralympics later that month, with Durham singing from a wheelchair.[6]

It's a song that has also enjoyed more bizarre cover versions than most. Fellow antipodean Nick Cave covered it in his typically stentorian fashion on the Bad Seeds' *Kicking Against the Pricks* covers album in 1986, while German disco stars Boney M did a version of it in 1982 that sounds precisely like you'd imagine a Boney M cover of 'The Carnival is Over' to sound.

Despite becoming the first global Australian superstars, the Seekers called it a day in 1968 following a farewell concert that was broadcast around the world and viewed by 10 million people. Durham's solo career enjoyed solid success in Australia, as well as intermittent international attention. Guy had a brief stint as a TV host before entering Victorian state politics, where he served three terms as a Liberal member of the uncharacteristically progressive government of Premier Dick Hamer. Potger put together the squeaky-clean New Seekers, who had a huge hit with the Coke ad jingle 'I'd Like to Teach the World to Sing'. And Woodley made children's toys and enjoyed a moderately successful career as a

---

6 An Olympic-closing Seekers performance of 'The Carnival is Over' was considered such a foregone conclusion that the final episode of the John Clarke/Bryan Dawe/Gina Riley satirical comedy *The Games*—written and filmed months earlier—ended with the trio (and Nicholas Bell) forced to impersonate the band performing the song.

songwriter and a less successful one as a solo artist, although he did co-write the much-broadcast 'I Am Australian' with Bushwackers frontman Dobe Newton for the Australian bicentenary. Durham would later cover the song.

There were also several Seekers reunions, with and without Durham (with lead vocals handled by Julie Anthony and former *Young Talent Time* star Karen Knowles during the non-Judith years). So while the rock'n'roll explosion was creating a wave of social change and youth-led upheaval in the mid-sixties, Australia's biggest band was making music that grandmothers could enjoy.

That would not remain the case for long, mind, because there were some long-haired teenage types who were set to change everything.

5

1966

Friday On My Mind

The Easybeats

*In which we meet the first truly world-class
Australian rock band of immigrants*

At the time of writing, Australians are working longer hours
for lower pay than they have done in decades, thanks to
stagnant wage growth, an exponential increase in property
prices and governments happy to nudge the age of retirement
up and up in the hope that more people will die off before
accessing pensions.

But in 1966 it wasn't considered a shameful insult to the
gods of productivity to suggest that jobs were a necessary evil
that had to be endured in order to enjoy the things that made
life worth living. Indeed, it wasn't even especially controversial
to dare suggest that one might turn up at work on a Monday,

sure, but even then already have Friday—not to mention the prettiness of one's girl—very much on one's mind.

There's another reason why 'Friday On My Mind' would have been considered dangerously subversive had it been recorded in 2017, aside from the lockout-flouting idea that one might actually seek to have fun in the city: it was made by a bunch of migrants—and working-class ones at that. The members of the Easybeats—and particularly the two who wrote the song: guitarist George Young (from Scotland) and Harry Vanda (born Johannes van den Berg in Holland)—seemed to be under no illusion that Australia was the egalitarian, classless paradise it purported to be even then. They knew that they were 'working for the rich man', and it made them feel justifiably angry and in need of release.

The band members first met in the migrant hostel in Villawood in the outer suburbs of Sydney.[1] Vanda and Young were joined by fellow Netherlander bassist Dick Diamonde (a stage moniker, slightly catchier than his birth name of Dingeman Adriaan Henry van der Sluijs) and two Brits: Gordon 'Snowy' Fleet and frontman Stevie Wright. By 1964 they were playing regularly in Taylor Square and found themselves signed to Albert Productions (with distribution through EMI).

Like every other bunch of teenagers in the English-speaking world, the five Easybeats were enamoured of the Beatles; however, unlike most of the other hastily formed beat combos, they took note not just of the sound, the haircuts and the

---

1   Then it was called the Villawood Migrant Hostel; these days it's known as the Villawood Detention Centre, in keeping with Australia's increasingly aggressive xenophobia regarding immigrants.

matching suits, but also of the names in the brackets after the song titles. The Beatles' greatest strength was that they wrote many of their own songs, and the Easybeats realised this was a powerful weapon they would be wise to add to their rock'n'roll arsenal. Their first single, 'For My Women', didn't do much, but 'She's So Fine' was a smash—and, importantly, both singles were written by Wright and Vanda. For a scene dominated by bands covering the latest hits from the US and UK, this was a significant development. Indeed, their debut album *Easy*—which appeared in September 1965—featured songwriting credits for all five members and marked the first time that an Australian rock'n'roll band had written an entire album themselves. They even wrote for other people, most notably Johnny Young and Kompany, who went to #1 with the Young/Wright penned 'Step Back'.

In 1966 the Easybeats were bigger than the Beatles in Australia, and figured that it was time to take their show global. They relocated to the UK (after another #1 with the *Easyfever* EP and its storming lead track, 'Sorry') and immediately discovered that no-one at EMI or in Great Britain in general gave the slightest of shits about them and their stupid colonial success.

Ted Albert, who had produced all their material to date, was shoved aside by the label, and the material the band had been working on was dismissed as unsophisticated. Their first UK single, 'Come and See Her', was a flop, which didn't exactly strengthen the band's hand. Wright's confidence was badly dented and Harry Vanda—who had been improving his shaky English in the intervening years—stepped up as the band's main lyricist. And not a moment too soon, since this was make or break for the band.

Then a song Vanda and Young had knocked up caught the ear of the band's new producer, Shel Talmy (who'd helmed records for the Kinks and the Who), and was deemed suitable for recording. That song channelled all the band's frustration at being subjected to the whims of their bosses into two minutes and forty-seven seconds of pure rock'n'roll genius.

Everything about 'Friday On My Mind' is perfect. That two-note opening riff, played at breakneck pace, starts the song with a tightly wound tension familiar to anyone sleeping through their Monday alarm. The slow burn of Wright's vocal, ably supported by the band's keening backing harmonies. Those slashing chord changes ahead of the chorus. The sheer stomping joy of the chorus. There's not a moment wasted.

It was an international hit: #1 in Australia, predictably, but also #1 on the Dutch charts, #6 in the UK and #16 in the US. It would also be widely covered over a remarkably long period. There've been several dozen versions thus far: the Shadows were first off the blocks in 1967, and David Bowie recorded it for *Pin Ups* in 1973. Gary Moore had a fairly dreadful hit with it in the eighties, and Vanessa Amorosi and Lee Kernaghan recorded it for the NRL in 2000.

It was the high-water mark for the band—and their only international success—not least because they started to fracture not long after.

Snowy jumped ship in 1967, missing his family back in Australia, and more ambitious singles like 'Heaven and Hell' and 'The Music Goes Round My Head' failed to set the UK charts alight. Drugs also entered the picture, especially for Wright,[2] but a bigger issue was the growing distance between the Vanda/Young partnership, which was establishing itself both as a writing team and a production house, and the rest of the band. After the Easybeats split in 1969, Vanda and Young would go on to work both as successful artists in their own right as Flash and the Pan, but have greater cachet as producers of the band formed by George's little brothers Malcolm and Angus. You may have heard of them.[3]

Wright returned to Australia and formed bands in Melbourne, Perth and Sydney before taking to the stage to play Simon Zealotes in *Jesus Christ Superstar* in 1972. He settled into a solid line-up with Stevie Wright and the Allstars (produced by Vanda and Young) for his solo album *Hard Road*, and had an unexpected #1 smash hit with 'Evie (Parts 1, 2 and 3)'. The stardom had largely evaporated by 1975's *Black Eyed Bruiser*, and from 1976 onwards he concentrated more heavily on heroin than anything musical.

This led to the most tragic part of the story: Wright admitted himself to Chelmsford Private Hospital in the late seventies, where he underwent deep-sleep therapy in an attempt to conquer his addiction. In total, twenty-four people died from the treatment, administered by Dr Harry Bailey, and while Wright escaped with his life he did suffer psychological

---

2 If you can get your hands on the harrowing biography *Sorry: The Wretched Tale of Little Stevie Wright* by Jack Marx, a) it's an amazing read, and b) it's worth a staggering amount on eBay, which makes me deeply regret lending my copy to someone years ago. Let this be a lesson, dear reader: never lend this book to anyone, ever, under any circumstances. In fact, you should buy six or seven spare copies just to be on the safe side.

3 . . . and they turn up in chapter 11!

trauma and physical brain damage that would affect him for the rest of his days.

A few Easybeats reunions were mooted, and the band finally did a well-received tour in 1986 with all five members in top form. However, it proved a one-off—Wright's health and addictions made it impossible for the band to continue, as did the production pressures on Vanda and Young. It seemed to hit Wright particularly hard.

After a difficult nineties Wright found some degree of peace with his family and the occasional gig (and he, Fleet and Vanda attended the 2005 ARIA Awards to accept the Easybeats' Hall of Fame nomination) before retiring from music in 2009. His well-lived-in body finally gave out on 27 December 2015.

They barely existed for five years and yet the Easybeats' catalogue is still staggeringly strong—especially the immortal 'Friday On My Mind'. In 2001 it was voted the best Australian song of all time in a poll marking the seventy-fifth anniversary of the Australian Performing Right Association (the folks who collect songwriter royalties), and you know what? It's really hard to argue with that result.[4]

---

4   That said, You Am I's performance of it that night (with Harry Vanda guesting) was astonishingly sloppy. Then again, it'd been a long night.

6

1969

The Real Thing

Russell Morris

In which Australia grows its hair and gets an injection of groovy

The psychedelic sounds of the US and England had hit Australia just as swiftly as ships carrying copies of *Sgt Pepper's Lonely Hearts Club Band* and *Freak Out!* could arrive in 1967, with bands like Taman Shud, the Wild Cherries and the Masters Apprentices doing their best interpretations of a southern hemisphere form of grooviness. By 1969 most of the psych acts were toughening up their sound, as you'll see in the next chapter,[1] but the style was about to go out with a bang with a song which was to utterly define its performer.

---

1   See? *Artfully constructed jigsaw puzzle!*

Russell Morris was an artist at a creative crossroads, having just left the band that had made him a teen heartthrob in Melbourne and trying to work out how best to fashion himself as a solo artist. 'The Real Thing' did that—boy, how it did that!—but the most immediately interesting thing about the song is not really the man who sang it but the other big credits on the disc: the songwriter and the producer, both of whom were significant figures in the Melbourne-centric music scene and about to become household names as lovable mainstream television stars.

The writer was one Johnny Benjamin de Jong, aka Johnny Young, later to host the talent quest variety show *Young Talent Time*. He'd already had a busy few years since relocating from Perth (where his Dutch family had emigrated) to Melbourne in 1966 with his band, Kompany. Having been a TV personality in Perth, hosting *Club Seventeen*, he soon got a gig as host of *The Go!! Show* after the previous host and future game show legend Ian Turpie quit. Things were looking up for Young and Ko.

Turps seemed to have been on to something, though: despite Young winning a Logie for Best Teenage Personality that year,[2] the show was axed not long after he came on board. Sick of this jerk nation and its lack of respect for Logie-winning teens, Young upped stumps to London to lick his wounds and share a flat with Barry Gibb, who was busily making the Bee Gees a global concern.

Gibb wrote Young some songs, including the minor hit 'Lady', but by 1968 Young was back in Melbourne not being

---

2 Why does the Logies no longer have this category? At the very least they could rename it Most Disaffected Millennial or something.

a superstar and writing for *Go-Set* magazine. However, if Young was hoping some of Gibb's hit-making magic would rub off on him, he was in luck. A song did emerge as Young absorbed bits and pieces of other songs of the day—including Donovan's 'Hurdy Gurdy Man' and Paul Revere & the Raiders' '(I'm Not Your) Steppin' Stone'—to create a song inspired by Coca-Cola's brand new slogan.[3]

Meanwhile the producer of the song, at least theoretically, was Ian 'Molly' Meldrum, a *Go-Set* journalist and Melbourne scenester who was shortly to become the most influential man in Australian music as host of the ABC's groundbreaking music show, *Countdown*.

Meldrum had discovered Morris's band Somebody's Image, which had developed a strong local following at dances and showcases despite having what was inarguably the worst name in all of Melbourne. He began managing the band, which had a minor hit with a cover of 'Hush' before Morris decided that he'd have better luck as a solo artist.

Meldrum wanted to make damn sure that he launched Morris's career with a stone-cold killer of a single, complete with ambitious plans to combine all the sonic flourishes that made Beatles tracks like 'Strawberry Fields Forever' and 'I Am the Walrus' so theatrical and epic. After hearing Young's song and deciding that it would work as the scaffold on which to attach the ornate cladding of his planned production, he spent months crafting Morris's masterpiece. One reason why it took so long was that Meldrum didn't really

---

3   This is true, incidentally. Young had apparently seen the 'Coke: It's the Real Thing' ad while he was in Britain and found it deeply distasteful.

know how studios worked. Engineer John L. Sayers did the heavy sonic lifting while the musical backing for the single came mainly from members of another Meldrum-managed band, the Groop, who celebrated their uncredited appearance on the single by splitting up with guitarist Don Mudie and frontman Brian Cadd forming Axiom.

Meldrum may not have been a technician, but he did know a hit when he heard it. Importantly, he also knew a hook when he heard it, and when Morris sang a stream of nonsense words to indicate a guitar line he wanted over the escalating chords after the chorus, Molly decided that it was staying. Thus the world was given one of pop music's classic lines of gibberish: 'ooh mau-ma mau mau'.

At six minutes plus the song was epic, with the hypnotic outro washed in whooshing flange effects that neatly predicted what producers unable to achieve a George Martin-style sonic effect would do for generations to come: load on the studio trickery with a trowel.[4] It was a huge hit, going to #1 and becoming the biggest-selling Australian single for 1969. It also became a local hit in several US markets including New York, thanks to the then-haphazard distribution system for records, although the UK was less well disposed to Morris's sub-Beatle psychedelia.

---

4 'Flange' is more accurately called artificial double tracking, where a sound is moved ever so slightly out of phase with itself to create a weird, otherworldly effect. While variations on the technique existed before, flanging was invented by EMI engineer Ken Townsend at Abbey Road Studios in 1966 after John Lennon had complained he was sick of doing double-tracked vocals and wanted a way to record it once and still get the same effect. When Lennon asked how it was achieved (on 'Tomorrow Never Knows', incidentally), producer George Martin, aware that Lennon knew nothing about technical matters, responded: 'It's very simple. We take the original image and we split it through a double vibrocated sploshing flange with double negative feedback.'

At first it seemed like Morris would continue on this star-making trajectory, with his second single—the sequel 'Part Three into Paper Walls'—also going to #1 (written by Morris and Young, and starting with the coda of 'The Real Thing'), but Morrismania had essentially burned out by 1973, at which point he relocated to the US to attempt to kickstart an international career. He returned to Australia a few years later, and still plays music to this day, but for most people this song is his sole claim to fame.[5] To be fair, it's a pretty amazing one to have.

While Meldrum might not have created the sonic masterpiece he was after with 'The Real Thing', it proved incredibly influential on Australian music. The thin, effect-heavy sound provided a template for modern Australian psych bands, perhaps most notably Tame Impala, the John Steel Singers, and King Gizzard and the Lizard Wizard, who would similarly harness the intoxicating power of a repetitive, slow-building, guitar-pedal-laden jam.

The song lived on too: Morris rerecorded it multiple times himself, and there were high-profile (and, let's be honest, pretty awful) covers by both Kylie Minogue and Midnight Oil. But nothing quite captures the sheer oddness of the original. Sing it with me: *Ooh mau-ma mau, m-mau-mau-m-mau . . .*

---

5 For a long time he toured as Cotton Keays and Morris with Daryl Cotton and former Masters Apprentices' frontman Jim Keays, who . . . hold on, they're in the next chapter! Why, what a ride this book is!

7

1970

Turn Up Your Radio

The Masters Apprentices

*In which a band from Adelaide invents the seventies
by looking back to the fifties*

Let's be clear: Adelaide is a really nice place.[1] It is, however, a bugger of a city in which to make a musical career.[2]

It's a good city in which to start out, with plenty of centralised venues and a cost of living that makes Sydney and Melbourne rent payers and mortgage holders cry tears of blood, but the fact is that precious few bands have managed to create a sustainable career while calling South Australia home. The list of bands and performers that began in Adelaide before heading east is impressive—the Angels,

---

1 I speak from experience.
2 I speak from deeply frustrating experience.

41

Cold Chisel, Sia Furler, the Superjesus, I Killed the Prom Queen—while the list of bands that began in Adelaide and stayed put to watch their careers wither and die is far, far longer and nowhere near as impressive.[3]

The first band to realise this was the Masters Apprentices, who are still celebrated in their hometown as the band that put Adelaide on the map, despite a) having got the hell out as soon as humanly possible, and b) all bar one of the original Adelaidean members had quit by the time the band hit their most critically and commercially successful period. And it's arguable that their definitive song was one of their final releases—the tender 'Because I Love You'. But let's instead focus on a song that made Australia rock, and that hasn't had every last drop of beauty drained out of it by bank and insurance commercials in the decades since: 'Turn Up Your Radio'.

Keays always described his band as having three eras: the garage era, the psychedelic era and the prog rock era. That's slightly misleading, since 'Turn Up Your Radio' is a three-chord stomper in the blues tradition which is pure garage rock, yet appeared in 1970 as the band hit their most musically ambitious period. And while it would be a massive stretch to call it punk, it was unambiguously intended as a middle finger to the band's Australian audience which still frustratingly considered them a pop act rather than a serious rock outfit.

The Masters Apprentices (deliberately spelled with no apostrophe in order to infuriate generations of subeditors) had formed in 1965, when surf instrumental combo the Mustangs

---

3   In chapter 44 you'll meet the band that changed all this, living in the Adelaide foothills while becoming Australian music pioneers. But don't skip ahead or you'll ruin the surprise.

took on a lead singer in the form of Scots immigrant Jim Keays.[4] He, guitarists Rick Morrison and Mick Bower, drummer Brian Vaughton and bassist Gavin Webb swiftly became local favourites in Adelaide. In September 1967, the band had been riding high as Australian teen idols to rival the Beatles (or, more accurately, to rival the Beatles' main competition; *Go-Set* writer and Melbourne DJ Stan Rofe had memorably declared: 'The Masters are to Australia what the Rolling Stones are to England, and The Doors are to America'). They were a Big Deal, and Adelaide was unable to contain them.

That year they relocated to Melbourne, losing Vaughton in the process.[5] Morrison was next to depart, passing out on stage with a collapsed lung. Bower suffered a nervous breakdown in Tasmania and quit. With the main songwriter gone, the band got by in the short term by accepting a song from Brian Cadd and Max Ross (of the Groop, whom you met last chapter) called 'Elevator Driver', as Keays settled in with new guitarist Doug Ford, formerly of the Missing Links. And then, just as things got settled, Webb quit with stomach ulcers.

Once the dust settled the band consisted of Keays, Ford, Glenn Wheatley (who joined as a guitarist but ended up on bass) and drummer Colin Burgess. Management problems

---

4 Keays had turned up at the age of five with his adoptive parents, in 1951, and been resettled in an Adelaide migrant hostel. Ten years later another Scottish immigrant family, the Swans, would follow the same path, with a couple of their sons going on to forge musical careers in their new homeland. You'll meet one of them in chapter 13.

5 Just to clarify, Vaughton decided to stay in Adelaide; they didn't physically lose him on the drive east or anything, just in case you were concerned he'd fallen out of the van in Bordertown and was never heard from again.

pushed Wheatley into the organisational role, prepping him for his future career as one of the nation's biggest managers-turned-tax-evaders,[6] and the band was tiring of its teenybopper image as its music, its image and its lifestyles became harder. That became clear on the release of its *Masterpiece* album, which was a bit of a mess of past singles and transitional tracks. They needed a bold new song that was also a statement of intent. Something to make it clear that they were no longer the cutesy-pie teen idols of yore. Something that could be recorded while falling-down drunk.

That song was 'Turn Up Your Radio', the single that launched the seventies and Australian rock generally.

It was by far the heaviest thing that the Masters had done to this point, despite being reduced to a one-guitar band: Ford's big chunka-chunka barre chords made clear that the jangling psychedelia of 'Elevator Driver' had been left light years back.

The falling-down-drunk part was covered by Keays, who claimed in his heftily titled autobiography *His Master's Voice: The Masters Apprentices, the Bad Boys of Sixties Rock 'n' Roll* that he had to be held up to the microphone to do his growling vocals. The boldness came in the massed brass section blasting out the song's infectious riff.

The weird thing was that the song was a celebration of nostalgia, which seems a strange thing to be celebrating in what is generally regarded as the most fertile period in rock music the world has ever seen. Yet here was Keays quoting

---

6 You'll meet his future charge in chapter 28. No peeking. Man, this chapter has a lot of foreshadowing packed in. ARTFULLY CONSTRUCTED JIGSAW PUZZLE!

'Rock Around the Clock' and singing about learning the lessons of 'a long time ago'—specifically, 1956.

It also inadvertently spearheaded what was to become a fertile sub-genre of music: songs with 'radio' in the title and lyrics bitching about how lousy today's music is compared with that of the past. It's a noble lineage which includes Elvis Costello's 'Radio Radio', Queen's 'Radio Ga Ga', REM's 'Radio Song', The Beach Boys' 'That's Why God Made the Radio', and songs called 'Radio' by Robbie Williams, Beyoncé, Darius Rucker and literally dozens of others. As the variety of epochs represented by these songs demonstrate, the lesson to be learned is that music was always better before, no matter what era one is listening in.

The song did the trick: it gave the floundering band a top 10 hit, it established the Masters Apprentices as a rock act and it gave the new line-up a clear path forward. The next album, 1971's *Choice Cuts*, was a hit on the back of the (ahem) masterful 'Because I Love You' (and, being something of a concept album, didn't contain 'Turn Up Your Radio'), but success proved short-lived: a disastrous move to London ended with little record company support, no opportunity to play, and the inevitable split on the release of their barely heard final album, *A Toast to Panama Red* in 1972.

Keays embarked on a career releasing solo albums and fronting Southern Cross; Wheatley went into management with Little River Band and John Farnham and, as alluded to earlier, went to jail for tax evasion in 2007; Ford worked around Europe with various musicians through the 1970s and early 80s; and Burgess returned to Australia, where he became the first drummer with AC/DC before embarking on a colourful career that included backing Tiny Tim on his staggeringly peculiar *Rock* album in 1993.

All four returned to the band for re-formations over the years. And while 'Because I Love You' was a radio staple and ad jingle, 'Turn Up Your Radio' lived on too. The song's rockin' simplicity made it a fun cover for garage bands, which included the Apprentices themselves. In 1995 they rerecorded it with another band that embodied the Australian rock'n'roll spirit, the Hoodoo Gurus, and a specially recorded cover of 'Turn Up Your Radio' featuring Sarah Blasko, Custard's Dave McCormack, Spod and other Sydney artists was the first track broadcast on Sydney's beloved community radio station FBi when it began broadcasting under its permanent licence in August 2003. In 1998 the Masters Apprentices were finally inducted into the ARIA Hall of Fame with fellow ex-Adelaide boys the Angels. Sadly, in 2014 the band at last definitively ceased to exist, along with Keays, who at age sixty-seven succumbed to pneumonia relating to multiple myeloma.

The song had sent a strong message: the sixties were over and the future of guitar bands was going to be a good deal heavier. The amps would be louder, the hair would be longer, the jeans would be . . . um, denimier?

Of course, rock wasn't the only thing going on, but it was clear that change was in the air. Even in the easy-listening mainstream things were getting surprisingly provocative . . .

8

1971

I Am Woman

Helen Reddy

In which two Australians in the US create a global feminist anthem

It's difficult to make clear just how unexpected 'I Am Woman' was. Helen Reddy was not known as a feminist, if she was known at all, and was certainly not considered a songwriter. Yet she was to be the first Australian to release a #1 single in the US, and the first to invent singalong women's liberation.

Reddy's career had been through some odd phases by the time 'I Am Woman' happened. She was born in Melbourne but lived in the US, where she'd moved after winning the Bandstand talent competition in Australia, whose first prize was a deal with Mercury Records in New York—a deal that turned out not to exist. But rather than return home, the freshly divorced Reddy and her young daughter stayed put, eking out a living with as many gigs as her lack of a work permit would allow, before marrying Jeff Wald after a three-day courtship. With Reddy now able to remain in the US, Wald became her manager and finagled a single deal with Capitol Records, and while the A-side of her debut single 'I Believe in Music' flopped, the B-side—'I Don't Know How To Love Him' from the ubiquitous *Jesus Christ Superstar*—became an unexpected radio hit in 1970. An album deal followed and Reddy, who wasn't really a songwriter, found herself a song short and hastily knocked up some lyrics which had come to her as she lay in bed one night—'I am strong, I am invincible, I am woman'.

In 2003 she explained to the *Sunday* magazine: 'I couldn't find any songs that said what I thought being a woman was about. I thought about all these strong women in my family who had gotten through the Depression and world wars and drunken, abusive husbands. But there was nothing in music that reflected that.'

Her lyrics needed music, though, so she called on another expat Australian. Ray Burton's band the Executives was trying its luck in LA and he would later go on to form the prog-jazz-fusion Ayers Rock—a band that occupies a very special place in my heart as producing the absolute worst garbage I have ever heard in all of my life.[1] He and Reddy were friends and

---

1   My late father owned their self-titled album and would play it more often than anyone who genuinely enjoyed music would ever choose to do. I hated it for a bunch of reasons, principally musical, but also because the album had the world's least necessary die-cut sleeve in which at first there appeared to be a picture of Uluru, but when you pulled out the inner sleeve you discovered it was . . . a larger picture of Uluru. Fuck you, Ayers Rock.

she tapped him to craft a suitably triumphant accompaniment for her stirring words.

She and Burton would later dispute ownership of the song (he accused her of writing him out of the history of the song; she vehemently denied his claim that he edited her lyrics) and there would be a related kerfuffle over royalties, with Reddy declaring she had bought Burton out of his share in 1972—a conflict that wasn't settled until 1988. However, with both it and 'Best Friend' credited to Reddy–Burton on 1971's debut album *I Don't Know How to Love Him*, 'I Am Woman' . . . well, did pretty much nothing.[2]

At least, at first.

A year after the album appeared the producers of the otherwise unmemorable 'women's lib' comedy *Stand Up and Be Counted* approached Capitol about using the song as its theme music. Because the version on the album was deemed too short to cover the entire opening credits Reddy rerecorded it, adding another verse, and Capitol figured that it was worth whacking it out as a single just in case the film was a hit.[3]

It was not—but the single was. Momentum started to build after Wald got Reddy daytime TV spots singing it (while visibly pregnant with her son, Jordan), which led to a grass-roots movement of women ringing radio stations demanding they play it. DJs were less thrilled by it; Reddy joked about how

---

2 'Best Friend' is the song Reddy performed as the habit-wearing nun Sister Ruth in the schlocky disaster flick *Airport 1975*. If you've not seen it and yet that trope still rings a bell it's probably because you've seen the beat-for-beat parody, *Flying High* (released as *Airplane!* in the US).

3 In the end the film used the original album version in any case. Thanks a bunch, film.

often she'd turn up at a radio station to be told, 'I can't stand this record! I hate this song! But you know, it's a funny thing: my wife *loves* it!' And it wasn't just activists doing the ringing either. As Reddy later wrote, 'I was able to connect with all kinds of women, women who had been initially turned off by some of the more strident feminist voices; or women who believed they were already liberated.'

The timing was especially good, though. Feminism was making great strides into the mainstream, with a new political awareness moving into the world of women's magazines—most significantly with *Ms* launching in the US and *Cleo* in Australia. It's almost a Bechdel test of a song in that it's all about women, but unlike most other songs about female empowerment, it's not defined in relation to men.[4] In fact, the only reference to males comes in the line '. . . until I make my brother understand' in the third verse, which was the one Reddy added for the rerecording. This is one of the reasons why the song has never really gone away: there's nothing in it that's aged especially badly. It had already been Reddy's regular opening song, but now it moved to the other end of the set as it became her signature tune.

And the song was a sleeper: three months after its (re) release in its new, single-version form, it reached #1 in the US and won a Grammy for Best Female Pop Performance—at which Reddy delivered the immortal thank you 'to God,

---

4 In case you're not familiar with the test: cartoonist Alison Bechdel invented it in 1985 in her comic *Dykes to Watch Out For*. A character states: 'I have this rule, see. I only go to a movie if it satisfies three basic requirements. One, it has to have at least two women in it who, two, talk to each other about, three, something besides a man. Last movie I was able to see was *Alien*.'

because She makes everything possible'. If ever a line called for a mic drop, that was it.

Her third album was named after the song and was also a major hit, setting her up as one of the biggest middle-of-the-road stars of the seventies. Her professional career took a hit in the early eighties after her marriage ended (Reddy alleged that Wald blackballed her in the music industry, in which he remained a significant player), and she officially retired in 2002—although she returned to the stage again in 2012 and has been working ever since, including singing 'I Am Woman' at the 2017 Women's March protesting the inauguration of Donald Trump as president of the United States.

While the song was clearly deeply important to her, Reddy turned out not to be super protective of it: she performed it at the 1981 Miss World contest (dismissing critics with: 'Let them step forward and pay my rent and I'll stay home. What I'm doing is advertising a product I wouldn't use.'). Even more insanely, the song was later used for various commercials, including a Burger King advertisement in the US in which the lyrics were changed to 'I Am Man' to launch their Double Whopper. And, predictably, it has proved a popular cover for female artists, as well as the odd male.[5]

---

5 Tex Perkins—a man generally respected for being a goddamn national treasure—did a version that's borderline offensive in its half-arsedness for the 2007 compilation *No Man's Woman* (recorded with his unfortunately named backing band, the Ladyboyz). A far superior version appeared in 2015 to close out Judith Lucy's ABC series *Judith Lucy Is All Woman*, with a killer line-up of Deborah Conway, Killing Heidi's Ella Hooper, Vika and Linda Bull, Bertie Blackman, Liz Stringer, Jen Cloher, former Frente! singer Angie Hart, Rebecca Barnard of Rebecca's Empire and Justine Clarke, among others. It's absolutely worth your time.

Reddy never wrote another hit, and none of her other successes had anywhere near the cultural impact of 'I Am Woman'. However, that one song inspired a worldwide rise in awareness of feminist issues—and no-one's ever gonna keep it down again.

9

1971

Eagle Rock

Daddy Cool

*In which rock gets a bit less self-important
and a good deal more feathered*

Now listen: at the risk of boasting about Australia's avian superiority, our nation has some freakin' excellent eagles. Most obviously the wedge-tailed eagle,[1] mighty avenger of the skies, but also such classic air fowl as the letter-winged kite, the spotted harrier and the elegant nankeen. And that's before you get on to our kick-arse range of owls.[2]

---

1   As any ornithologist will tell you, the wedge-tailed eagle is named in honour of Wedge Antilles, the Rebel pilot who covered Luke Skywalker during the first Death Star run and landed the successful hit on the power regulator in the second Death Star's core.

2   There's no other place in the book to say this, so I'm taking the opportunity here: mopokes are awesome.

This, however, is not what 'Eagle Rock' is about.

According to an interview with the song's author, Ross Wilson, the tune that was to inspire generations of Australians to turn around at least once was inspired not by a bird but by a photograph.

'It came from a *Sunday Times* lift-out magazine A–Z on music,' he explained in the ABC's 2001 television series, *Long Way to the Top*. 'In the before-blues section there was an evocative photo of rural black Americans dancing in a dirt-poor juke joint—the caption was along the lines of *some negroes "cut the pigeon wing" and "do the eagle rock".*'

It's a song about dancing—and, like all classic songs about dancing, by dancing they mean sex. It also has a venerable lineage since, as Wilson noted, the eagle rock is a dance with a significant history behind it—you might accurately consider it to be here to stay.[3]

Musically it's based around a gloriously simple riff that anyone with a reasonable grasp of guitar can play (it's basically fingerpicking an A major chord). And, perhaps most importantly, it's a song that reportedly encourages men to get together and drop their pants. This makes sense if you remember that Daddy Cool was effectively a joke band, at least at first. All four members—singer/guitarist Wilson, lead guitarist Ross Hannaford, bassist Wayne Duncan and drummer Gary Young—were members of a proper serious group, the progressive rock project Sons of the Vegetal Mother. As the name suggests, this was obviously a far more commercially viable

---

3 It's name checked in 1913's 'Ballin' the Jack', the ragtime hit that contained the line 'Now do the Eagle Rock with style and grace'. Which, incidentally, is the best way to do it.

prospect than some silly little dance combo. Kids just *love* vegetables, right?

Since S of the VM contained up to eleven members at a time, it wasn't a great addition for multi-band gigs with limited time to get one act offstage and another on, so they tended to play happenings of various progressive rock kinds and put on their own shows, figuring it would be easiest to also perform as their own support act. Wilson, Hannaford, Duncan and Young shared a love of fifties doo-wop and decided they'd create a nice simple good-time band to run through a few party favourites before Mum's Vegetable Offspring did the important big boy music. Needing a name, they christened themselves 'Daddy Cool' after the B-side of 'Silhouettes' by the Rays, thereby showing their hip fifties-savvy blues credentials. (A credibility challenged by the cheesy cover version of that very song which Drummond had taken to #1 for seven weeks in 1971, right at the time the band was developing a name.)[4]

In a massive shock to the band and to literally no-one else, the fun, lighthearted and danceable side project turned out to be more popular with audiences than the theatrical multi-movement prog stylings of Motherson V-Gs. This fact was made crystal clear when both bands played at the three-day Myponga Pop Festival, held about sixty kilometres from Adelaide in the middle of a dusty paddock on the Fleurieu Peninsula, since one was an immediate hit with the audience and the other was a prog band. Footage of their triumphant

---

4 Drummond was one of several names that the Adelaide-born band Mississippi made novelty singles under before dropping their singer, expanding their line-up and becoming Little River Band.

performance would feature heavily in the film clip for 'Eagle Rock'.[5]

This was Daddy Cool's debut single, released in May 1971, and set a number of records: it held the #1 spot for longer than any other Australian single up to that time (ten weeks), was the biggest-selling Australian single of 1971, and was lead single for *Daddy Who? . . . Daddy Cool*, which was the first Australian album to hit #1 on the national charts and to sell more than 100,000 copies.[6]

The song and the band's cartoon character outfits also caught the attention of Elton John and his songwriting partner Bernie Taupin. It inspired John to write his own animal-referencing dance song about better rock-themed times of the past—and just in case anyone wasn't clear on the link that led to 'Crocodile Rock', Taupin wore a 'Daddy Who?' badge for his picture on the single's parent album, 1972's *Don't Shoot Me I'm Only the Piano Player.* And the influence didn't stop there: years later Benmont Tench of Tom Petty and the Heartbreakers would reminisce on a *My Favourite Album* podcast about Petty playing him Daddy Cool in his bedroom when the pair were teenagers in Gainesville, Florida.

The fact that Daddy Cool was never really intended to be a band might also explain why they lasted less than three years, splitting up in 1972 after two albums—although they then re-formed in 1974 and split again the following year,

---

5 Incidentally, the fairly disastrous festival was the first Australian performance for Black Sabbath, who headlined and enjoyed what seemed like a fairly unique experience for Myponga performers in that they were actually paid.

6 This isn't quite as magnificent an achievement as it sounds, since there wasn't really a national album chart before *Go-Set* started running one in May 1970, compiled by Ed Nimmervoll.

with various reunions and break-ups ever since. Wilson in particular seemed frustrated by the somewhat limiting format of Daddy Cool and explored more expansive sonic canvases, first with Mighty Kong and then the smooth, chart-topping sounds of Mondo Rock before embarking on a solo career.

It also heralded a move towards good-time boogie in Australian music, one embraced by pop star and TV host Billy Thorpe and his latest version of the Aztecs. He'd enjoyed massive hits during Beatlemania (including the impressive achievement of keeping the band off the top of the charts during its one and only Australian tour, thanks to his hit 'Poison Ivy'), but his fortunes had waned along with the sixties. The year after 'Eagle Rock' was released, Thorpe hit it big with what was to be his signature tune, the shuffling, eagle-evoking 'Most People I Know Think That I'm Crazy'— and, like Daddy Cool, his defining moment was to come at a music festival. This time it was Sunbury, where he was hailed as a conquering hero—at the same time as a young band called Skyhooks was being booed offstage.[7]

In 2001 'Eagle Rock' was voted the second-greatest Australian song of all time in the APRA seventy-fifth anniversary poll, pipped by 'Friday On My Mind'—which you already know, assuming that you're reading the book in order.[8] It was also adopted by numerous ball-fleets of the sport-making arts, some sensible (the West Coast Eagles) and some not (the Sydney Swans—the inappropriateness of which actually inspired a petition demanding the song be changed).

---

7 Foreshadowing.
8 You don't have to, by the way. There's no test . . . OR IS THERE?

But one of the weirdest legacies of the song happened far from the sports-hole, allegedly in the bar of the University of Queensland, where a group of students from the Mining and Metallurgical Association decided to drop their pants and dance to 'Eagle Rock'. This tradition extended to other Australian universities, including the Australian National University, which took action when a group of men surrounded some women and danced pantslessly at them to the song at an event in 2017—except that the action taken was against the playing of the song rather than against threatening sexual behaviour, which seemed to be the larger issue.

Daddy Cool still sort of exist, technically, and were all around to be inducted into the ARIA Hall of Fame in 2005. Sadly, both Hannaford and Duncan boogied into the great unknown in 2015.

But back in the seventies Wilson also started a sideline as a producer, which meant that he had a hand in helping another team of costume-loving Melbourne upstarts create some Australian classics of their own—as you'll discover presently.

10

1974

You Just Like Me Cos I'm Good in Bed

Skyhooks

*In which a bunch of costumed Melburnians become
public enemies one-through-five and prove that
the quickest route to popularity is to get
The Man to ban you*

Maybe it was the fact that two of their number ended up as cuddly mainstream media mainstays on commercial television. Maybe it was the deadening effect of their brief 1990 reunion. Maybe it was because they were so strongly connected with a specific place and time. Whatever the reason, Skyhooks are seldom given their due as Australian cultural pioneers, and they deserve a serious reappraisal.

As the previous chapters may have indicated,[1] Australia was gradually, if tentatively, starting to realise that it might just have a culture of its own. Cues were still taken from the US and Britain, but there were the first exciting rumblings of an independent nation. Most obviously, the election of Gough Whitlam in 1972 had ended twenty-three years of conservative rule in Australia and his bold, progressive, far-too-much-to-successfully-manage agenda was to come to an abrupt halt in November 1975. But for the first time since Ben Chifley, the nation had a prime minister with a strong vision of what an independent Australia might look like, as opposed to the Queen-worship of Robert Menzies,[2] or Harold Holt's 'all the way with LBJ' support for US intervention in Vietnam.

And while songwriter Greg Macainsh was looking at the studious, jeans-wearing prog and boogie bands that were boring him to tears around the Melbourne traps, he got to wondering why it was considered completely reasonable for American and English artists to name-check locations in their songs—Soho, Detroit, Memphis, Waterloo—but barely any Australian artists were doing so. As he started putting Skyhooks together, he was determined that they would be different.

So while the band's music owed much to American rock'n'roll and their heavily costumed look was inspired by the explosion of glam rock in Britain, their songs were proudly Melbourne-based, with titles like 'Carlton (Lygon

---

1   You really do have to read this in order to get the whole impact. This wasn't just flung together willy-nilly, you know.

2   That's the House of Windsor monarch, not the theatrical British rock band. Their first album didn't come out until 1973 in any case.

Street Limbo)', 'Balwyn Calling' and 'Toorak Cowboy'. This was a genuinely big step towards overcoming what the writer A.A. Phillips had identified as the 'cultural cringe' in a 1950 essay, the term coined to describe Australia's bizarre and damaging inferiority complex with regards to its own ideas, identity and, especially, art—a theme touched on by Donald Horne in his wryly titled (and often misunderstood) 1964 classic, *The Lucky Country*.

Of course, the idea that Australia had an issue with its own identity was not new. Henry Lawson had railed against this back in 1894, prefacing his *Short Stories in Prose and Verse* with a screed that included the observation:

> The Australian writer, until he gets a 'London hearing', is only accepted as an imitator of some recognized English or American author; and, as soon as he shows signs of coming to the front, he is labelled 'The Australian Southey,' 'The Australian Burns,' or 'The Australian Bret Harte,' and lately, 'The Australian Kipling.' ... But mark! As soon as the Southern writer goes 'home' and gets some recognition in England, he is 'So-and-So, the well-known Australian author whose work has attracted so much attention in London lately'; and we first hear of him by cable, even though he might have been writing at his best for ten years in Australia.

And this must have been enormously comforting for subsequent bands like the Go-Betweens and the Saints, secure in the knowledge that they were merely following in a proud and well-established tradition of Australian artists being contemptuously ignored in their homeland until after the British press or American audiences confirmed their value.

Interestingly, the northern hemisphere's Australia—known locally as Canada—suffers from an almost identical cultural malady, and while they don't have a pithy name for it like we do, they make up for it by creating derogatory terms for governmental attempts to promote Canadian culture. For example, the compulsory blocs of Canadian-only music promoted on radio from the seventies onwards were derisively termed 'the beaver hour', even though only 35 to 40 per cent of Canadian music is specifically about beavers.[3]

But enough of cringes and amphibious rodents; back to Skyhooks.

Less than three months after the band's line-up had solidified with Macainsh, drummer Freddie Strauks, guitarists Red Symons and Bob 'Bongo' Starkie and finally frontman Shirley Strachan (replacing original singer Steve Hill, who quit after the band were booed offstage at the 1974 Sunbury Pop Festival at which Billy Thorpe and the Aztecs made such an impression with their jeans and prog-flavoured boogie), Skyhooks went into the studio to cut their debut album, produced by the jeans-clad boogie-progger Ross Wilson, he of Daddy Cool.[4] And it was to be the definitive Australian album of the era, painting a portrait of life in the inner city that was as much a critique as a celebration.

The sex and drug references in Macainsh's lyrics led to six of the ten songs from *Living In The 70's* being banned from Australian commercial radio. And thus Skyhooks was

---

3　All albums by Styx, Anne Murray and Wolf Parade are entirely and exclusively about beavers. FACT.

4　See how it all fits together?

to learn a lesson that many other grateful artists would learn: heavy-handed censorship can be incredibly lucrative.[5]

There's been a very convincing argument made that the defining event that turned hip hop music from a niche music style to the dominant popular musical form in the US was the introduction of parental warning stickers warning about bad language and anti-social themes. Turns out that young people aren't dissuaded from listening when albums come out with a nice clear indicator that this is a record of which their parents will not approve.

The smut and sleaze of the lyrics also made them the perfect adversary for the clean-cut chart-topping pop music of fellow Melburnians Sherbert, led by the perma-grinning Daryl Braithwaite;[6] Sherbert were the clean-cut Beatles to Skyhooks' dangerously decadent glam rock Stones.

And this was all catnip to rebellious young music fans, who sought the album out because of the controversy, and thus Skyhooks set a new record for Australian music sales: over 225,000 copies of the album sold between release and the end of 1975.

'You Just Like Me Cos I'm Good in Bed' neatly summed up Skyhooks' other greatest quality: they loved taking the piss. It's a one-joke song on a record that came alive on stage, but it's also smirkingly subversive: the much-repeated title is welded to a premise about the singer being forced into sex

---

5 In fact, getting banned is a great way to prove your cultural cachet. Frankie Goes to Hollywood's 'Relax' only went to #1 in the UK in 1984, months after release, because BBC1 DJ Mike Read took it off air having noticed that it was clearly about hot gay sex.

6 . . . who turns up again in chapter 34, as it happens.

fifteen times a week in a gender reversal of rock music's familiar narrative of sexual pursuit, typically represented by a lascivious male protagonist pursuing a grimly compliant female. It's sold via Strachan's winking delivery, but it hasn't exactly aged well—there's a reason why Missy Higgins did some editing for her jaunty 2005 cover of the song,[7] wisely leaving out the reference to getting raped every weekend.

But the song did mark one of the most important developments in Australian music history: at 11 am on 19 January 1975,[8] it became the very first song played on the air by the brand-new Sydney-based youth network Double J, in an act of defiance intended to show The Man just where he could stick his ban. As Double J producer Ron Moss told Dr Liz Guiffre for her 2015 Whitlam Institute paper, it was 'the perfect launch song, it was a bit naughty, and something that would never get played on Australian radio'.

And as you will see, Double J was to be a little bit important in just about everything that was to come.

---

7 The cover by the then-unknown Higgins, incidentally, was commissioned by Triple J to mark the station's thirtieth anniversary.
8 If Triple J needed a new not-Australia-Day date for the Hottest 100 broadcast, then declaring that the date is actually the nearest barbecue-friendly Saturday to the first date of broadcast would give a reasonable amount of cover without making any dramatic changes to the current process. Just saying.

11

1975

It's a Long Way to the Top (If You Wanna Rock'n'Roll)

AC/DC

In which rock unambiguously becomes the sound of Australia, and a mythology is created

When the Easybeats were changing the face of Australian music, two people were paying especially close attention: George Young's little brothers Malcolm and Angus.

They witnessed the attention their sibling enjoyed from uniquely close quarters, since their house was occasionally under siege from fans—on one occasion Angus even had to climb over the back fence to get into his own home after police assumed he was a fan and shooed him away—and presumably reached the same conclusion as generations of homely men before and since: *If I play the guitar, I will get attention from girls.*

And it turned out they were good at playing guitar—very good, in fact. It came as a lovely surprise to George when he returned from the UK in the early seventies and heard the band Angus and Malcolm had created, named after the electricity warning on their mother's sewing machine. The boys weren't great, but they unambiguously had *something*.

Despite the meat-and-potatoes rock AC/DC was soon to define, they actually started off as a glam band in the Skyhooks mould. In fact, the schoolboy outfit Angus Young wore was but one of a range of costumes the group adopted at various times, as they went through multiple line-up changes before becoming the lean rock machine that took over the world.[1] You can hear the competent but tentative early band on the sole single recorded with original vocalist Dave Evans, 'Can I Sit Next to You, Girl?', but it's mainly instructive to illustrate the evolution that took place in the year between that and 'It's a Long Way to the Top'. This was mainly due to the arrival of one Ronald Belford Scott, better known by the nickname 'Bon', who had been working through many of Australia's third-tier rock acts.[2] He was initially concerned that the brothers were too young for a singer of his experience, while they were concerned Scott was too old for their youthful rock energy. Thankfully, however, their mutual reservations proved short-lived.

The song's parent album, *TNT*, appeared in December 1975 and was in many ways the first 'real' AC/DC album. Scott had

---

1 Among the members who passed through the Dacca was former Masters Apprentices sticksman Colin Burgess. ARTFUL JIGSAW PUZZLE.
2 Including an Adelaide band called Fraternity, who replaced him with a singer who'll appear in two chapters' time . . .

only joined the band two months before they recorded *High Voltage* in November 1974, released the following February, on which he had hastily added lyrics to music that was already completed by the brothers Young. But things moved fast after Scott's arrival: he streamlined their sound, provided the band with a frontman who was the charismatic equal of their dervish guitarist and gave the band a lyrical point of view that was to define them long after his tragic death.

The other big changes between *TNT* and *High Voltage* were that the band settled on the rhythm section that was to define the Scott era—bassist Mark Evans and drummer Phil Rudd—and Malcolm and Angus Young set in place their permanent guitar dynamic. Previously there had been a degree of fluidity to the Youngs' partnership, but *TNT* set the parameters that were to be followed from that moment on: Malcolm played rhythm guitar, Angus played lead, and that was that.

From the opening chords, *TNT* marked an enormous leap forwards for the band—and they knew it. The title track, 'High Voltage' and 'The Jack' all remained in the live set for the next thousand years,[3] but the indisputable masterpiece was the agenda-setting opening track: 'It's a Long Way to the Top (If You Wanna Rock'n'Roll)'. As a showcase of what AC/DC now was and would be for decades to come, this was a masterclass in every regard. The driving force is Malcolm Young's pumping chords, which gives Evans loads of room to throw in little runs and riffs on bass (which Vanda and Young turned down in the mix: there was a definite Young-bias in all

---

3 Confusingly, 'High Voltage' is on *TNT* rather than the album of the same name. Released in June 1975, it was recorded with George Young on bass and Tony Currenti on drums, prior to Evans and Rudd joining.

the albums that the duo produced for the band), while Rudd sits just ever so slightly behind the beat, giving the song a swagger that perfectly complements Bon's vocal.

It's also remarkable to note that Angus Young, the planet's premier histrionic guitar wizard, is incredibly restrained on the song. There's not really a guitar solo per se, just a series of tasty licks acting more as punctuation than as text. But the song did have one stroke of utter genius that more than made up for the lack of frantic fretwork: bagpipes.[4] The Youngs hailed from Glasgow, while fellow Scot Scott was born in Forfar and lived in Kirriemuir before his family moved to Australia, so the idea of pipes being a stirring extra element to give the song some oomph was etched into the band members' cultural DNA. It was George Young's idea, George having been told that Bon had played in a pipe band as a teenager. And it was a great idea, except for one fairly important problem: Bon didn't play bagpipes in said band, in which he had been a drummer. Because he was Bon Scott, though, he decided that the obvious solution was to learn to play bagpipes. So that's exactly what he did—and he played them live for the next few years, too, until he put his pipes down onstage too close to the audience, who promptly ripped them apart in what seems like a very natural fight-or-flight response to being confronted with bagpipes.[5]

Music aside, there are Scott's lyrics, which are among the most meta in rock'n'roll history: a song by a working rock

---

4 Please note that this is possibly the only sentence ever written that contains both 'stroke of utter genius' and 'bagpipes'.

5 This is not the only Australian classic to feature a bagpipe break for no obvious reason: you'll meet another such song in chapter 28.

band about how much it sucks to be in a working rock band, performed with utter conviction and triumphant, defiant joy. AC/DC might have been dismissed in certain circles as being dumb music for dumb people, but this was searingly clever stuff.

The song was accompanied by a perfect video clip that had been knocked up for *Countdown*: the band performing the song on the back of a truck edging its way down Melbourne's Swanston Street with the massed pipes of the Rats of Tobruk marching with them. It harkened back to a more innocent, less public-safety-obsessed time, as every band who attempted to shoot a similar clip would discover to their considerable legal chagrin.

'It's a Long Way' was the band's biggest Australian hit, cracking the top 10 (a feat it wouldn't accomplish again until after Scott's death by misadventure on 19 February 1980).[6] It's also been covered literally dozens of times, by everyone from W.A.S.P. to the Wiggles.

Despite this being one of the band's signature songs, AC/DC didn't touch it live after Bon's death. There are two schools of thought as to why this is: one is that new frontman Brian Johnson felt that it was Bon's signature song and refused to sing it as a sign of respect to his fallen predecessor. Another, more mundane explanation is that bagpipes are a bastard to tune (the band played the song in A major live, but on record they're tuned up half a step to B flat major to match the intonation of the pipes) and going through fiddly tuning at every gig was more trouble than it was worth.

---

6 The official finding was 'acute alcohol poisoning', but 'passing out drunk in a car on a below-freezing London night' is equally accurate.

In any case, the song was and remains the definitive ode to the rockin' arts and was the tune that set AC/DC's course to world domination, as well as cementing Australia as the true home of no-nonsense rock.

Speaking of which, there was another band getting ready to change the world up in Brisbane: and, buddy, that's a lot harder than it looks . . .

12

1976

(I'm) Stranded

The Saints

In which punk music gets invented in inner-city Brisbane . . . almost

In 1976 punk was invented. And it very, very nearly happened first in Australia—but, importantly, didn't.

Sure, there are people who will argue sniffily that the MC5 or Iggy and the Stooges or the New York Dolls were the first punk band, or that the *real* first punk record was the Kinks' 'You Really Got Me' or Ritchie Valens' 'La Bamba' or any number of other tiresome theories that fall under the exam-ready umbrella: 'But ultimately what *is* punk, really? Discuss.' But anyone who attempts to embark on such a conversation is not your friend and does not have your best interests at heart.

Punk was invented in 1976, although it was happening simultaneously in multiple sites around the world: in the UK, in Germany, in Australia and in the US, where their first punk single rather annoyingly came out before Australia's and thereby ruined what would otherwise have been a perfect narrative for this chapter.

See, any time you read about '(I'm) Stranded' you'll immediately be told that it was Australia's first independent single and that the Saints—and, by extension, Australia—beat all the UK punk bands. And that's sort of true, as it goes: '(I'm) Stranded' was released on the band's own Fatal Records label in September 1976. For context, the first UK punk single— the Damned's 'New Rose'—came out in October, the Sex Pistols' 'Anarchy in the UK' in November and the Clash's debut 'White Riot' was released in March 1977.

The reason that everyone makes the point that Australia beat England to punk is partly because we still have a massive inferiority complex when it comes to the motherland and thus overstate the importance of every tiny, meaningless victory over the Brits, but mainly because the first unambiguous punk single—'Blitzkrieg Bop' by the Ramones—beat the Saints by over six months.

It's also important to qualify the claim that the Saints were the first band to release an 'independent' single in Australia. Yes, it was made without the help of a record company, as the band paid a vinyl-pressing plant to press copies of the single, but that idea hadn't occurred to them from out of nowhere. Guitarist Ed Kuepper had worked as the North Queensland sales rep for Astor Records, which had run a sideline in 'custom pressing'. Hobbyists from the hinterlands would send in tapes of their country and western recordings, which Astor would press into singles in its own plant. The artists would then put these limited-run singles into regional jukeboxes and revel in being a tiny, very local-ised celebrity. Kuepper realised that he could do the same with his rock'n'roll band—although, perhaps inconveniently, he only had this revelation after he'd left the job.

It's also worth noting that Australia's punk sound was being invented simultaneously in Sydney, and if there'd been a month's delay at the pressing plant then history would be celebrating Radio Birdman's *Burn My Eye* EP as Australia's first punk record. Mind you, Brisbane had a better claim to it: Sydney was a cosmopolitan city with a thriving music scene; Brisbane, meanwhile, was effectively a police state. By 2017, of course, those situations would be largely reversed.[1]

The Sydney live scene was pumping in the seventies, as the pub rock explosion started to take off. By contrast, gigs were hard to come by in Brisbane as the government of Joh Bjelke-Petersen brought in repressive laws that treated gatherings of young people as though they were violent protests requiring brutal police action—most of the Saints gigs were at parties and in squats (and drummer Ivor Hay's house, which they named Club 76), since live venues were thin on the ground. When it came time for the band to relocate to the UK, it

---

1 Seriously, go out to see some bands in Brisbane's Fortitude Valley. Then go out and try to find any bands at all in Kings Cross or Darlinghurst. The Sydney lockout laws pretty much killed the live scene—but they did great things for those plucky property developers who really contribute so very, very much to our national culture. Shine on, you greedy diamonds!

wasn't like it was a hard decision: the music scene in Brisbane pretty much guaranteed an arrest and a likely beating.

It's not hard to see why no record company was interested in releasing the single. At a time when bands like Sherbert and Little River Band were dominating the charts, this was a furious slab of Kuepper's distorted guitar and Chris Bailey's laconic, near-spoken vocals over the rhythm section of Hay and bassist Kym Bradshaw (whose tenure in the band would be brief; he turned up in time to record this single and the first album and then left, to be replaced by Algy Ward).

Not only is the sound pure punk rock, the subject matter is too: Bailey's lyrics paint a picture of disaffected youth feeling alienated from their society and everyone in it, and the video of the band performing in an abandoned house just added to the mystique. (The clip was directed by Russell Mulcahy, then a cameraman at Channel 7 and later to enjoy worldwide acclaim as the director of *Razorback* and *Highlander* among many, many films; he became the go-to video clip director of the 1980s, directing almost all of Duran Duran's video clips during their imperial period.) The opening shot showed Ivor Hay kicking the door open, which was rich in new-generation symbolism, and a shot of the scrawled '(I'm) Stranded, The Saints' above the fireplace would become the cover of their debut album.[2]

The band sent copies of the single out for review, but it was ignored by pretty much everyone—except, amazingly, Jonh

---

2   Despite the band being from Brisbane, the video was actually shot in the inner-Sydney suburb of Darlinghurst. An abandoned terrace house with band-themed graffiti in Darlo would still sell for about $2.4 million at the time of writing.

Ingham,[3] who declared it 'Single of This and Every Week' in the UK music magazine *Sounds*.

His gushing review was remarkable enough, but the band was about to get even luckier. As punk took off in Britain, EMI was feeling on the back foot after undergoing a very embarrassing parting of the ways with the Sex Pistols. Despite having signed the Pistols to a two-year deal and releasing the aforementioned debut single, the band's public behaviour—especially, but not solely, enthusiastic swearing on live television—made them too hot to handle. Capitulating to public pressure (including bans of 'Anarchy in the UK' on TV and radio, and packers at the pressing plant refusing to touch Sex Pistols records), EMI dropped the band—who signed briefly to A&M a few months later, and then to Virgin when A&M also got cold feet—and therefore desperately needed a new band to burnish its tarnished punk cred. Hence the UK office informed its reps in Sydney, who had never heard of the Saints and had zero interest in punk music, to get to Brisbane post-haste and sign them to a three-album deal, effectively unheard.

Sadly, the dream of making the Saints EMI's new punk saviours didn't quite come off. For one thing, the band was never really punk so much as a garage band with a love of soul and R&B (as their fearsome covers of Motown classics like 'River Deep, Mountain High' would demonstrate), and when they arrived in London it was to an enthusiastic record company showing off 'Saints suits' (green shirts, spiky hair)

---

3 Not a typo: that's his name. Maybe there was a touch of parochialism at work, though, since while he was working in the UK (and had begun writing in the US under the tutelage of legendary music critic Robert Christgau), he was Australian-born. Maybe he saw the postmark and got homesick enough to give the single a spin.

with which it planned to market the band, a look which was immediately vetoed by the horrified Brisbanites.

That soured relations with the label, and by the time the band came to make its second album, 1977's *Eternally Yours* (led by the magnificent brass-section-sporting single 'Know Your Product'), EMI's ardour for the Saints had cooled completely. They were dropped after 1978's equally excellent *Prehistoric Sounds* failed to set the charts alight, although by that stage Kuepper and Bailey's working relationship had soured; the former quit the band and returned to Australia to explore a more jazzy musical furrow with the Laughing Clowns before embarking on an excitingly idiosyncratic solo career.[4] Bailey still fronts the Saints, through a vast number of different line-ups and records of varying degrees of necessity. But those first three albums—and especially the debut single—changed the face of Australian music.

The sound hasn't especially dated either, and the sentiment is as timeless as ever, which might explain why '(I'm) Stranded' is still covered by young bands to this day. That door the Saints kicked open never closed again—as you shall see in the chapters to come.

---

4 The Laughing Clowns also recorded a song entitled 'Eternally Yours' which, like 'Ghost of an Ideal Wife' and a bunch of Kuepper's solo material, was absolutely on the longlist for this book, damn it.

13

1978

Khe Sanh

Cold Chisel

*In which Australia's complicated relationship with Vietnam,
and the entire geographical region in which our continent
sits, is summed up in four toe-tapping minutes*

Despite the band being best known and revered as the
nation's most uncompromising rock'n'roll animals, the most
beloved Cold Chisel songs are not by any stretch the hardest-
rockingest ones.

'Flame Trees' is a heartfelt ballad, 'Breakfast at Sweethearts'
is a slow reggae, and 'Khe Sanh'—arguably their masterpiece
and most timeless composition—is unambiguously a country
tune. From the jaunty rhythm to the honky-tonk piano of its
composer Don Walker and the tasty countrified licks of guitarist Ian Moss, the only thing that stops it being something

Slim Dusty could have happily covered was Jimmy Barnes's howling, urgent vocal.

Cold Chisel was never just a rock band. It was formed in Adelaide by a weird amalgam of individuals bringing their influences and experiences from all over the planet. There was the studious Queensland-born Walker, about to attempt to put the band on hold to complete his physics studies, Alice Springs blow-in Moss and Polish immigrant Les Kaczmarek on bass (replaced a year later by Adelaide local Phil Small).[1] The final pieces of the puzzle were singer Jimmy Barnes (born James Swan)—a deeply troubled Scots immigrant who'd grown up on the wrong side of the tracks in the housing trust tracts of Elizabeth, the northern suburbs' shitburg that was once meant to be South Australia's second city but actually became a dumping ground for immigrants and poor people— and drummer Steve Prestwich, whose family had moved to Elizabeth from Liverpool only a few years earlier.

And there was alchemy in that mixture of musicians,[2] although the clincher was that Barnes (who'd briefly been the frontman of a band called Fraternity, when its leader singer Bon Scott quit to be in that group from chapter 11) could sing like a demon. It was his supernatural vocal power

---

1 Kaczmarek died of liver failure in 2008, but his legacy lives on in the stands at every Port Power game: he co-wrote the AFL team's theme song.

2 There's nowhere else to ram this impressive fact, so: it's worth noting that while the band initially relied on the songwriting of Don Walker, it is one of the very few bands in history where every single member wrote at least one signature hit. While Walker was responsible for 'Khe Sanh', 'Breakfast at Sweethearts' and the lion's share of the band's material, 'You Got Nothing I Want' was by Barnes, Prestwich wrote 'Forever Now' and 'When the War Is Over' (and the music that became 'Flame Trees', after Walker wrote lyrics to the song), Moss contributed 'Bow River' and Small gave the band 'My Baby'.

that transformed the band from their prog-lite roots as an Adelaide-gigging cover band named Orange into Australia's most dangerous live act.

What's especially amazing is that 'Khe Sanh' wasn't the culmination of a band finding its feet and capturing a uniquely Australian story articulating our nation's troubled relationship with South-East Asia—it was an early Don Walker number from the very first Cold Chisel album.[3] More specifically, it was far and away the best song on what was a fairly inauspicious debut.

The band had developed an enviable live reputation by the time it was signed to WEA in 1976 and started work on its debut album in 1978. And, as with so many great Australian bands, Chisel struggled to capture the power of its live shows in the sterile confines of the studio, not especially helped by the fact that Walker laboured over his songs, which often took months to complete. However, with 'Khe Sanh' that meticulousness was entirely warranted. In seven impression-istic verses Walker portrayed a haunted Vietnam veteran unable to settle after returning to Australia, suffering from what we'd now diagnose as post-traumatic stress disorder and trying to numb himself with hard drugs and sex tourism. Walker had based the song on young men he'd known who returned from Vietnam as very different men from the ones who had left, most notably an unnamed neighbour from Grafton and

---

3 Odd fact: the model on the front cover of Chisel's debut album was one Micki Braithwaite, then-wife of Daryl—about whom you'll learn more in the chapter on 'The Horses'. In later life she worked as a personal assistant to media heavyweights Alan Jones and Eddie McGuire, but tragically lost a short battle with cancer in 2007.

Adelaide guitarist Rick Morris,[4] but the narrator of the song could have been anyone, so universal was the experience.

And there's nothing celebratory about the song, and certainly no suggestion of great valour or pride in service. The Battle of Khe Sanh raged from January to July 1968, but wasn't even that big a deal for Australia—the RAAF supplied a small amount of air support with Canberra bombers from the Number 2 Squadron, but otherwise it was almost exclusively a US operation, significant enough to a) almost become the US's second use of a nuclear device in wartime, which thankfully didn't happen, and b) to be name-checked in Bruce Springsteen's 'Born in the USA'. However, Australian combat engineers—known as sappers—did have the hellish task of clearing the area of mines after the siege ended, a point made in the opening line of the song.

One other big advantage to the tune was that it was also, as Walker announced to the band, 'really easy' to play, since it was basically the same chord progression over and over again. Easy, that is, provided you weren't Barnes, who had to learn a short story's worth of lyrics in the space of an afternoon before giving the song its first public performance. Originally it was far faster, turning the lyrics into a tongue twister, before the band realised that it worked best slowed down and given a country twang.

The recording—produced by Peter Walker, who also contributed some guitar to the track—has been tweaked over the years. The original version was edited down without the piano intro

---

4 Morris was best known for playing with the rock band Salvation Air Force—not to be confused with the Canadian Christian outfit that also inexplicably and mistakenly thought this was a good name for a band.

and a new lead vocal for the US release of the *East* album in 1980, and Barnes rerecorded the vocal again in 1985 for release on the *Radio Songs: A Best of Cold Chisel* compilation—and that's the version that gets played on radio to this day.

Given the song's resonant place in Australian culture it's bizarre to remember that 'Khe Sanh' wasn't remotely a hit. It only reached #41 on the national charts as Chisel's debut single (although it did reach #4 in the South Australian charts, back in the days when such things existed), although this was principally because the song was banned from radio for containing references to sex and drugs, with the line referencing open legs and closed minds apparently too inflammatory for the delicate sensibilities of the radio listeners of 1978. With commercial radio closed to them, that left Double J as the only station to playlist the song.[5] That said, there was some vindication of the lowly chart placing in 2011, when it was rereleased and roared all the way to, um, #40.

Most importantly, it presented Don Walker as a songwriter with a rare skill for telling complex stories—specifically Australian stories—in a few well-chosen lines. He'd become more economical in future compared with the seven verses here, but he'd never lose that eye for detail.

It wasn't the only Australian song to explore the damage the Vietnam War did to Australia—as you will see in a few chapters' time—but it was among the best, and certainly the one most often sung by drunk men hugging one another. That's a weird and special thing.

---

5 The Js love for Cold Chisel might seem a little incongruous now, but it was utterly sincere. In fact, Chisel's 'Never Before' was the first song Double J played to mark its switch from AM to FM in 1980.

14

1979

Shivers

The Boys Next Door

In which a teenager's snide joke becomes the lovelorn anthem for a generation and launches the career of our dark poet laureate

In 1975 a Melbourne teenager named Rowland S. Howard wrote a two-chord song for his short-lived punk band, the Young Charlatans. It was a satire on his high school classmates who were mooning and spooning over their tragic teen romances, and Howard found their confected emotion deeply tiresome and insincere—beginning with the narrator shrugging that he'd commit suicide, if it better suited his style.

As performed by Howard and co. the song was a droll, snide backhander at these overdramatic adolescent romantics who read *Romeo and Juliet* as an instruction manual rather than a cautionary tale. And then Howard learned a hard lesson: sarcasm really doesn't translate in song. What was intended as a sly joke has become one of the most covered Australian songs ever, thanks in part to its simplicity but mostly to the melodramatic way in which it was eventually recorded—to its composer's initial horror and eventual begrudging acceptance. And that was largely because of the man whose performance was to define the song: a chap named Nicholas Edward Cave.

Howard met Cave when the latter's band, the Boys Next Door, were building a reputation in Melbourne's inner-city venues. The two forged a quintessential male friendship, in that it was based on a good deal of rivalry. Both, for example, were in love with singer/songwriter Anita Lane; Rowland had been her pal all through high school, but it was Cave who swept her off her feet. This could be seen as a forerunner of their parallel careers: Howard would be admired—rightly—for being objectively special, but Cave would inspire genuine worship.

Despite some misgivings about joining a band where he wasn't the primary songwriter, Howard became the second guitarist alongside Mick Harvey in the Boys Next Door and immediately changed the band from adequate to electrifying. You can hear the transformation on the band's only album, 1979's *Door, Door*. Side one, without Howard, is perfectly decent new wave that would probably be termed 'punk-funk' by more annoying contemporary writers, while side two, with Howard, points towards what the band would achieve after their move to the UK and their transformation into the Birthday Party.

Despite this being Cave's band, the album's only single was also the song that closed the album: 'Shivers'. But if the Young Charlatans played it as a joke, the Boys Next Door laid on the amateur dramatics. For a start, there's the funereal pace. There's the addition of Cave's stately piano. There's Howard's new way-up-the-neck guitar line, whose two-note movement was possibly meant ironically but actually sounds appropriately power-ballady. And, most of all, there's Cave's show-stopping vocal performance. It's odd that Howard didn't sing lead himself, since he'd performed it live at Boys Next Door gigs (with Cave on borderline-inept rhythm guitar), but in the studio Cave stepped up instead.[1] His stentorian delivery turned the chorus from a snide slam mocking an inamorata so vain that she's practically a mirror into a poignant cry of unrequited love. It might have been meant as a parody of love-gone-wrong songs, but played straight it was a perfect—indeed, genuinely beautiful—example of the genre. It's Cave's sheer commitment that made the song work; in lesser hands the permanent shiver would sound downright ridiculous if sent running down the narrator's spi-yi-yi-yi-yi-yi-yiyiyiyine—but Cave sold it beautifully.

Speaking of committing, the low-budget performance video is notable for Cave emoting wildly in the foreground while the rest of the band look distinctly embarrassed in the background. Harvey, bassist Tracy Pew and drummer Phill Calvert look

---

1   There have been multiple explanations as to why Cave sang it rather than Howard, which can be read as a barometer of the Howard/Cave relationship at the time. When they've been at odds, the story was that Cave demanded that he sing it; when things have been more friendly, Howard agreed that it made sense since Cave was the singer. Either way, it was the right decision—although the Howard-sung live version on 2014's *Six Strings That Drew Blood*, a posthumous compilation of Howard's work, is a rough gem.

sheepish in their attempt to exude studied indifference, but the impossibly youthful Howard looks downright mortified.

'Shivers' was by no stretch a hit and troubled the charts not at all, but by the time the song was actually released in Australia the band was already way beyond caring about such things; they'd moved to London, rechristened themselves the Birthday Party, upped sticks to the cheaper and more accepting Berlin, and left the Boys Next Door behind in favour of a groundbreaking musical experiment that ended two albums and a scant few years later as the creative and chemical differences between Howard and Cave became insurmountable.

Howard went on to play in Crime and the City Solution and form These Immortal Souls, while Cave and Harvey created the loose affiliation that became Nick Cave and the Bad Seeds. The Birthday Party, the Boys Next Door and 'Shivers' seemed destined to become footnotes—except that 'Shivers' refused to die.

First it appeared on the soundtrack of Richard Lowenstein's cult movie *Dogs in Space*, set around the 'little band' scene of Melbourne, both in its original version and in a laconic onscreen cover performed by Marie Hoy and Friends. The weirdest version, however, came in 1992, when pub rockers the Screaming Jets did a somewhat countrified cover of it on their second album *Tear of Thought* and turned it into an unexpected top 20 chart hit. Given that the Jets looked very much like the sort of people who would have beaten up Howard in high school, this seemed especially incongruous.

In recent years Courtney Barnett released her own version as a special seven-inch single for Jack White's First Man

Records in 2016, while the US indie supergroup Divine Fits did their own version on their 2012 debut, *A Thing Called Divine Fits*. For what was intended as a two-chord joke, it's a song with an astonishingly long reach.

For a long time Howard all but disowned the song, seething that people misunderstood the intent and Cave had compounded the insult with his over-the-top performance. But as time went on, and as the ruptured friendship between the two was mended, his opinion of the song softened. By the time of Howard's tragic early death from liver cancer on 30 December 2009, 'Shivers' had periodically returned to his live set in an arrangement that split the difference between his sarcastic early performances and the Boys Next Door's stately version. By the end, however, it was left to the ages.

'Thankfully people have stopped calling for it in concerts,' he told Fairfax's Simon Sweetman that October, in one of his final interviews.

> I have just tried, perhaps finally successfully, to divorce myself from the song. It's impossible for me to re-create what I was trying to do when I wrote that song so whilst I can see that people have an attachment to it, I don't. I feel like, when I did use to do it in shows, I was doing a cover of some song that had been around forever. And I guess that is a strange way to feel about a song you wrote, so yeah, I am happy to not have to do it these days. I don't like to think about it.[2]

As the song said, he had no room for cheap regrets.

---

2   There's nowhere else to put this, so here will do: some Australian music festival—Meredith, specifically—should institute an annual Australian classic cover which all performers are encouraged to include in their set. 'Shivers' would be a perfect option for the first year, then 'My Pal' by God, then 'At First Sight' by the Stems . . .

15

1980

Shaddap You Face

Joe Dolce Musical Theatre

*In which Australia creates a worldwide comedy
accent monster*

In the 1970s Carlton was the epicentre of a vibrant artistic
scene. Musically it had spawned the likes of Skyhooks, the
Sports, Jo Jo Zep and the Falcons, and Ross Wilson's bands
Daddy Cool and Mondo Rock, among many others, but rock
was only part of the story. Independent theatre La Mama had
opened in 1967 and the Pram Factory had followed a couple
of years later. Community radio station Triple R started at
RMIT, where the art school was also housed, and a wealth of
experimental and cabaret venues popped up amid the established live music rooms. And one of the performers therein,
rubbing shoulders with the likes of the Captain Matchbox

Whoopee Band and Dada experimentalist Syd Clayton, was a blow-in from Ohio named Joe Dolce.

Dolce had performed music theatre and cabaret in his home country before moving to Australia in 1978 with his then-wife, Zandie Acton,[1] and was soon ensconced in the local scene with his live show, Joe Dolce Musical Theatre, in which he would take on various personas for his songs. At first he was something of a provocateur: Australia's less-than-stellar treatment of immigrants, particularly refugees, became immediately apparent to him, and inspired his first Australian single, 'Boat People', but his earnest political material did nothing commercially. What people did respond to, however, was a character called 'Giuseppe', a well-intentioned immigrant from Sicily trying to do right by his family, despite their overbearing nature and broken English. It was a character Dolce could perform with confidence, being the eldest son of Italian-American parents. One of Giuseppe's numbers was a playful little trifle based on his mother's admonitions about it not being so bad, the niceness of the current place, and reflecting on the importance of face-up-shaddapping.

It's incredibly easy to ignore the impact that Joe Dolce's greatest and only hit had, because it was the very epitome of the novelty song. The plot is simple and silly: a man looks back on his mother's advice about not being a troublemaker, and the kid grows up to be a big star who proceeds to sing about that very piece of advice in *the song he is playing right now*. It's a triumph of accent comedy postmodernism.

---

1 Sister of fashion designer Prue Acton. The marriage didn't last, but Dolce has been the creative and romantic partner of singer/artist Lin Van Hek pretty much ever since.

'Shaddap You Face' was recorded in 1980 and Dolce initially assumed that people would understand he was performing a character and not attempting to give a nuanced and sensitive portrayal of the immigrant experience, and also that he was obviously making a wry comment about stereotypes in the context of a cabaret performance. And when it very quickly became clear that no, no-one appreciated those subtleties at all but were still buying the single in vast, shed-sized amounts, he figured that was also fine.

He performed the song on *Countdown*, with Molly Meldrum miming the accordion in a pink muscle shirt, a weird beret and a pencil moustache. He went on *Top of the Pops* in the UK. He and his mandolin did the rounds of music shows and breakfast TV all over the planet.

Before you sneer that it has no place in this list, be advised that 'Shaddap You Face' held the record for the biggest-selling Australian single for decades. Depending on how you calculate it (whether digital sales count, for example), it still holds the record now.[2] It's estimated to have sold over 6 million copies worldwide, with almost half a million of those sold in Australia, where it comfortably topped the charts—a feat it also achieved in eleven other nations.

Weirdly enough, it appears that his home country understood the song's intent best of all. It was only a very minor hit in the US, but became a firm favourite on Dr Demento's

---

2 If you count downloads, the biggest-selling single by an Australian artist is either Kylie Minogue's 'Can't Get You Out of My Head' or 'Somebody That I Used to Know' by Gotye featuring Kimbra. The confusion is because sales are not calculated consistently in all places, which makes comparisons between territories and eras slightly rubbery.

nationally syndicated comedy and novelty record show, becoming one of his most popular songs of that year.

There were also multiple cover versions in several different languages.[3] Hell, it was even covered by Andrew Sachs in his *Fawlty Towers'* character of Manuel, which didn't exactly speak to the song's credentials as a respectful take on immigrant culture.

Lightning didn't strike twice, though. When Dolce realised that no-one was distinguishing between him and Giuseppe, he figured he'd keep giving the people what he assumed they wanted, and thus his follow-up singles were a cavalcade of zanily diminishing returns. First there was an in-character cover of Jimmy Soul's insipid 'If You Wanna Be Happy', followed by less-successful novelty songs like 'Pizza Pizza' and 'You Toucha My Car, I Breaka You Face': singles which he knew were pale copies of his hit, as well as also being completely bullshit songs in their own right.

'It was destroying my belief system, trying to conform to what the mass market understood "Shaddap You Face" to be about,' he told *The Guardian* in 2002. 'The general mass will always remember only the broadest strokes. If I had done that persona my whole life, people would have believed it was actually me.'

Wisely, as the units stopped shifting and with the world still failing to appreciate the myriad subtleties and layers of 'Shaddap You Face', Dolce chose to step back and concentrate on his theatrical and artistic work, funded by the proceeds of

---

3 Even British band EMF—responsible for the one-hit wonder 'Unbelievable'—covered it in the 1990s, although its version bore no relation to the original other than that both are audible.

his worldwide smash which still, bafflingly, enjoys airplay and use in commercials all over the globe to this day. And if Dolce didn't get a second bite of the accent-comedy apple, it spoke well of Australia that no-one else did either.

Subsequent attempts at three-chord singles based around people hilariously struggling with English didn't take off—not even that of Mark Mitchell's also-not-okay Greek character Con the Fruiterer[4]—who did his own godawful novelty single in 1989. Thankfully 'A Cuppla Days' peaked at #49 on the Australian charts before deservedly vanishing off the face of the earth.

And Dolce got a little defensive about the song from time to time, including during a fight with another Carlton superstar. As he rightly pointed out to *The Age* in 2005, supposedly in response to an earlier jibe from his old Carlton comrade Skyhook's Shirley Strachan about being a one-hit wonder: 'It wasn't a hit. It was a phenomenon. Better to have one phenomenon than 10 piddly little hits.'

Of course, it's possible to do both. And that's what happened in our next chapter.

---

4   In a rather less cringeworthy piece of comedy, Dolce appeared on an episode of *The Micallef P(r)ogram(me)* in 1998 performing a grammatically correct version of the song.

16

1981

Down Under

Men at Work

In which Australia celebrated being regarded as a cartoon to everyone else around the world

If there is a single song that most typifies Australia in the minds of damn near everyone on the planet, it's a perky little number about vomiting and stealth marketing of sandwich spreadables: Men at Work's 'Down Under'.

The quintet had formed in Melbourne when singer/ songwriter Colin Hay, who had emigrated to Australia as a teenager, met guitarist Ron Strykert. They started working on songs together, gradually accumulating the rhythm section of drummer Jerry Speiser and bassist John Rees, and the band's secret weapon in multi-instrumentalist Greg Ham, whom Hay had met at high school. They started gigging around

Melbourne and eventually became the highest-paid unsigned band on the circuit.

While record companies started sniffing around the band, they formed their own label to self-release their debut single, the pleasantly nondescript 'Keypunch Operator', about which no-one cared in 1980. Of more interest was the B-side, a far weirder song called 'Down Under'.

This original version was based around a sliding, jazzy bassline and a back-and-forth riff between Ham's flute and Strykert's guitar, with double-tracked vocals and a tempo about half that of the future single version. The chorus is still potent, but oddly monotone—and the jokey call-and-response bits in the verses did little to improve what seemed like a throwaway joke turned oh-so-zany novelty song. However, it was slated for a revisit after the band drew the attention of Columbia's Australian A&R manager Peter Karpin, who signed them to a deal. He was immediately rewarded with a #2 hit, 'Who Can It Be Now?', while producer Peter McIan took the stoned jam of 'Down Under' and performed some life-saving surgery: ripping out the bassline, stripping back the guitars, speeding up the tempo and driving Hay to deliver a vocal which jumped up the scale as the song went on, from muttering at the bottom of his range at the beginning of the song to belting out the third verse.

Although Australians took the song to heart as a celebration of our larrikin patriotism and keen passion for taking drugs in exotic locales,[1] Hay's take on the lyrics is rather more nuanced,

---

1   The 'zombie' in the first verse refers to particularly potent marijuana, while the 'den in Bombay' suggests the narrator was reclining in an opium haze. Or maybe just hanging out in Bombay with someone named Dennis.

noting the references to colonisation. (The Men weren't entirely sanguine about their country of origin, acknowledging that it was built on plunder, though that subtlety was largely over-shadowed by the reference to Vegemite sandwiches.)

'It's quite a dark song, actually,' Hay told *Songwriter Universe* in a February 2017 interview. 'People don't really pick up on that, which is not really my job to point out. It's not a song about waving a flag, it's really a song about the plundering . . . of the natural wealth of a country for short-term gain.'

The video clip was mainly shot in the sand dunes of Cronulla, south of Sydney, and the band enthusiastically dialled up the wackiness, thereby continuing the theme of 'Who Can It Be Now?' and giving the nascent MTV another clip to put on high rotation (as much because it had precious little else to play as for any particular fondness for the tune).

The song was a huge, inescapable hit. It topped the charts in the US, the UK, New Zealand, Denmark, Germany, Ireland, Switzerland and Italy, as well as—predictably—Australia, where it was #1 for nine weeks. The parent album, *Business as Usual*, was also a #1 smash. And its longevity was unprecedented: eighteen months after release it got a second lease on life when it became the unofficial soundtrack to *Australia II*'s historic win in the 1983 America's Cup.

However, the band did not really survive its success. A second album, *Cargo*, was another huge global smash when eventually released in 1983, though not quite to the extent of *Business as Usual*, and the internal discord was growing. Extensive touring didn't help, and when the band reconvened in 1984 Hay informed Rees and Speiser that they would no longer be required for the upcoming recording of *Two Hearts*. Strykert quit midway through recording, leaving Hay and Ham the only members of Men at Work. The overproduced, underwritten album deservedly flopped, and Ham bailed during the band's 1985 tour. And that was that.

Despite the massive success of Men at Work, the members discovered that the enthusiasm for the band in no way extended to the individual constituents. Hay launched a solo career, but as he told *Rock Cellar Magazine* in May 2012, 'After we broke up, it became apparent to me that Men at Work didn't build a foundational audience. That audience didn't transition over to my solo career. Men at Work had massive radio success, but when that goes away and the band breaks up, then the audience seems to disappear as well.'

Thus, Hay and Ham would periodically re-form Men at Work over the next few years, but the original line-up would never play again—and the relationship between Strykert and Hay became downright poisonous. Yet the worst was to come when a question in a TV quiz show started a court case that was eventually to cost the band millions.

It started innocently enough, with a 2007 episode of ABC's *Spicks and Specks* asking: 'What children's song is contained in the song "Down Under"?' The answer was 'Kookaburra' (aka 'Kookaburra Sits in the Old Gum Tree'), and the owners of the rights to said song, Larrikin Music Publishing,[2] launched a copyright suit claiming that Ham's

---

2 The song itself was written by a schoolteacher named Marion Sinclair in 1935. She only registered the song in 1970, and the rights to it were bought by Larrikin for $6100 when her estate was sold off following her death in 1990.

flute riff was the melody line. To the surprise of pretty much everyone Larrikin won in 2010, and the band then lost an appeal in the Federal Court the following year. The settlement was far less than Larrikin Music had wanted—5 per cent of the song's Australian royalties from 2002 onwards, which came to about $100,000—but the four-year case still cost both sides an estimated $4.5 million in legal fees. 'So they didn't really win,' Hay said, 'they just lost less than us.'

Ham took the outcome especially hard, feeling that the case had undermined him as a musician. He told reporters: 'I'm terribly disappointed that's the way I'm going to be remembered—for copying something.'

In April 2012 he was found dead in the North Carlton home to which he'd downsized after selling his house and studio nearby following the end of his marriage.[3] An autopsy found that he'd suffered a heart attack. Hay still blames the stress of the court case for his friend's too-early demise at the age of fifty-eight.

The song, however, remains immortal. The international reception of 'Down Under' highlighted how the world—and especially the US—perceived Australia as a bunch of stereotypes loosely bundled into a caricature. Recognising this, our nation seemingly shrugged, went, 'Rightio, then,' and began pandering to it—most obviously with the massively successful *Crocodile Dundee* films, and to a lesser extent with Yahoo Serious's *Young Einstein*, as well as Paul Hogan's tourism ads, which confused millions of Aussies who had no idea why

---

3   This studio was where Archie Roach recorded his debut album *Charcoal Road* (1990), incidentally. That comes up later.

Americans suddenly expected them to chuck another shrimp on the barbie for them.[4]

Of course, Australia was having a hard enough time trying to work out how it felt about itself at the time—which brings us neatly to the next song . . .

---

4 Not only did Australia not screen the ad and therefore not know what the hell Americans were talking about for a good long time, there's the important fact that we call them prawns. *Shrimp*? Crazy talk.

17

1982

True Blue

John Williamson

*In which an unabashed patriot questions
the notion of nationalism*

There are plenty of Australian country music superstars—indeed, Australia's biggest musical export of the 00s was the ruggedly good-looking Keith Urban—but John Williamson is closer to the classic Australian country music of Slim Dusty than the US-influenced country rock of, say, Lee Kernaghan. Part of the likeness is his sheer output, which comes close to matching the mighty Slim—including compilations, Williamson has made over fifty albums since 1970—and part is that he's never shied away from combining the sincere with the playful. While he has celebrated Australian mythology in songs like 'Diggers of the Anzac (This is Gallipoli)' and 'The Breaker', generations of Australian kids have grown up on songs like 'Old Man Emu', 'Rip Rip Woodchip' and 'Goodbye Blinky Bill'.[1]

'Old Man Emu' was also the song that launched Williamson's career: he played it on the national talent quest program *New Faces* and won. Stardom beckoned as it became the fourteenth-biggest selling single of 1970 and led to his self-titled debut album, which flopped miserably.

Fortunately, what could have been a one-off novelty hit ended up launching Williamson's TV broadcasting career. He spent the next few years in Newcastle hosting the music program *Travlin' Out West* and releasing singles no-one bought.[2]

In fact, the seventies were a pretty lousy time for Williamson's music. He tried a number of different approaches, from the US-influenced country of 'Comic Strip Cowboys' (complete with ten-gallon hat) to the 'rock with a reggae influence' of his band Sydney Radio, which involved Williamson dressing as a sad clown called Ludwig Leichhardt. Oddly enough, this didn't capture the public's imagination.

Williamson wisely decided to abandon his forays into new wave and get back to his roots, playing solo shows with his acoustic guitar and a custom-designed stage/PA contraption he could plonk in the corner of suburban pubs that weren't necessarily equipped for live music. He played mainly country covers and Australian bush ballads, adding more and more of his own material as he became more confident, and sold

---

1   Williamson handed the rights for this song over to the Port Macquarie Koala Hospital, where it raises much-needed funds for this unique veterinary service. If you find yourself in the Port, pop by and purchase one of their awesome t-shirts.
2   Although there's no way I would not have bought the 1972 single 'Misery Farm' had it crossed my path, purely because it was credited to Williamson and his then-band Lumpy Pumpkin.

cassettes out of his car as he built up a local reputation. And then came the call that changed everything.

In 1982 legendary advertising and TV entrepreneur John Singleton asked Williamson to compose a theme song for a TV show he was working on, *True Blue Aussies*, which captured the essence of dinkum bonza mateship. The show never made it to air but the song rapidly became a live favourite. 'True Blue' made its first appearance in 1982 as a new track on a compilation of older material entitled *True Blue: The Best of John Williamson*, but the version that most people know is the superior 1986 rerecording.

In the US, country music has long been the music of American nationalism—indeed, straight-up jingoism. That's also been true of Australia, but Williamson wanted to do more than just celebrate his love of his homeland: Singleton might have required nothing more than a quick tune about Straylia and mateship, but Williamson wanted to tease out exactly what that meant. The result is a series of questions without answers—indeed, as he makes clear, he's asking you.

It helps that Williamson's stock in trade is unpretentious sincerity. There's nothing knowing or arch about his work: the emotions are simple, clear and uncluttered. The music is also marvellously simple: big first position open chords, the sort of song that any young guitarist would be able to play after a weekend with an acoustic and a chord book.

The result is something unique: a patriotic song that gently questions easy definitions of patriotism. You can feel his contempt for those who seek either to trivialise or commercialise it: the original version of the song contained the line 'or is it just Vegemite?', but he amended it in subsequent releases (due to his desire to protect the song from being, as he put it, 'commercialised')—occasionally to 'Mightymite', the Australian-owned Vegemite-like alternative product, but more often asking if she'll be right, as on the 1986 rerecording for his breakthrough album, *Mallee Boy*.

That Williamson was reluctant to ally the song with commerce seems a weird concern given that it became a household anthem as the jingle for the Hawke government's Buy Australian Made campaign in the 1980s. That was also courtesy of Singleton, who made the deal on Williamson's behalf. 'I didn't charge the Australian Made campaign a cent for using it in their television commercial but it gave the song thousands of dollars worth of advertising for weeks,' Williamson wrote in his 2014 autobiography, *Hey True Blue*. 'And it gave me a hit. But I was a mug for not getting a fee. No doubt Singo made heaps.'[3]

In 2003, during a session for yet another rerecording of the song (this time for the *True Blue Two* best-of), Williamson explained to Capital News what the title meant. 'If you are "true blue" you are an honest person to be trusted, your word is your bond, you love Australia and respect the nature of the land, you feel Australian and are proud of it, you care about others, you are a really good mate. "True blue" is something that is truly, unmistakably Australian—like shouting a beer in a pub, or a kelpie dog.'[4]

---

3 They later had a falling out over Singleton hawking 'True Blue' to Harvey Norman. Williamson took out a $60,000 advertisement in the *Sydney Morning Herald* insisting he had nothing to do with the campaign.

4 How one would shout a beer in a kelpie dog is not made clear.

The line between patriotism and nationalism is thin and, if anything, has become a lot thinner since 'True Blue' was written. Even so, it's a song that no nationalist group or political party has been able to commandeer for its own ends, partially because Williamson has been enormously protective of the song, and possibly also because those groups are not well known for asking deep questions about the value and basis of their beliefs. The upshot is something utterly unique: an anthem to Australian patriotism, performed by an unabashed patriot in the most patriotic musical genre on the planet, that asks questions about the very notion of patriotism. As alternative national anthems go, 'True Blue' is probably the most unexpectedly meta.

And as Australia started to wrestle with the question of its own identity in an increasingly interconnected world, and as it started to acknowledge some long-ignored truths about its less than noble history, 'True Blue' was and remains one of the most potent summaries of the Australian character—not for what it says, but for the strangely vulnerable way in which it says it.

18

1982

Great Southern Land

Icehouse

*In which the stresses of touring lead a homesick Sydneysider
to capture his homeland in synthesised sonics*

When Iva Davies wrote his classic ode to our vast continent, he did so in a place renowned for its timeless beauty, its endless vistas, its mighty panoramas of natural splendour: Leichhardt, in Sydney's inner west.

Davies' house was opposite a bus stop, so every ten minutes or so his home demo sessions for what was to be Icehouse's second album—or, technically, debut?[1]—would be interrupted by an idling bus, and Leichhardt's sought-after position under the flight path meant that the rumbling of traffic was relieved

---

1 This becomes clear in a few paragraphs, trust me.

by the roar of landing planes: the perfect scenario in which to craft his tale of mountains and oceans and endless aeons of deep time.[2]

It was a challenging time for Davies, as he was following the enormous success of his band's first album, but had also mislaid the band in the interim. Flowers had been a popular Sydney covers act before the classically trained Davies figured that this songwriting lark couldn't be too difficult and began synthesising a sound that owed more than a passing debt to the new wave heroes dominating the UK charts—most notably David Bowie and Gary Numan. And he was rewarded with hits right out of the gate: 'Can't Help Myself' went top 10, followed by 'We Can Get Together' and 'Walls', and immediately attracted international interest—which meant that the quartet had to change its name in 1981 thanks to an extant Scots combo of the same name. The solution was an elegant one: the band's debut album was called *Icehouse*, by Flowers, so they just swapped the band and the album and voila: Icehouse's debut album *Flowers* didn't even need new cover art.

The newly renamed band toured the US, Canada and Europe, at which point it started shedding members. A single, 'Love in Motion', was recorded effectively solo by Davies in London, setting the template for what was to become *Primitive Man*.

Touring had been difficult for Davies. He found it gruelling and lonely—a condition not helped by his vanishing bandmates—and he found himself deeply homesick. He'd also been

---

2 This book was written a few hundred metres away, on and around Parramatta Road in Stanmore. You can pretty much feel the majestic natural beauty coming off the page in palpable waves, right?

under pressure to write while touring behind *Flowers/Icehouse*, so by the time he landed back in Sydney the record company was already tapping its metaphorical watch and asking where the demos were.

If you combine Davies' touring homesickness with the urgent need to create his own universe in Leichhardt, you come some distance to understanding how 'Great Southern Land' could exist. He later described some of the images he had in his mind for an October 2012 piece in *The Australian*, writing 'Uluru . . . seemed to have formed in my mind as a great anchor, at the centre of a huge land mass, pinning the continent to the core of the Earth. It slowly revolved in my mind like the hub of a great wheel, from which spun out all the haphazard features of a unique landscape, until they eventually sprawled into the surrounding sea.'

It was also a reaction against the cartoonish patriotism spurred by the 1982 Brisbane Commonwealth Games. Davies was put off by 'what seemed to me like a lot of jingoism and fanfare', he told *The Music* in 2012. 'I wanted to write something that would offset the kind of postcard, souvenir model of Australia and get to something that was much more to the core of the place.'

One of the things that makes 'Great Southern Land' so timeless is that while it draws on the continent's vast geological past—the mountains turning to rocks, the rocks turning to sand—it also is clearly set as much in the present, with Davies referencing rainy days in the harbour contrasting with the unspoiled bay, suggesting they're the same location at different times.

But if the lyrics are largely impressionistic, they're also beautifully served by the music beneath them: long synth notes drawn out like streaked clouds, the syncopated clapping sticks subtly reminding the listener whose land this is, echoed in the land's own warning of the betrayals that are to come, because this is ultimately a song of colonisation.

The Great Southern Land was known to exist in some form by the time Captain James Cook opened his sealed orders and set sail to 'discover' it in 1788; by that stage a number of European explorers had made landfall on the northern and western coastlines, and there were literally hundreds of nations extant in Australia for thousands of years before that. But the land itself predates not only its European inhabitants, but its Aboriginal ones. This is a land whose memory predates humankind altogether.[3]

The song set the tone for *Primitive Man* as its opening track and, unsurprisingly, was a hit in Australia and nowhere else. The video clip was shot in a chalk quarry outside Sydney, which was presumably intended to capture the desolate beauty of the red centre except without the 'red' bit, the upshot being that it looked more like a *Doctor Who* episode than an Australian travelogue.

It also featured Davies in a central role, supported by the three slightly out-of-focus other members of the band who'd been recruited once recording had been completed. Many

---

3 The song doesn't *specifically* articulate the idea that Australia should have been left to the stewardship of diprotodons—the hippo-sized predecessors of koalas and wombats—but it's heavily implied. Okay, it's not implied at all, but I choose to interpret it that way. To be clear, I also choose to interpret literally all other songs as having a strong pro-diprotodon subtext.

of these players would be hugely important to the way the band developed, particularly guitarist Robert Kretschmer and English bassist Guy Pratt, but it was also clear that this was entirely Davies' game now.

'Great Southern Land' remains one of the greatest evocations of the sheer ancient emptiness of Australia. While other songs would capture the vast distances of our nation—the Triffids' 'Wide Open Road',[4] or the Cruel Sea's 'This is Not the Way Home',[5] for example—'Great Southern Land' is unique in its suggestion that the land in question couldn't care less about the people inhabiting it: it was here before we arrived, and it'll still be here long after our bones are ground into nothing.

The single got to #5 in Australia but failed to chart significantly elsewhere—fortunately, Europe was about to fall in love with 'Hey Little Girl', so it didn't make that big a difference. It is, however, still Australia's favourite Icehouse song—or was in 2007, when it was voted as such in a Triple M poll.

The song enjoyed a second wind in 1988 thanks to a key sequence in the surprise Australian cinema hit *Young Einstein*, written by and starring Yahoo Serious,[6] who married it to a series of visuals of the Australian landscape that seemed far more suitable than a burning stick-filled quarry just waiting for a mob of Cybermen to march into frame.

Oddly enough, it was also a bout of homesickness that was to create our next Australian classic, as you shall see . . .

---

4   Which you'll learn about in chapter 26!
5   Which really deserves a chapter but doesn't get one. Sorry.
6   While the film was a hit, the biggest cultural effect it had was arguably the staggeringly good all-Australian soundtrack, which also featured Models, Mental as Anything, the Stems, Paul Kelly and . . . look, it was a really good soundtrack, okay?

19

1983

Cattle and Cane

The Go-Betweens

*In which Far North Queensland is transformed
into a mysterious and beautiful wonderland
through the power of homesickness*

Let's start with the obvious first question. The rhythm of most of the Go-Betweens' elegiac ode to Queensland childhood runs as follows: 'This is the verse pattern. 5/4, 2/4, 4/4. Three bars. The chorus is 4/4. Verse and chorus separated by half bar. The confusion lies in the different time signatures between both verse and chorus and that damned half bar separating them.'[1]

That is the official and definitive word from Lindy Morrison herself, who had to work out a drum pattern to drive along

---

1 If any music theory person is reading this and sniffing, 'Pah, it's 11/8 time before modulating to straight time,' then you're wrong.

the bizarre piece of music her band had just decided to create. How the hell she was able to develop a part to such an absurdly non-intuitive rhythm is a testament to just how extraordinary a musician she is, but also to the genius of the late Grant McLennan, whose song it (mostly) was.[2]

The trio of Morrison, McLennan and singer/guitarist Robert Forster had followed the classic Australian band technique of moving to the UK in the hope that success would ensue, crashing mainly with their friends, the Birthday Party. Their debut album, 1982's *Send Me A Lullaby*, had been generally well received but little sold, and the UK move was also about solidifying the band's relationship with distributors Rough Trade since their Australian label, Missing Link, had made clear that it wouldn't be financing another record.

The band found the UK exactly as warm and welcoming as every other band in this book had done—i.e. they were somewhere between largely ignored and deliberately abandoned—but at least they had some friends there who could offer company, support and the warming numbness of heroin.

Legend has it that 'Cattle and Cane' was written by a deeply homesick McLennan in a squat in London: specifically, in Nick Cave's room, in which the Black Crow King was crashed out on a mattress in the corner. McLennan was supposedly quietly fiddling around with Cave's acoustic guitar when the riff came tumbling out. He initially envisioned it as a song

---

2 It's worth pointing out that the band was mucking around with time signatures a lot at this point: for example, 'A Bad Debt Follows You', the first song on *Before Hollywood*, is in 7/8. 'Cattle and Cane' didn't come out of nowhere, in other words.

for his mum about the property she, Grant and his stepfather called home in the middle of Far North Queensland, and while he had thought of 'Cattle and Cane' as a poem rather than a song, it's one of the most perfect marriages of lyric and music.

Leaving aside the cinematic beauty of the images—cane fields, cinder-filled skies—the loping, off-balance rhythm beautifully matches the gait of a child running over uneven ground of fields and pathways on his way home from school.

The lyrics are melancholy and wistful, but don't dip into nostalgia. The three verses by McLennan cover three phases of his life to date in a series of images—the primary schoolboy scrambling through cane fields, the adolescent in boarding school losing his late father's watch in the showers, the young man at university discovering a bigger brighter world—and then the fourth phase of his life: Robert Forster, playing himself.

In a lesser band the sudden appearance of Forster would seem intrusive, but it works both musically and biographically. At face value, Forster's contribution seems almost hip hop— reinforcing the message of the main lyricist like the world's most polite hype man—but as far as the theme goes, Forster's appearance in the song, as with his appearance in McLennan's life, changes everything.

His bandmates recognised just how significant a work of art it was too. Forster compared McLennan's lyrics to those of Banjo Paterson or Slim Dusty in their evocation of the Australian landscape, and Morrison told the ABC that it was 'a master song'.

'Cattle and Cane' became the lead single of *Before Hollywood*,[3] the first truly great Go-Betweens album, and set the standard for what was to come: a more or less even split between Forster and McLennan songs,[4] which demonstrated just how complementary were their very individual talents. By the time of its release the band had taken on a bassist, Robert Vickers, who appears in the video the band made for *Countdown*, and they were rewarded with an alterna-hit in the UK, where the single reached #4 on the independent charts, and absolutely nothing whatsoever in Australia, where the single and album failed to chart.

Time, however, was more kind to the song. It was voted one of the Top 30 Australian Songs of All Time by APRA in 2001,[5] and appeared in the first three of Triple J's Hottest 100s (debuting at #11).

While the Go-Betweens were destined to remain more loved than financially rewarded, they were regularly cited along with the Smiths, REM and New Order as one of the most important bands of the eighties. And the absence made the world's hearts grow fonder.

---

3 Fans are well aware of this, but it's worth noting: every Go-Betweens album during the 'classic', pre-reformation era had a double L in the title: *Send Me a Lullaby, Before Hollywood, Spring Hill Fair, Liberty Belle & the Black Diamond Express, Talullah* and—okay, this is a stretch—*16 Lover's Lane*.

4 The Go-Betweens were the first band where the solo albums really made me aware of how vital the absent members were: Forster's solo albums seemed arch and brittle without McLennan's more emotional pop sensibility, and McLennan's solo albums seemed cloying and over-sweet without Forster's wry intellectualism. They're still pretty damn amazing records, to be clear, it's just that the Go-Betweens were always more than the sum of their parts.

5 Just as an aside: only the top ten of the APRA top 30 songs were presented in order; the other twenty—including 'Cattle and Cane'—were bundled up chronologically.

Forster and McLennan even pulled off the near-impossible task of making a comeback record worth listening to when they re-formed the band in 2000, eleven years after their split.[6] However, anyone wondering whether the wounds from the break-up were still raw had their answer when noting that Morrison was not invited back for *The Friends of Rachel Worth*, and neither were the other two members of the final line-up— bassist John Willsteed and multi-instrumentalist Amanda Brown.[7] The 'new' line-up, which included bassist Adele Pickvance and former Custard stickman Glenn Thompson, made two more excellent albums before McLennan died suddenly of a heart attack on 6 May 2006 at the age of forty-eight.

'Cattle and Cane' is not an easy song to play, but UK Go-Betweens obsessives the Wedding Present covered it during their Hit Parade era (which involved recording a single every month for a year, with a cover version on the B-side) and Jimmy Little included it on *Messenger*, the album you learned about in chapter 3.

Two years after the release of 'Cattle and Cane', another song with a similar story from a similar landscape would appear, though told from a very different perspective. Instead of being a nostalgic look back at a rural Queensland childhood from

---

6   Fun fact: the reformation was brokered by the genius Scots singer-songwriter and massive Go-Betweens fan Lloyd Cole, who asked Forster and McLennan to tour with him. The world owes you a debt, Lloyd.

7   The bitterness of the Go-Betweens' break-up was exacerbated by the end of Morrison and Forster's long-term relationship the previous year, while Brown ended her relationship with McLennan as a result of the band's sudden dissolution. Forster's autobiography *Grant & I* confirmed the long-held theory that most of McLennan's first solo album, *Watershed*, was written about Brown.

lonely England, it was by an English migrant remembering his parents' marriage dissolving in the oppressive humidity of the hills near Bundaberg. The visual motifs are even similar—lightning cracks over cane fields as silent herds of cattle graze off in the distance—but while McLennan's memories are filled with wide open skies and the warmth of coming home, Mark 'Cal' Callaghan remembered the smell of the Hardiflex walls of his cheap family home, filled with rented furniture, radiating the heat of the day back into the house as they attempted to find a moment's solace in sleep. Bizarrely, that song by GANGgajang,[8] 'Sounds of Then',[9] ended up being used on a Channel 9 promo and a Coke commercial, while 'Cattle and Cane' never broke into the mainstream consciousness to anything like that degree. Maybe it was better that way.

---

8   The name is supposedly the sound a guitar makes when playing a chord and is definitely not a barely concealed reference to ganja, oh no no no no no no.
9   By the time it became the fifth single from GANGgajang's self-titled debut album it had acquired the parenthetical title '(This Is Australia)' after the band presumably realised that no-one would identify it otherwise. You'll learn a similar the-obvious-title-is-in-the-parentheses lesson in chapter 38.

20

1983

I Was Only Nineteen (A Walk in the Light Green)

Redgum

In which Australia is stirred to acknowledge the fallout from Vietnam and the cost of following other countries into ill-advised wars

Remember back in chapter 13? There's a reason that the character you met in the Cold Chisel song is living a life of quiet desperation, unsupported and unmoored: it was a staggeringly common outcome for Australians who returned from the Vietnam War. They were not hailed as heroes or feted for keeping our nation safe, as the country had the growing suspicion that following the US into Vietnam had all been a terrible mistake. And that desire to forget extended to those who served.

The war had very little impact on the teenaged John Schumann until the older brother of a school friend—a soldier named Robert Castin—was killed in action and it dawned on him that he would shortly reach the age of conscription. Fortunately his birthdate didn't come up in the conscription ballot, but the experience of those who fought niggled at him as he formed his folk band, Redgum, while studying at Flinders University,[1] and the niggle increased when he started encountering returned servicemen he'd known as a teenager. That put the seed of the song in his head, the desire to capture the Australian experience of returning from Vietnam. And then . . . well, someone beat him to the punch.

'I remember when "Khe Sanh" came out I thought it was an absolutely sensational song,' he told Radio National's *The Real Thing* in 2016. 'I thought, "Oh, that's it, Don's done it. And I don't know what made me put "Khe Sanh" to one side and write my own.'

'I Was Only Nineteen' is based on a true story, for the most part. It's the story of Mick Storen, older brother of Denise—the 'Denny' mentioned in the opening line of the song—who was to subsequently marry Schumann.

Mick had a few stipulations before sitting down and speaking to Schumann on a matter which he'd largely been unable to talk about even to his own family: when the composition was finished he'd hear it first and have the right of veto;

---

1 Schumann and I are both philosophy graduates of that noble institution, and stirring examples of just how little a philosophy degree enhances one's future employability. In fact, we did the exact same mix of subjects, both married women named Denise, and are firm believers in the masculine power of the human beard. If it turns out that we're also Highlanders, it's going to end explosively.

specifically, he was concerned that the song be neither flippant nor a load of propaganda in the vein of Staff Sergeant Barry Sadler's cringeworthily patriotic 'The Ballad of the Green Berets'. If Storen didn't approve, or thought that the song failed to capture the facts as he remembered them, Schumann would agree to discard it.

Storen and Schumann met at Denny's place in Cherry Gardens in the Adelaide foothills and, over an afternoon of beer drinking, Mick opened up about the whole thing: his enlistment; his training; the passing-out parade in Puckapunyal (a still-active army training facility just outside Seymour in south-eastern Victoria); volunteering for the 6th Battalion based in Townsville; shipping out on HMAS *Sydney* to the Nui Dat base in Vietnam and seeing combat; and, finally, his return to Australia as a very different man. John recorded their conversation, and later listened to it on his first-generation Walkman ('the size of a brick') as Redgum toured the country.

The resulting song was written in a single burst in the backyard of the house in North Carlton where Schumann was living at the time. When he was next in Adelaide, he played it for Mick.

It was a shock. 'I had anticipated he was going to do some generic song, not my personal history,' Mick said in the aforementioned *Real Thing* interview.

The subtitle 'A Walk in the Light Green' refers to military maps that rendered terrain as dark green (jungle, no defoliants, probably about as safe as areas in an active war zone could get) and light green (signifying the use of defoliants— most often Agent Orange—where one should expect active combat and minefields). A walk in the light green, therefore, was one in which any single step could be your last.

The shrapnel Mick took in the back was also real, although he absolutely felt it ('it was a hot little zap'). The only bit that deviated from Storen's own experience was the part of the song about Frankie who supposedly stepped on a mine. Frankie was a real person—his name is Frank Hunt, and he appeared with Redgum and Schumann multiple times after the song was released—though he didn't kick the mine himself. He was, however, badly wounded when his squad skipper Peter Hines stepped on a landmine on 20 July 1969—minutes after the Apollo astronauts made their historic first steps on the moon—and endured over thirty operations and over a year and a half in hospital, barely surviving his injuries.

Storen didn't want to disrespect the memory of Hines by referencing him directly in the song, but suggested Frankie's name after Schumann had put a 'Tommy' in the lyrics as an all-purpose army name. He wasn't, however, due to go home in June; that was just a good rhyme.

After Schumann tracked him down in Bega, Frank too gave the song his blessing (and happily took responsibility for treading on the song's mine as a way of protecting the reputations of the deceased). Having worked with veterans' charities since returning from combat, he realised the song would be a great way to encourage those who were struggling to seek help and support—and that's exactly what happened.

The song also helped in rather more tangible ways as the royalties were donated to the Vietnam Veterans Association of Australia. At least, Schumann and bassist Hugh McDonald decided to donate the royalties since they were the only members of Redgum who played on the track. Schumann had thought that the hurdle to the song's release would be the people whose stories he was attempting to tell, but it turned out the biggest obstacle was that Redgum nearly didn't record the song that was to define them, with the rest of the band boycotting the song for political reasons.

The song was released as a single in late February, and the impact was immediate—which came as a huge surprise to everyone, including Schumann, who was on his honeymoon with Denny as the single went to #1. The parent album *Caught in the Act* went top 3, thereby saving the band's floundering career and papering over the internal politics and personality differences that were threatening to scuttle the band.

Such was the public response to the song that in May 1983 the Hawke government launched the Royal Commission on the Use and Effects of Chemical Agents on Australian Personnel in Vietnam. In 1985 the inquiry concluded that there was no link between the chemicals and the health complaints of Australian and US servicemen. Veterans groups protested the result. The matter became front-page news again after the US National Academy of Sciences published research in 1993 linking defoliants to a range of horrifying conditions, including several cancers and leukaemia. It took until 2014 for the Australian War Memorial to agree to amend the official history of the war to take this new information into account.

The song was also taken up by the anti-war movement generally, and taught Australia that following the US into foreign conflicts brought nothing but tragedy and suffering—a lesson that meant Australia would subsequently only ever go to war every single time the US asked us.

It was also embraced by the veterans' movement and was responsible in no small part for the long overdue Welcome Home parade that was finally held in 1987. The song also enjoyed a renaissance in 2015, when the Herd covered it for Triple J's weekly segment Like a Version—and so popular did it prove that this new version came in at #18 on that year's Hottest 100.

As for Redgum, their sole #1 single was the high-water mark. There was another hit—the tongue-in-cheek cod reggae of 'I've Been To Bali Too'—but then Schumann announced he had a solo deal and quit the band. The remaining members struggled on for another few years without their lead singer and main songwriter (recording the godawful safe sex anthem 'Roll It On Robbie', which is about as non-folk as can be imagined, not least since it's a masterclass in eighties synth stabs) before splitting in 1990. But 'I was Only Nineteen' far outlasted the band. As Schumann put it: 'It's a hymn, and you don't fuck around with a hymn.'

21

1984

Throw Your Arms Around Me

Hunters & Collectors

*In which the nation's most resolutely masculine band
discover their sensitive side and give Australia
a song to hug along to*

The weirdest thing about 'Throw Your Arms Around Me'—
the song that will be on the gravestone of Hunters & Collectors
and is the alternative national anthem for several generations
of Australians—is that almost every cover version of the song
(and there are many) does a better job of capturing the song's
fragile beauty and heartfelt sentiment than did the band that
created it. That is, until the fourth time they recorded it.

To say the song wasn't typical Hunters & Collectors fare
in 1984 is a massive understatement. Since forming in 1981
out of the ashes of various art school bands in Melbourne,

the group had released two albums of pounding, artsy, Krautrock/Talking Heads-inspired rock under the direction of co-founders Mark Seymour and Greg Perano. After one fight too many the band dissolved and Seymour reconvened it with almost everyone from the original line-up bar Perano and made 1984's *The Jaws of Life*, a stripped-down and more rock-focused album that did little to improve the band's fortunes and convinced its UK label that there was no point in paying any attention to Hunters & Collectors from that moment on.

As a result, the band decided it'd attempt to make its next album one that radio stations might want to play and that people might even want to buy. With that vague idea in mind, it recorded a wildly out-of-character number as a one-off single: a love song—a love song!—that Seymour had written about the dying relationship that was to inspire most of the next record. This song was a plaintive declaration of devotion called 'Throw Your Arms Around Me', and when it appeared in November 1984 the band's bold experiment in being direct and emotionally honest defied all expectations by doing absolutely nothing to improve its commercial malaise.

Well, that's not entirely true: it very quickly became a singalong live favourite, but the band seemed to struggle to reconcile its thumping, abrasive, thundering style to the aesthetic of this gentle three-chord strummer. The version that opened the following year's live album, *The Way to Go Out*, saw the band continue to pull at the song, trying to get it to move, unable to settle into it. But it clearly knew that there was something magical there, so it had another bash at it for 1986's *Human Frailty*, which was, as promised, commercial and polished—by H&C standards at least. It was also the first album that really showed the band's power and songcraft, most notably on the throat-grabbing opener and first single 'Say Goodbye', in which the band's great strengths of a killer rhythm section, a face-punching horn section and Seymour's anguished and emotive voice came together in perfect concert.

And yet even on this masterpiece album, 'Throw Your Arms Around Me' still doesn't *quite* work. Maybe it's the minor thirds John Archer keeps throwing into the bassline,[1] that undercut the simplicity of the unadorned sentiment and unfussy major chords of the song; maybe it's the fact that the band is still playing it uncomfortably fast and not giving it a chance to stretch out. Either way, when it became the second single off the album it peaked at #38 before vanishing. The album, however, reached #10 and kept on selling.

The now commercially-viable band continued to be a potent live draw and 'Throw Your Arms Around Me' was still a central song in the band's sets. In 1989, the year that Triple J held its first ever Hottest 100 poll of the best songs of all time, it was voted #2, making it the highest-rating Australian song,[2] and it attained the same position the following year, and then slipped to #4 in 1991 before the Js limited the Hottest 100 voting to songs of the previous twelve months so that the whole thing wasn't just the same playlist in a slightly different order.

---

1 Yes, it's that.
2 In 1989 and 1990 Joy Division's 'Love Will Tear Us Apart' was #1; in 1991 it was Nirvana's 'Smells Like Teen Spirit'.

In 1990 the band finally recorded the song the way it perhaps should have always been done—gently, semi-acoustically, with a slow build to a glorious coda—as the promotional track for their career-spanning best-of *Collected Works*. As no-one ever says, fourth time's the charm.

The thing about the song was its universality: although it was about a very specific relationship, that feeling of desperate carnal desire and bravado—even (or perhaps especially) when knowing that this is a fleeting moment that may well never be repeated—spoke to anyone, from the doomed and lovelorn to the horny and opportunistic. That's the genius of the song's lyrics: a sexual invitation becomes something powerfully sacred. That's because Seymour touches on a human truth so simple as to be primal: our time on earth is fleeting, so we must take our joys as and when we can. As Robert Herrick put it in 1648, gather ye rosebuds while ye may. Or, to put it more bluntly: life's short, let's fuck.

Seymour also acknowledges the power of 'Throw Your Arms Around Me', telling Barry Divola in a May 2017 interview for *Rolling Stone* that it would be the one song he couldn't conceive of letting go.[3] 'It's just so completely out of character for Hunters & Collectors,' he pointed out. 'It's an outlier in my own work. What's incredible is it worked in that really masculine environment. There's a huge amount of Celtic styling in that song. I'd been listening to a lot of Van Morrison at the time. That song's so important to me. It's so special. It's really a part of me.'

---

3   Like most H&C material, the song is credited to the entire band, but let's be honest: Seymour wrote it.

It's also part of the culture in general.[4] Cover versions abound, from Crowded House (featuring Seymour's younger brother Nick) to Pearl Jam to the Doug Anthony All Stars. And, as mentioned above, all these versions intuitively seem to grasp the nature of the song better than H&C did for the best part of a decade.

But as long as there are Australians with an acoustic guitar, a few drinks under their belts and a solid dose of homesickness, you can guarantee that someone will make them call your name and shout it to the blue summer sky.

---

4   It wasn't a one-off either, although it took the Hunnas a little while to write a track that matched its potential. It wasn't until 1992, after two more albums failed to make the hard-touring band an international concern, that they succumbed to record company meddling for what was to be their least-fun-to-create album: *Cut*. It was a long and stressful process that nearly split the band, and during the process Seymour would write a bitterly cynical song comparing the band's fruitless attempts to crack America to Napoleon's equally doomed attempt to lead an army against Russia, and in so doing created another anthemic Australian classic in 'Holy Grail'.

22

1985

What You Need

INXS

In which one last-minute decision to salvage an otherwise average album makes the international career of Australia's biggest-ever band

There was a moment when INXS very audibly said goodbye to their home country and started looking overseas. It comes right at the end of their third album, 1982's *Shabooh Shoobah*, and is their first truly classic song. It's called 'Don't Change', and if you're not already tearing up a little bit at the mere mention of its name then, damn it, you're not a true Australian.

If INXS had spontaneously combusted in 1983, then 'Don't Change' would still have guaranteed that they'd be remembered forever in their homeland, but given everything that followed, the song can—and should—be interpreted as

131

a loving but definite farewell. It sounds like it's directed at a friend or a lover, but it works equally well if you assume that it's INXS telling Australia that while they've really valued the time they spent together, the nation deserves a band that was capable of loving it the way it *deserved* to be loved. There's a reason it remained their standard closing number until the end: it's one of the greatest full stops in Australian musical history.

Having bid their homeland adieu, the next step was the US and Europe, where the band did its first international touring in support of the album. The decision to be the biggest band in the world had crystallised, and the next album was made with the assumption that listenership would not be limited to a hometown audience. From the outset 1984's *The Swing* sounded excitingly international. And it should have done: it was the band's first album made outside of Australia. The producer, Nick Launay, was English,[1] and Chic mastermind Nile Rodgers had already completed the album's breakthrough lead single 'Original Sin' in a pre-album session with INXS in New York. These were sounds for the dance floors of the northern hemisphere, not the beer gardens of the northern beaches.

The influence of Rodgers and Launay in the studio had taught INXS the lesson that all great bands eventually learn, from REM to Radiohead to Midnight Oil to U2: not everyone

---

1 Launay had just finished work on two other iconic Australian albums: Midnight Oil's career-making *10–1* and Models' *The Pleasure of Your Company*, which is hands down my favourite Australian album of all time by my favourite Australian artists of all time. And are they in this book? No, they are not, because much as I tried to find ways to argue that 'I Hear Motion' and 'Barbados' and 'Atlantic Romantic' were pivotal songs in Australian cultural history, I just couldn't make a convincing-enough case, despite their being obviously awesome. That's the sort of hard-nosed objectivity and respect for the process I brought to this book, damn it.

has to play at once. The cluttered, dense arrangements of the early albums were replaced by sleek, spacious production that gave room for each of the players to stretch out a bit—no mean feat for a six-piece band, especially one that contains a saxophone. Learning to shut up and trust that the others will do some of the heavy lifting made INXS sound orders of magnitude better, especially when said lifting was done by the meat-and-potatoes rhythm section of drummer Jon Farriss and bassist Garry Gary Beers.[2]

The album also marked the dominance of the songwriting partnership that was to dominate the band's fortunes from this point forward: that of keyboardist Andrew Farriss and singer Michael Hutchence. While other members would contribute songs and collaborate in various combinations, it was tacitly understood that Hutchence/Farriss would be responsible for most of the big boy singles from now on.

The album was deservedly their most successful to date and the infernally catchy 'Burn For You' proved that 'Original Sin' wasn't a fluke. The years of road miles meant INXS was electrifying live, and it was regularly blowing headliners off stage during its support slots through the US. *The Swing* was getting rave reviews all over and Hutchence was being hailed as a proper sex symbol of the Mick Jagger stripe. The moment had come, INXS had arrived, and the expectations for the next move were impossibly high—and since the UK had already succumbed, by the time the band came to make *Listen Like Thieves* it had the US firmly in their sights.

---

2 Fun fact about Garry Gary Beers: his name. That's literally it. Apparently it was a schoolyard joke because people didn't know how many r's it had. See also: people who pretentiously use their middle initial.

After spending the best part of 1984 on tour, INXS reconvened in Sydney in March 1985 with UK producer Chris Thomas—most notable for his work on Pink Floyd's *The Dark Side of the Moon*, the Sex Pistol's *Never Mind the Bollocks ...* and, later, for helming Pulp's breakthrough single 'Common People'—and set about making the album that would propel them into the stratosphere. They had the moxie. They had the fire in their bellies. The only problem was that they didn't have the songs.

It's hardly a shock given the sort of schedule the band was working to—they'd finished an exhausting year of international touring less than three months before entering the studio—but you can still hear it on the album today. No matter how you cut it, *Listen Like Thieves* is basically a really kick-arse EP with a hell of a lot of filler—especially compared with its predecessor, *The Swing*, and the album that was to follow, 1987's nearly-all-killer *Kick*. Sure, it's got 'This Time', 'Kiss the Dirt (Falling Down the Mountain)' and the title track, but as for the rest of the album ... look, no-one's going to cite the barely third-rate 'Same Direction' or the cheesy synth instrumental 'Three Sisters' as INXS's creative pinnacle unless they're being deliberately provocative—and your life will be the richer without such people in it.

More problematically INXS didn't have The Song, the sit-up-and-take-notice lead single that would set the agenda for the album and give radio a reason to get excited. Thomas told them as much during recording, making clear that the band was currently set to release a decent but unspectacular record that would quite possibly kill them, given INXS's new international status and the scrutiny the album would consequently receive. That was a courageous move, since most hired guns would be a little more circumspect about telling their employers that their efforts weren't up to scratch, but if that decision arguably made Thomas the inadvertent catalyst of INXS's later success, his next would make him the accidental architect of their future sound.

Legend has it that as the sessions drew to a close Thomas was listening to some of Andrew Farriss's unused demos in the hopes of finding something that might be bashed into a single, and he was struck by a song with the inspirational title 'Funk Song Number 13'. At that point it was little more than a repeating bassline, but Thomas was hooked, reportedly exclaiming. 'I could listen to that groove for ten minutes!' Thus entranced, he instructed Farris and Hutchence to go and turn it into a proper song.

It took the band two days in the studio to write and rehearse the track, now retitled 'What You Need', and the final studio day was spent recording it. And it changed everything.

Every element was perfect, from the inspired opening, where the band appears to be getting settled (complete with a nod to 'A Hard Day's Night' in that open-tuned chord) before Jon Farriss marshals them in with his building-sized drums ahead of Hutchence's authoritative, attention grabbing *'Hey!'* But it was the overall effect of the band locking together that was to have such a lasting influence on its sound for the rest of its existance. Not only was this The Song for the new album, it was pretty much The Song for the imperial phase of INXS.

Here was Hutchence as the declarative frontman, speaking directly to the audience. Here was the rhythm section showing off every lesson Launay and Rodgers had taught them about what makes people dance. And here was the sonic template that the band would follow for its biggest international hits from this point onwards—'Need You Tonight' and 'Suicide Blonde', for example—which, like 'What You Need', were extended dancefloor grooves rather than the classic verse-chorus-verse-chorus-bridge songs of the 'Burn for You' or 'Don't Change' mould.

Weeks later it was in the US top 5, starting the band's extraordinary run of American hits. It was helped by a groundbreaking rotoscoped stop-motion video clip courtesy of Richard Lowenstein (later to direct Hutchence in the fascinating failure *Dogs in Space*[3]) and Lynn-Maree Milburn, for which they'd subsequently share an ARIA Award for Best Video. The album went to #1 in Australia with four times platinum sales, and only barely missed out on going top 10 in the US (peaking at #11) and selling double platinum: the beginning of INXS's reign as one of the world's biggest bands.

Years later, Andrew Farriss would tell *Classic Rock*: 'The band's performance on that track is amazing. We absolutely nailed it. But it is amazing that often the simplest songs—unbelievably simple songs—that take you the shortest time and just happen, are the ones that become the huge hits.'

And that's undeniably true, but there's one thing he's leaving out: sometimes it also takes having someone brave enough to tell you to lift your game, and then you being egoless enough to respond, 'You know what? You're right. Let's go.'

---

3   You read about it before: it's the film that has 'Shivers' in it, twice.

23

1985

Blackfella/Whitefella

Warumpi Band

*In which a band from the middle of the nation brings
reconciliation to the national consciousness and starts
the process that will eventually take Aboriginal
land rights to the airwaves*
(Aboriginal and Torres Strait Islander readers please note that
this chapter contains the names of deceased persons.)

The Northern Territory settlement of Papunya is a tiny
community 240 kilometres north-west of Alice Springs in
the red sands of the Western Desert.[1] Its population hovers
around the 300 mark, and has the distinction of being the

---

1 If you're thinking of popping by, be advised that a (free) permit from the
Central Land Council is required to travel to or through Papunya as it is freehold
Aboriginal land under the Land Rights Act. Just a heads-up.

furthest town from the Australian coastline in all directions, being a mere thirty kilometres south-west of Australia's Continental Pole of Inaccessibility. In other words, it's literally the furthest town inland no matter what direction you travel from.

In 1980 local brothers Sammy and Gordon Butcher Tjapanangka met Victorian country boy Neil Murray, who'd moved to the region as a teacher and occasional truck driver.[2] Sammy played guitar and bass, Gordon played drums and Murray was a tasty guitarist, so they started jamming—and since they needed a frontman, the Butchers volunteered their brother-in-law, an eye-catchingly charismatic singer and didgeridoo player named George Rrurrambu Burarrwanga.[3]

They were mainly a country and blues-rock act, those being the most popular musical genres in the region, and in those pre-internet, barely-a-landline days the band had a DIY approach to touring: loading their gear into a ute, driving somewhere, setting up and playing for whoever happened to be around. They started off doing sets of covers before composing their own material. Their 1983 debut single, 'Jailanguru Pakarnu (Out from Jail)', was sung in

---

2 Murray was teaching in two settlements at the time: Papunya and Kintore, a twelve-hour drive due west along a road subject to flooding, which should put your commute into perspective—not least because you want to be very careful about being stranded by floods in the region since waterways tend to contain saltwater crocodiles. In fact, the 2016 Kintore Street School Croc Race (a fundraising event in which rubber crocodiles are raced down the Katherine River) was cancelled after sightings of an actual, giant, non-rubber croc.

3 During his life, he was known as George Rrurrambu, and after his 2007 death he was referred to as George Burarrwanga for Yolngu cultural reasons. He was born Kumanjayi Rrurrambu II Burarrawanga and was also known as George Djilaynga. Dude had a bunch of top-quality names, in other words.

Luritja,[4] a dialect of Wati, the Western Desert language, although Burarrwanga himself was an Arnhem Land man of Elcho Island—a place closer to Papua New Guinea than Papunya. But it was their second single—sung in English—that transformed the band's fortunes.

'Blackfella/Whitefella' was the sort of punchy, straightforward reconciliation anthem the Clash would have written if they were a country-influenced majority-Indigenous band from Central Australia: short, to the point, and insanely catchy. Written by Murray and Burarrwanga, the initial spark came from Murray's happy discovery that he was welcomed and valued in the Papunya community, despite being a non-Aboriginal blow-in.

The message was one of unity and respect, but the chorus made clear that this wasn't merely about congratulating oneself for one's own broadmindedness. Consisting of one single repeated line—a demand that the listener must stand up and be counted—it made clear that being open-minded about race wasn't just a question of individual choice; countering racism meant being outspoken about it. And it wasn't just about European–Aboriginal relations either. Burarrwanga insisted on adding 'yellafella' in there as well, and although it was intended to include those of mixed heritage, it had the bonus of making the song span just about everyone. Any concern that this was a very male sort of message was alleviated by the call for more brothers and for more sisters, if things were ever to improve.

---

4 Interestingly enough, it seems as though the language was named from the outside: *lurinya* is an Arrernte word for foreigner or outsider, as was possibly applied to the Western Desert speakers who were moving—not necessarily of their own volition—onto Arrernte lands near Alice Springs.

Warumpi Band was not the only Indigenous group playing in Central Australia, but it was one of the few to tour to the eastern capitals. This made the band's debut album, *Big Name, No Blankets*, a must-have for the socially aware, and it was on that tour that the group was seen by Melbourne music writer Clinton Walker (who began the journey to his seminal book on Aboriginal music, *Buried Country*) and Midnight Oil in Sydney, beginning a friendship that was to have major ramifications for both bands.

For the Warumpi Band, it meant signing to Powderworks— the Oils' label—and gaining a whole new audience; for the Oils it meant a co-headline tour of desert towns in 1986, captured in the documentary also entitled *Black Fella/White Fella*, that inspired the band to make its finest record.

In the great tradition of rock'n'roll, however, success almost sounded the death knell for Warumpi Band. Murray saw the opportunity for the band to take things to the next level, only to discover that the Butchers weren't really interested in a career that would take them away from their homes for too long and Burarrwanga had family business that prevented him touring much. They even passed up the opportunity to support their heroes Dire Straits in Brisbane, which particularly disappointed the guitar-obsessed Sammy.

The line-up changed multiple times, with Murray and Burarrwanga the only constants, and there were a couple of actual break-ups in between until their final album, 1996's *Too Much Humbug* (a title that gives some indication of the delays and distraction that caused them to take nearly a decade to record their follow up to 1987's *Go Bush!*). This album featured a more confident rerecording of 'Blackfella/Whitefella' that did more justice to the song's propulsive live energy, but it didn't lend a similar propulsion to the band's trajectory; they ground to a halt for good in 2000.

Murray had a successful solo career (his 1989 breakthrough album, *Calm and Crystal Clear*, featured Midnight Oil's Peter Gifford and Jim Moginie on bass and guitar respectively) and Burarrwanga also kept performing, even making a reggae-inflected solo album, *Nerbu Message*, in 2000, before being felled by cancer in 2007 at the age of fifty.

'Blackfella/Whitefella' enjoyed an extended life via idiosyncratic covers by Jimmy Little, Missy Higgins and Emma Donovan, and Warumpi Band's legacy lives on in the solo work of Neil Murray as well as artists like Christine Anu (a member of Murray's band the Rainmakers), who turned Warumpi's 'My Island Home' into an unexpected hit in 1995. But perhaps the biggest effect was in helping to prime Midnight Oil to focus on Indigenous issues—as you'll read presently.[5]

But more generally it's possible to trace a line from Warumpi Band to every Indigenous artist who refused to tailor their art to mainstream—or, to put it another way, white—sensibilities, from the unvarnished truths of Archie Roach, to Dr G Yunupingu recording in Yolngu languages,[6] and the uncompromising hip hop of artists like Briggs and Trials, many of whom you will meet in chapters to come.

---

5 Well, unless you stop reading now, or take a really long break. But you're digging this so far, right?
6 Dr G Yunupingu was also from Burarrwanga's home of Elcho Island, as it happens.

And as Australian society slowly continued its journey towards addressing the structural racism meted upon the nation's first inhabitants, it was important to have a rallying cry. It didn't matter what your colour, you needed to stand up and be counted.

24

1985

Working Class Man

Jimmy Barnes

*In which a Scotsman releases a true Australian classic,
written by an American*

In 1984 a frustrated Jimmy Barnes stepped out from the
shadow of Cold Chisel with his debut album, the bare
bones rock assault of *Bodyswerve* (named after a move in
soccer—or, as it's known in Barnes's birthplace of Scotland,
sportsball),[1] which was a massive success. And that, obviously, wasn't enough.

Perhaps *Bodyswerve* hadn't distanced Barnes from the band
quite enough—and after the acrimonious way Chisel had
disintegrated during the fraught and unhappy recording of

---

1   I really don't care for sport.

1984's *Twentieth Century*, and the subsequent farewell tour, he wanted to make it very, very clear that he was going on to bigger and better things. Sure, the album gave him two huge hit singles—'No Second Prize' and 'Daylight'—but both had begun life as Chisel songs. Barnes clearly had an audience, but he needed to be something other than That Guy What Was In That Band People Liked. *Bodyswerve* wasn't going to make him that, and it was hard to see how it was going to happen in Australia. Cold Chisel had never managed to break the US, and Barnes felt like this was unfinished business for him.

Thankfully, the album attracted the attention of Geffen Records—specifically, Geffen's head of A&R, Gary Gersh. He thought the US was just waiting to fall in love with Jimmy Barnes and all this would take was for America to get something that was very like *Bodyswerve*, but more American.

The answer was obvious: make *Bodyswerve* again, only this time make it more Americanier. The plan was to take the best—or at least the most American radio-friendly—moments on the first album and remix them for maximum Yank appeal, and then get some top-flight new material to complete the album. The upshot was that *For the Working Class Man* had five brand new songs, including material from local writers. Bruce Springsteen's guitarist "Little" Steven Van Zandt contributed 'Ride the Night Away' and classic rock songwriter Chas Sandford penned 'I'd Die to Be With You Tonight',[2] and when Barnes decided to try Jonathan Cain's 'American Heartbeat' Gersh thought they could go one better by getting Cain to knock up a song with Barnes's own audience in mind.

---

2   He also wrote John Waite's 'Missing You', which is a goddamn *mighty* tune.

Cain was the keyboard player in soft rock chart-toppers Journey—the band that gave the world the cartoonishly triumphant 'Don't Stop Believin' (which Cain co-wrote)—and Gersh hoped he would sprinkle some chart-topping magic on his new signing.

'So I heard a couple of songs that he had done in Cold Chisel and I heard his voice and I had the title in my head and sort of waited until the last minute to finish it,' Cain told Shane Pinnegar of *Xpress Magazine* in 2013. 'So maybe it was like a week before he got to the States to record, Gary kept calling to say, "Is Jimmy's song done yet?" and I said, "It's coming!" And I was out with my dog by the Bay where Steve Cropper supposedly wrote "Dock of the Bay" with Otis [Redding] and . . . I wrote the song in half an hour with my German shepherd.'

The central inspiration for the song was Cain's father—the very same one who told him not to stop believin' during his lean times as a struggling musician—though there are some really odd lines in the song which reflect the fact that Cain is American but knew he was writing a song for an Australian artist.

For a start, while Australia does indeed have cyclones rather than hurricanes, they are more common in our tropical north, not racing across our 'mid-western skies'. Also, Australia doesn't have a mid-west, and while simple men with hearts of gold can certainly be found in Australia, few would choose 'complicated' as the definitive adjective for our land.[3]

The other line that sounds a little off to Australian ears comes in the bridge, when Barnes declares the character of

---

3 Although as this book demonstrates, we're a hell of a lot more complicated than we like to pretend we are. Oh, Australia, you have so very, very many issues . . .

the song 'believes in God and Elvis', which worked as signifiers of solid working-class US values but don't really translate to Australia, a secular nation of notoriously low church attendance and personal faith, in which Mr Presley would probably not be nearly as venerated by the average working man as, well, Jimmy Barnes.

Then again, it also has echoes of the other Barnes-sung classic in this book with its reference to a subject who served in Vietnam and remains unhappy with Uncle Sam—which is at least a more healthily outward-facing response to the traumas of war than the self-destructive behaviours of the protagonist in 'Khe Sanh'.

With the new tracks and old ones remixed and remastered by US superproducer Bob Clearmountain (who mixed Springsteen's *Born in the USA* and David Bowie's *Let's Dance*, and would go on to mix INXS's *Kick*), Barnes's US debut was complete. Most records made under these sort of magpie conditions wouldn't have a hope of working as a cohesive whole, but *For the Working Class Man* somehow hangs together as a unified piece of work, carried by the power of Barnes's voice, enthusiasm and charisma—and, if his own reports are anything to go by, truly heroic amounts of drugs and alcohol.

In Australia it was released as a mid-price album, reflecting the fact that it wasn't entirely new to local audiences, and became the fifth Barnes-related album to go to #1 in as many years.[4] Bizarrely, however, the single that gave the album its title stalled at #5.

---

4   Those albums are Cold Chisel's live album *Swingshift* (1981) and the final two Chisel studio albums *Circus Animals* (1982) and *Twentieth Century* (1984), then the Barnes solo albums *Bodyswerve* (1984) and *For the Working Class Man* (1985).

The video was a celebration of sweaty masculinity and poor occupational health and safety protocols, with Barnes standing in steel smelters and before large burning cane fields wearing a sleeveless white t-shirt and no protective gear. Hopefully the union had a stern word with him.

In the US, however, the album was retitled *Jimmy Barnes* and did basically nothing. This, as it turned out, would largely be the case with all things entitled Jimmy Barnes: while he would build up a global audience over the coming decades, he would remain largely a cult figure outside Australia while hailed as a conquering god-hero inside it.

The song also gave the title to his shockingly excellent (and best-selling) 2016 autobiography *Working Class Boy*, which became a bestseller with its harrowing tales of childhood neglect and abuse in Glasgow and Adelaide as the child of penniless alcoholics.

'Working Class Man', meanwhile, is undeniably Barnes's signature song and a stone-cold Australian classic. Written by an American.[5]

---

5 You can read a similar story of how an American song became an Australian classic in chapter 34.

25

1985

Man Overboard

Do-Ré-Mi

*In which Australian feminism calls bullshit
on gaslighting*

One of the things you've probably noticed by now is that a lot of the most successful songs in terms of sales and cultural impact are, for want of a better word, odd. It's one thing to write a good, catchy song, but for it to have that certain something it needs to make the listener go '. . . what was that again?' Maybe it's a singalong flute riff, or a sudden bagpipe break, or a time signature that would make most drummers burst into tears—or, perhaps, just a bunch of words that wouldn't normally appear in a polite pop tune.

'Man Overboard' was a top 5 hit for Do-Ré-Mi in 1985 despite not having a chorus, and is easily the highest-charting

Australian song to contain 'pubic hair', 'penis envy' and 'anal humour' in the lyrics.

Describing it as a feminist anthem is blindingly obvious, but more specifically it's a savage takedown of a very common dynamic in heterosexual relationships whereby the male half leaves all the emotional labour to the female half. In the song, the protagonist refuses to accept being used by a partner happy to make a booty call and then make his excuses and depart, to make fun of her insecurities in public and then demand that she excuse his childish behaviour because he's the *real* victim here. And this was decades before the internet made being a furious man-baby such a popular way to respond to any hint of female independence.[1]

Even so, there's no guarantee that anyone would have heard it because the original version was . . . well, a bit shit.

The song was first recorded for Do-Ré-Mi's second EP, *The Waiting Room*, in 1983, and was wildly different to the version that is rolling through your head right now. The entire lyric is there, as is the basic structure, but almost everything else is far inferior to the version that was to come. For example: the vocal melody is far more subdued than Deborah Conway's subsequent bravura performance, Stephen Philip's guitars slash aimlessly and the rhythm section barrels along at a pace that made the song's dense lyrics sound impenetrable while the hooks of the song—the melody of the title line, the simple, hypnotic guitar riffs—are completely absent. To be honest, it's hard to hear the genius single that's buried under the frantic mess.

---

1 I'd put a shout out to the nation's proud men's rights activists here, but evidence suggests they're not exactly big on reading books. Or history. Or reading.

Then again, Do-Ré-Mi was basically a punk band when it formed in 1981 after Melbourne group the Benders split up, leaving singer Conway and drummer Dorland Bray at a loose end. They decided to move to Sydney to form a new band with Helen Carter, bassist with punk band Friction.

While working on their first self-titled EP the trio enlisted Carter's friend Philip—who was better known as Vivi Sector, guitarist with Sydney's pioneering DIY punk band Thought Criminals—to add some guitars; by the time the EP was out, he was a full-time member.

Six months later the band released *The Waiting Room*. It garnered a lot of attention, not least from the UK-based Virgin Records, which signed the band and flew its members to London to record their debut album under the supervision of British producer Gavin McKillop. And what a great idea that turned out to be.

Domestic Harmony showcased a vast leap forward in the band's confidence in their sound, their writing and—most dramatically—Conway's vocals. And that confidence was perhaps most clearly visible in the radical deconstruction of 'Man Overboard'.

See, bands occasionally will go back over old material and give a spit and polish, but they rarely do so in such a forensic way. Sometimes a song will develop on the road, sometimes the sketch laid down for a B-side transforms into a fully-fledged classic with a bit of perspective, but for the most part once a song is released, that's the definitive version. Bands tend to move forward creatively and don't typically look back at material they've already worked on, but when it happens, it's also incredibly confronting to be told: 'You have a great song in here, except that you completely missed it.'

Generally this sort of outside perspective only comes from a producer or the record company, because only people in a position of power could force a band to go through the excruciatingly uncomfortable process of second-guessing their creative instincts. Countless bands have split up in the studio under this sort of high-pressure self-examination, while others have been permanently crippled as fault lines emerge between those members who prove essential and those who find their parts being tweaked or rerecorded by more competent players.[2] Given that most bands start as gangs of friends rather than musical colleagues of a uniform standard, discovering the weaknesses and inadequacies of one's self and one's closest pals in the unforgiving confines of the studio can be emotionally and personally devastating.

Do-Ré-Mi, however, had the internal fortitude to consider what they did with 'Man Overboard' with a critical eye and were rewarded with stunning results.

The band would wisely ditch the a cappella introduction, retaining the lyrics as a spoken word piece for Conway to recite as the band settled into a groove behind her. Slowing the song down to a walking pace shuffle had another major benefit: it made Carter's growling bassline the foundation of

---

2   In the eighties this most often took the form of drummers not even appearing on their own albums, being replaced by the ubiquitous drum machine. This not only sidelined the players who are so often the heartbeat of the band, it also dated the albums in question. Much as I love the mid-eighties Go-Betweens records, the replacement of Lindy Morrison with a machine does not enhance them.

the song, freeing up Philip to abandon his chords and instead add impressionistic guitar flourishes.

What's remarkable about listening to the song now is how immediate it sounds: the production is crisp and punchy, perfectly balancing the mix of organic sounds (Conway's front-and-centre vocal, Bray's bongos, the sudden appearance of trombones from guest player Roger Freeman) and the highly processed (Philip's guitar noises, which still defy easy categorisation, the synths from future Marillion frontman Steve Hogarth).

It was a huge hit in Australia, climbing to #5 on the national charts and carrying *Domestic Harmony* with it. Much ink was spilled dissecting the song's meaning in the music press, and Conway became a bona fide star.[3] It set an unachievable standard to follow, though, with none of the other singles coming close to matching the success of 'Man Overboard'.

Domestic Harmony was followed in 1988 by a second and final album, *The Happiest Place in Town*,[4] produced by Martin

---

3 The band consistently presented themselves as a four-part collective, but Conway was always the focal point. It's not that big a surprise: while the other members maintained punk's distrust of the mainstream, Conway had been an actor and model prior to getting into music, and had also performed the lead vocals for the ABC's musical drama *Sweet and Sour*.

4 Just as an aside: there is no greater indication of internal discord in a band than the sudden appearance of very specific songwriting credits from a band that has hitherto credited everything to the entire group. If a band want to make it work, individual members cut their own internal deals while publicly crediting everything to the band (for example, Radiohead) or just credit everything to everyone and assume that it'll even out over time (REM's model); bands that want to split in a flurry of bitter recriminations make a point of leaving the drummer out of the songwriting credits and bitterly calculating what percentage the bridge counts for. Basically, the abrupt appearance of individual members' names inside the songwriting brackets is a huge red flag with SOMEONE WAS GETTING ROYALTIES WITHOUT PULLING THEIR CREATIVE WEIGHT emblazoned across it, and that sort of resentment never bodes well for a band's longevity.

Rushent—best known for his synth-pop productions in the early eighties, most notably with the Human League—which seemed an incongruous choice for the band, and the resulting album was not a roaring success: lead single 'Adultery' was a moderate hit, but follow-ups sank like stones. When Virgin announced it wanted a Conway solo album before considering a third Do-Ré-Mi album, the band promptly split—and have bucked convention by never reuniting.

Philip and Carter formed two bands, Lupi and Underfelt, neither of which captured the public imagination, and Bray joined Ghostwriters with Midnight Oil's Rob Hirst. Conway, meanwhile, embarked on an impressively varied solo career (not with Virgin), and enjoyed a huge hit with the jubilant 'It's Only the Beginning'.

When asked about the band in 1997, Conway didn't seem especially nostalgic. 'I'm far more in control of my voice now and it has improved immeasurably,' she told Anil Prasad at *Innerviews*. 'I play guitar on stage, which I never did in Do-Ré-Mi, and that has altered the way I perform. I always felt straightjacketed as a frontperson in Do-Ré-Mi. There were three other people's views to represent and a band persona to convey which wasn't entirely mine.'

Even so, 'Man Overboard' stands as an unassailable classic after three decades and counting, in what's either a stirring tribute to the band's insightful song craft or a sobering reflection on how little Australian male attitudes have improved. Actually, that's unfair: it's both.

26

1986

Wide Open Road

The Triffids

*In which a band create one of the most evocatively
Australian songs ever from the other side of the world*

The 1980s were a big time for Australian expats to leave
their home country and settle in the UK to experience proper
poverty without all that pesky support network around them.
Fortunately there were other Australian bands around ready
to offer friendship, knowledge and, um, other stuff.[1]

The Birthday Party had relocated to London in 1980 and
the Go-Betweens followed suit shortly thereafter, as did the
Mount Gambier-via-Adelaide-via-Melbourne iconoclasts the
Moodists. So when the Triffids, Perth's elegant maestros of

---

1   Heroin. We're talking about heroin.

dark, symphonic pop, decided to head to the mother country they at least had some like-minded colleagues with whom to meet up.

The Triffids were unique in that they not only got gigs in the UK, they also got significant media acclaim. While the other antipodean bands were struggling to get noticed the Triffids were getting berths at major festivals and becoming a legitimate live draw—moderate in the UK, but decent-sized in the Scandinavian countries, which fell in love with David McComb's appealing combination of Nick Cave's baritone bellow and Robert Forster's intellectual lyricism married with the thin, hawkish good looks of both.

However, they couldn't manage to land a record deal. Their previous albums had come out through Australian indie label Hot and were distributed through Rough Trade in the UK, but the songs McComb had composed while the band was living in Melbourne—a vague song cycle about youth, innocence being eroded, isolation, distance and loss—would require more than the meagre advances an indie label could provide.[2]

A tour with Echo and the Bunnymen provided an intro to Gil Norton, the producer of the British band's massive *Ocean Rain* album, who was fast becoming the person all the cool kids were tapping for their records—he would shortly go on to record the Pixies' *Doolittle* and James's breakthrough single 'Sit Down'—and the Triffids decided that rather than wait

---

2 The band had relocated from Perth to Sydney but decided to make their home in Melbourne instead. This plan was abandoned, drummer Alsy MacDonald recalled, when punters threatened to kick their heads in after an ill-fated gig opening for singlet-wearing pub rock stars the Uncanny X-Men, at which point London seemed like a physically safer bet.

for a label to give them the resources they needed, they'd pay for the album they wanted to release and use that as their calling card.

The result was *Born Sandy Devotional*,[3] and while there wasn't a dud song on it, there was clearly one song that declared itself the linchpin.[4] It opened side two, and it was called 'Wide Open Road'.

The song was written in Melbourne, with that cross-country drive from Perth fresh in McComb's mind, and while David occasionally declared that the song wasn't specifically about Australia, he would also admit that it was about a very particular section of the Nullarbor Plain the band had often driven across en route to shows in the east—specifically, the stretch of the Eyre Highway between Caiguna and Norseman.

It is a song rooted in Australian landscape, as is the rest of the album, which deals with the surf and blasting heat and faded colours of Western Australia. The fact that it was on an album titled *Born Sandy Devotional* meant people immediately and correctly assumed it was about the huge skies and vast distances of Western Australia. They could hardly be expected to think otherwise: the album's iconic front cover is an aerial shot of Mandurah, which was a tiny beachside town in 1961, when the photo was taken, and is now Western Australia's second-largest city (and effectively a southern suburb of Perth).

---

3 The enigmatic title was, according to a 2006 *Melody Maker* interview with David McComb, 'the name of a song which didn't make it onto the record, which is about someone called Sandy'.

4 It was a meticulously planned record, not least because the band could only just afford the number of multitrack tapes they were going to need. As a result, there are no outtakes or leftovers; only the ten tracks that are on the album were recorded.

The album was universally praised, and 'Wide Open Road' became an instant classic. It's the story of a man driven mad with despair and anger in the fruitless pursuit of a lost love, barrelling through the flatlands in search of someone who doesn't want to be found. As with all of David's lyrics, it's remarkable how much is expressed in so few words, and they're perfectly supported by a masterclass in musical minimalism.

In fact, it's hard to think of another song in which six people play so little. The way the simple elements coalesce—Jill Birt's ethereal keys, Evil Graham Lee's eerie pedal steel, big brother Robert McComb's jangling guitar, Alsy MacDonald's martial snare bursts—is gorgeously evocative, and makes the song all but impossible to cover. That hasn't stopped people attempting it: fellow West Australians the Panics did it in 2007 for Triple J's Like a Version, and Weddings Parties Anything gave it a jaunty bash in 1998. The Church were perhaps most successful with their 2007 take on acoustic album *El Momento Siguiente*, and Steve Kilbey later replaced the absent David McComb when the Triffids performed it at their 2008 induction into the ARIA Hall of Fame.

The bit you just read—in which David is absent—gives some indication of what was to come in the aftermath of this record. The Triffids might have been the Australian Band Most Likely To Make It as far as the *NME* was concerned, but it didn't actually translate into, well, actually making it. 'Wide Open Road' got to #26 in the UK but didn't crack the Australian top 50, and that huge record deal didn't quite eventuate—at least, not at first.

The band did sign with Island, but not before returning to Australia and making the lo-fi album *In the Pines* in a shearing shed in rural Western Australia, and neither of the two subsequent albums—*Calenture* in 1988 and *The Black Swan* the following year—were commercial smashes.[5] Exhausted by the constant travelling and with David wanting to make a solo record, in 1989 the band agreed to a six-month break, which rapidly became permanent.

Robert McComb became a teacher, MacDonald became a lawyer, Birt an architect. The making of David's solo album, *Love of Will*, became a long, drawn-out affair, eventually appearing in 1994, and in the interim he joined the loose side project the Blackeyed Susans—as did Lee and bassist Martyn Casey, the latter quitting in 1990 to join the Bad Seeds.

Like so many of the Australian musical contingent who made the move to London, opiates had become part of the picture for David (in part to alleviate the pain of an accident that had crushed several of his vertebrae when the band was in the UK). Ill health and poor self-care led to a heart transplant in 1996, and in 1999 he was involved in a car accident in Melbourne; three days later, on 2 February 1999, he died at home.[6] He was thirty-six years old.

'Wide Open Road', however, has remained immortal. In Triple J's inaugural Hottest 100 in 1989 it came in at sixty-eight, rising to forty-nine the following year, and was voted

---

5   Although, amazingly, *Calenture*'s lead single 'Bury Me Deep in Love' was used as the wedding music for Harold and Madge in a 1988 episode of *Neighbours*. Seriously. Amazing.

6   The coroner's report, released the following year, determined that McComb had died from 'acute heroin toxicity', plus complications arising from the heart transplant.

one of the Top 30 Australian Songs of All Time by APRA in 2001.

Maybe McComb hasn't really left us at all. Maybe he's still somewhere out there on the flatlands.

27

1986

Don't Dream It's Over

Crowded House

*In which we acknowledge that it would be a lot easier
for everyone involved if we'd made this a book about
the songs that shaped Australasia instead*

Okay, let's make something clear: sometimes it's important to make a distinction between Australia and New Zealand, and sometimes it is not.

Yes, Australia has a rich history of claiming New Zealanders as honorary Australians, much to the disgust of said New Zealanders, who already hail from a perfectly good country and don't care for the implied slight. Yes, Australia missed its chance to keep New Zealand as part of New South Wales when the first British governor was sent there in 1832,[1] and

---

1   Fun fact: New Zealand was part of New South Wales when Arthur Phillip was made governor. Since it doesn't appear to have been any closer to Sydney back then, that would have been a hell of a long commute.

probably should have said something before the Treaty of Waitangi was signed in 1840. And yes, Neil Finn is unambiguously from New Zealand—he even references his birthplace, Te Awamutu, in the third line of Crowded House's first single, 'Mean to Me', just in case that little fact had somehow slipped notice.

However, Crowded House isn't easily described as a New Zealand band. For a start, it was formed in Melbourne. What's more, thanks to bassist Nick Seymour and drummer Paul Hester, it was two-thirds Australian (three-quarters, if you count the presence of former Reels guitarist Craig Hooper in the Mullanes, which . . . but we'll get to that). Besides, if you're going to determine the origin of a band on the basis of the nationality of its members, these days Crowded House is American,[2] thanks to the presence of multi-instrumentalist Mark Hart and drummer Matt Sherrod, which kinda weakens the argument.

But hell, 'Don't Dream It's Over' is a goddamn Australian classic and it's going in this book regardless of petty arguments over whether or not the band that created it was technically Australian. I'm writing the thing, and I can determine my own goddamn criteria.

So: Australian combo Crowded House was formed in 1984 when Australian Paul Hester and honorary Australian Neil Finn were wrapping up the Enz With a Bang farewell tour

---

2 Fun fact: Crowded House was also the name of a thoroughbred stallion that won two of his nineteen Group One races from his 2006 debut until becoming a breeding stallion in 2011. And that's well and good, but why the owners overlooked the obvious by failing to name him 'Crowded Horse' has yet to be adequately explained.

DON'T DREAM IT'S OVER 163

for Split Enz, a New Zealand band of which they were both members and . . . *damn it, if Split Enz are unambiguously from New Zealand—goddamn, it's even in their name!—how can Crowded House be Australi . . . Look, don't overthink this. Just keep going. You got this, APS.*

Right. Moving on.

Split Enz was splitting and enzzing and Finn and Hester had determined that they wanted to form a new band together. Nick Seymour, little brother of the Mark that you met in chapter 21, fronted up to Finn at the after party for the tour's Melbourne show and asked if he could audition,[3] and thus he and guitarist Hooper joined the band, which was at that point called the Mullanes because Neil Finn is terrible at naming bands.[4]

The Mullanes immediately signed a US deal with Capitol on the basis of Finn's work with Split Enz and the well-deserved confidence that he had more hits like 'Message to My Girl' and 'I Got You' percolating in his brain.

Hooper didn't stick around too long, and the remaining trio decided not to replace him before they decamped to the Hollywood Hills to work on their debut album with producer Mitchell Froom, bringing Enz keyboardist Eddie Rayner along for the ride.

---

3 Seymour's main rival for the gig was a bassist named Wayne Stevens. It would have kept things within the extended Split Enz family, since Stevens had played in the Swingers—you remember: they did 'Counting the Beat'—which was the band formed by Phil Judd after he quit Split Enz in 1980 and thereby necessitated the abrupt hiring of Tim Finn's little brother Neil to replace him. In the Swingers, Stevens had adopted the name 'Bones Hillman', which might sound a little more familiar—and don't fret, for a few years later Bones was to get a pretty sweet gig with the band in chapter 30.

4 'Mullane' was his mother's family name and is also Finn's middle name. What it definitely is *not* is a killer name for a band.

Capitol did have one immediate priority as the band created its debut: it needed a different name quick smart. And the band came up with an alternative, and thus the band of Neil Finn, Paul Hester and Nick Seymour became . . . the Largest Living Things.[5]

Capitol wisely suggested they try again and, when the band came back with a name based on their poky living arrangements in their rented apartment, gave whatever is the record company equivalent of a shrug and decided it would have to do.

The recording of the album was not without conflict; Crowded House's internal dramas were never far below the surface, thanks to Finn's fearsome ambition and desire to escape the shadow of his big brother Tim, who had formed Split Enz and had already embarked on a successful solo career. And Neil wasn't above stepping on people's toes to get what he wanted either. Indeed, he's the only member of the band to play on 'Now We're Getting Somewhere', with Hester and Seymour being kicked out of the studio to be replaced by session players (the drums are played on the track by the legendary Jim Keltner and the bass by Jerry Scheff). From the get-go, there was no doubt who was the daddy in this particular House.

And yet the band's singular chemistry is what makes 'Don't Dream It's Over'. It perfectly showcases the strengths of the band, with Hester laying down a solid groove that would seem incongruous for a ballad but provides a perfect bed for a

---

5   Honestly, how can someone so magnificent with words be so terrible at coming up with a decent band name?

gorgeously fluid bassline from Seymour, which in turn beautifully complements an understated Hammond solo by Froom. From the outset, this was clearly a classic in the making.

Astonishingly enough, it was also the *fourth* single released from the album rather than, as you would assume, the absolute and obvious first. 'Mean to Me', 'World Where You Live' and 'Now We're Getting Somewhere' all got a guernsey before someone at Capitol presumably went: 'Hey, this perfect song with the singalong chorus that makes grown men openly weep at its sheer undeniable beauty? What say we release it as a single, just for funsies?'

Finn didn't labour over the song either. 'I wrote that on my brother's piano,' he later told *Goldmine*. 'I'm not sure if I remember what the context was, exactly, but it was just about on the one hand feeling kind of lost, and on the other hand sort of urging myself on: don't dream it's over. That one actually fell out literally, without me thinking about it too much.'

Helped by the gorgeous video, made by a promising young director named Alex Proyas (who would go on to direct *Dark City*, *The Crow*, *I, Robot* and the massive 2016 flop *Gods of Egypt*), 'Don't Dream It's Over' became the band's biggest hit in the US, reaching #2 in the singles charts,[6] and #1 in Canada and New Zealand—but not Australia, where it topped out at #8. That's what happens when you save a perfect song for single number four: by that point everyone already has the album. (That said, the album was not an immediate smash in

---

6   For the record, the song that robbed them of a US number one was 'I Knew You Were Waiting (For Me)' by George Michael and Aretha Franklin.

Australia either: it did finally get to #1, but it took a year to do so.)

It was another song celebrated in the ARIA Top 30 Australian Songs of All Time by APRA in 2001, coming in at #7 on the Australian list and #2 on the New Zealand one, and if not even ARIA can work out which country Crowded House belong to it's downright unreasonable to expect this book would somehow do it.[7]

While Crowded House would go on to become massive stars in the UK, Australia and New Zealand, they proved a one-hit wonder in the US. Relations with Capitol deteriorated when *Temple of Low Men* failed to match the success of *Crowded House*. 'Don't Dream It's Over' has endured there too, though: it was used in an episode of *Glee* and was covered by a slew of artists, perhaps least necessarily by US Christian combo Sixpence None the Richer (who also gave the world a genuinely ghastly version of the La's 'There She Goes').

The song has always been a celebration of hope over adversity, but it acquired even greater poignancy when Ariana Grande and Miley Cyrus performed it together at the One Love Manchester concert on 4 June 2017, responding to the terrorist attack that killed twenty-three people leaving an Ariana Grande concert in the city on 22 May. Those lyrics of resilience and unity had never sounded more powerful.

---

7 So there.

28

1986

You're the Voice

John Farnham

In which a washed-up teen idol becomes the biggest-selling Australian artist of all time, and creates an alternative national anthem to boot

Given John Farnham's exalted position as a national treasure it's hard to fathom the fact that before *Whispering Jack* became the highest-selling Australian album by an Australian artist of all time,[1] absolutely no-one gave a shit about him.

Born in the UK, his family had moved to Australia when he was ten and he'd played with various Melbourne bands before coming to public prominence with his 1967 novelty

---

1   Only one album has sold more copies in Australia: Meat Loaf's *Bat Out of Hell*. What the fuck, nation?

single 'Sadie (The Cleaning Lady)'. The song was a #1 hit and Little Johnny Farnham was voted *TV Week*'s King of Pop for five years running, beginning in 1969. However, the hits started to dry up in the mid-seventies and Farnham decided to concentrate on his television career, starring in the one-season sitcom *Bobby Dazzler* and only singing in stage musicals.

By 1980 he was considered old hat, but the first seeds of his eventual renaissance were sown when he finally found a manager who understood his potential: former Masters Apprentices bassist Glenn Wheatley. The pair met when both were managed by Darryl Sambell, with whom Farnham had split. Wheatley immediately took control, giving Farnham a top 10 hit with his power ballad cover of the Beatles' 'Help!', but that appeared to be a one-off, as subsequent singles sank without trace.

The next big idea was to plonk Farnham in the space vacated by Glenn Shorrock in Little River Band in 1982, where he got to preside over a significant decline in their commercial fortunes and an uptick in internal disagreements. By 1985 he'd jumped ship—but the experiment united him with someone who would have a significant impact on his future success: keyboardist David Hirschfelder, who joined LRB around the same time as Farnham.

Another significant thing happened around this time: while on a US trip Farnham was at a jazz club where a friend told the MC that there was a star in their midst. 'Ladies and gentlemen, we have an Australian great in the house tonight,' he subsequently announced. 'Maybe he'll step up and give us a song. Here he is folks: Jack Phantom!'—which, to be fair, is a great name.[2]

To his credit Farnham very reasonably thought this was hilarious, and he adopted the nickname. Then one fateful night, while some locals played pool in a pub, he started doing mock commentary of the game in the style of *Pot Black*'s legendary snooker caller 'Whispering' Ted Lowe. In that moment Whispering Jack Phantom was born: all he needed was an album.

And that was a problem, because no-one was willing to stump up the cash for a comeback record by a man best known at the time as a pop culture punchline. Wheatley had faith, though, and mortgaged his house to raise the $150,000 they needed to get the album done. Farnham, for his part, had been all but wiped out by a series of bad business decisions. He was acutely aware that this album was his last chance to save his career and financial future.

They started accumulating songs during 1985, knowing that this record needed to be an all-killer-no-filler effort— and since Farnham wasn't really a songwriter,[3] that meant casting a wide net.[4] Even as it was taking shape Wheatley and Farnham had a nagging feeling that there was something

---

2 This excellent story comes from Jeff Apter's equally-excellent biography of Farnham, *Playing to Win*.

3 Farnham has written and co-written many songs over the years, but they tended to be B-sides and album tracks rather than his big hits. That said, two songs on *Whispering Jack* credit Farnham as a writer: the closing 'Let Me Out' is his, and he co-wrote 'Going Going Gone' with Hirschfelder and producer Ross Fraser.

4 For many years now I have been waging a one-man campaign to have 'Advance Australia Fair' replaced as our national anthem by *Whispering Jack*'s far superior opening track, 'Pressure Down'. I'll admit the going has been slow thus far, but I assume that as soon as we become a republic it'll be the new president's first decree.

important missing: the album needed a real rallying point, a statement of intent. An anthem. Maybe with some bagpipes or something.

Meanwhile a UK singer named Chris Thompson was attempting to kickstart his moribund solo career. He'd been fronting Manfred Mann's Earth Band and performed as The Voice of Humanity in Jeff Wayne's hilariously over-the-top musical version of H.G. Wells' sci-fi classic 'The War of the Worlds', but was at a bit of a low career ebb when he went into a session with a couple of fellow songwriters signed to the same publishing company: Maggie Ryder, a jobbing singer and songwriter who'd worked with the likes of Brian May and Eurythmics, and Andy Qunta, a British-born keyboard player who had joined Icehouse in 1982 and toured and recorded with them ever since. The trio began work on what Thompson had conceived as a protest song, inspired by the hundred thousand plus marchers who had descended on London demanding nuclear disarmament. Thompson had intended to be among them but had overslept, and was therefore feeling a bit guilty as well as inspired.[5]

The trio worked for a grand total of four hours on 'You're the Voice', trying to capture the spirit of a mass movement to a marching beat. Ryder came up with the vocal melody line for the chorus, Thompson came up with the 'whoa-oa-oa-oa' bit, and then none of them could come up with any decent lyrics.

Thompson then reached out to Keith Reid, the chap responsible for just about all of Procol Harum's lyrics, including those

---

5   Let this be a lesson to anyone who plans to get along to a protest and then bails at the last minute: it's absolutely acceptable, provided that you then write a chart-topping smash hit song about it.

of 'A Whiter Shade of Pale',[6] and tasked him with fixing up the song.

'He came up with some very important lines, like "We're all someone's daughter, we're all someone's son",' Thompson told News Corps' Cameron Adams in 2016. 'He got rid of what I called the "yuck" lines.'

Doris Tyler was working as label manager with the Wheatley Organisation when, according to one version of the story, she crossed paths with Icehouse, who were working on what was to become *Measure for Measure*. She mentioned that Wheatley was still looking for The Song for John Farnham, at which point Qunta pulled out a cassette with Thompson's recording thereon.[7]

Bizarrely, Thompson initially refused permission for Farnham to record the song. He had grown up in New Zealand and knew Farnham as the 'Sadie' guy and didn't want his precious song sullied by a novelty hit has-been—and besides, he planned to cut the song himself for his upcoming album with Atlantic. Except Atlantic hated the thing and said no.

The version that Farnham demoed was almost note for note what Thompson had demoed, but he made one big change to the original version. As a man with ears and a modicum of human taste, he very correctly felt that the choice of a bass solo after the second chorus was a terrible, terrible idea. But

---

6 Well, let's be honest: the *real* writer of 'A Whiter Shade of Pale' is Johannes Sebastian Bach, but he's not around to fight for his publishing rights.

7 There's another slightly more plausible version, which was that the song had been sent to Wheatley for consideration and Tyler happened to be the person who went through the tapes, but the other version is far more exciting. Also, assuming the more mundane version is the correct one, why would Thompson send a tape in and then refuse to let the song be used?

what could replace it? The answer was taken from Farnham's supposed favourite song, which you met in chapter 11.

Yes, because of 'It's a Long Way to the Top (If You Wanna Rock'n'Roll)', 'You're the Voice' got bagpipes. And they're real, too, by the way: while a lot of the album was made using the then-cutting edge technology of the Fairlight computer, the bagpipes are not a sample.[8]

It was the final song recorded for *Whispering Jack*, although there was some eleventh-hour drama when a cold-ridden Farnham rerecorded the vocal in one desperate final take to give it the necessary urgency and passion that made the song so compelling. But the effort was worth it: they knew they had a hit, they knew they had an album that any record company would fall over itself to release, and so Wheatley started shopping it around.

And no-one wanted it.

'Every label passed on it,' Wheatley told Adams. 'I had to release it on Wheatley Records because I couldn't get anyone to take the punt. I knew people at radio would still have a problem playing a John Farnham song, they'd still think of him as Johnny Farnham. I had a few stations straight up tell me: "We'll never play a John Farnham song, he's the 'Sadie' man." So I put it out on a white label without his name on it.'

By this time, Farnham was a complete wreck. He'd poured everything into the album and was acutely aware that if it wasn't a success it would not only spell the end of his own career but would probably bankrupt the Wheatleys as well.

---

8 What *is* a sample is that thumping *whoomp!* percussion sound in the verses, which was a car door slamming in the demo version and the door of Wheatley's Porsche slamming in the final version. Try it with your own Porsche at home!

Finally, 2DayFM agreed to playlist it after a performance on *Hey Hey It's Saturday*, and then the audience requests started coming in. A no-budget video was made, featuring Farnham emoting in front of a fake band that included Hirschfelder and a bunch of miming ringers: James and Vince Leigh from Pseudo Echo on unconvincing guitar and drums respectively,[9] and Greg Macainsh from Skyhooks on bass. It also boasts appearances from future senator Derryn Hinch and his then-wife, the actor Jackie Weaver, because hey, why not?

'You're the Voice' slowly rose up the charts, eventually getting to #1. *Whispering Jack* came out and did the same, staying at #1 for a staggering six months.

It not only saved Farnham's career, it relaunched it completely—and created a template for other mid-career artists who were keen to rejuvenate themselves. It's not much of a stretch to suggest that without Farnham there'd have been no nineties-and-beyond renaissance for other Australian seventies superstars like Daryl Braithwaite, Ross Wilson and Renee Geyer.

The song also inspired a young UK band named Coldplay, who played it in early rehearsals and would later perform it with Farnham at the 2009 Sound Relief concert. On a rather less pleasant note, racist nut jobs Reclaim Australia started using the song at their hate-rallies in the two thousand-teens, which Farnham spoke out against in no uncertain terms.

9　James Leigh was far better known as a keyboard player than a guitarist, but this was just before Pseudo Echo's career-scuttling 'rock' period, leading to their album *Race*, for which they wore denim, strapped on guitars and ditched the hair gel, the synthesisers and their entire audience.

Great successes and dramas were to follow: there were more hit albums, more massive tours—but also a lot of controversy about his failure to retire after his 'The Last Time' retirement tour in 2002,[10] and the fallout from Wheatley's conviction and imprisonment for tax evasion in 2007. But throughout it all, 'You're the Voice' became another alternative Australian national anthem.[11]

Thompson eventually recorded his own version in 2014. And this time he also put in bagpipes.

---

10 A disgruntled fan attempted to sue Farnham for deceptive marketing for continuing to tour after 2002. The ACCC failed to take any action.

11 ... although that should be 'Pressure Down', just to be clear.

29

1987

I Should Be
So Lucky

Kylie Minogue

*In which Australia creates a
global pop starlet*

Their imperial period might have only lasted a few short years, but between about 1986 and 1989 it looked like the UK writing and production trio Stock Aitken Waterman (SAW) were the future of pop music.

Their combination of upbeat synthesised songs (using largely the same sounds from one artist to the next) and pure weapons-grade pop sensibility gave them a total of more than two hundred #1 singles around the world. Nowadays they evoke more nostalgia than admiration, although the oddly enduring internet prank of 'rickrolling' has meant their work has become immortal in the digital age.[1]

The trio formed in 1984 when former DJ and major label A&R man Pete Waterman set up his own production company, PWL, and hired Matt Aitken and Mike Stock, two jobbing musicians from Mirage, a lounge band working the hotel and cruise ship circuit. The plan was to form an all-in-one hit-making company with songs, production and promotion all carried out in-house—and they immediately had two top 20 hits right out of the gate with Divine's 'You Think You're a Man' (#16) and Hazell Dean's 'Whatever I Do (Wherever I Go)' (#4).

While the first few massive hits were with acts that had strong opinions about their music and actually wrote (or co-wrote) their own material, such as Dead Or Alive with 'You Spin Me Round (Like A Record)' and Bananarama (who enjoyed hits with 'Love in the First Degree', 'I Heard A Rumour' and the enormous smash cover of Shocking Blue's 'Venus'), the trio realised they'd be even more efficient—and not have to share any songwriting royalties—if they just brought in attractive vocalists to put a face and a voice to material they'd already written out. And then they were advised about an Australian soapie star who had both a voice and a face they should check out.

---

1   In the unlikely event that you've not encountered it, 'rickrolling' is the act of making someone inadvertently watch the video for Rick Astley's 1987 classic 'Never Gonna Give You Up', normally via a disguised hyperlink to the clip. Occasionally it takes on a slightly more sophisticated form by slyly evoking the song's title or chorus. Indeed, there was a minor furore over Melania Trump's much-derided 2016 speech at the Republican National Convention, which contained the lines: 'He will never, ever give up. And most important, he will never, ever let you down.' Was the speechwriter for the future First Lady rickrolling us? We will never know. And also: yes, absolutely.

I SHOULD BE SO LUCKY

Kylie Minogue was a superstar in Australia thanks to her role on *Neighbours* as the plucky gal mechanic Charlene Mitchell. In fact, it's easy to forget how short her *Neighbours* tenure was—she first appeared in April 1986 and farewelled the show in July 1988—but in July 1987 her marriage to Scott Robinson (played by Jason Donovan) broke viewership records in both Australia and the UK. That same month she recorded her debut single for Mushroom Records—a cover of Little Eva's 'The Loco-Motion' (retitled 'Locomotion')— which went to #1 for seven weeks. Someone at Mushroom had the bright idea to team Minogue up with those British chaps who were having all those hits, which seemed a smart idea. Calls were made, and Minogue was promptly dispatched to the mother country to make her next single.

That single was 'I Should Be So Lucky', and the legend goes that it was written under less than opportune circum- stances. Depending on who you believe, it was either written in ten minutes or forty, but everyone agrees it was done in frantic haste because everyone at PWL had completely forgotten that the diminutive Australian soap star was coming to the studio.

Pete Waterman tells the story in *1000 UK Number One Hits*: 'I was at home one Friday afternoon when I got a phone call from Mike Stock at the office who asked if there was something I had forgotten to tell him. "A small Antipodean called Kylie Minogue?" prompted Mike. "Oh yes, I forgot, she's in town." Mike said, "No, she's in reception."'

When Stock told Waterman they couldn't apologise and reschedule since she had to return to Australia to continue filming *Neighbours* the following day, Waterman scoffed, 'She should be so lucky,' And thus did inspiration strike.

Minogue did her performance inside of an hour, and the hook 'lucky lucky lucky' was supposedly an improvised joke during recording that stayed put.

The lyrics were based on Stock figuring that Minogue's dream run of professional success must have come at some sort of a cost, which he decided was probably romantic.[2] And while the lyrics were not especially noteworthy, like a lot of SAW numbers what sounds musically simple is actually fiendishly complex.

'Anyone who thinks Kylie Minogue's "I Should Be So Lucky" is easy should try to play it,' a defensive-sounding Stock told *The Guardian* in 2010. 'It's in four keys, all of them really awkward, and you can't even strum it unless you're a really good musician.'

The video was shot in Melbourne—at Channel 7, which seems traitorous for someone on a Channel 10 program—and was a showcase of the many ways in which Kylie could be styled. In that sense, it set the scene for all the videos to come.

It went #1 in Australia and the UK, and Finland, and Germany, and Japan, and Switzerland, and Hong Kong, and Ireland. It even went top thirty in the US—although it didn't match the top 3 placement of 'Locomotion'. In fact, it would take until 2001 and 'Can't Get You Out of My Head' for Minogue to enjoy another bona fide US hit.

However, this song was the first of an unbroken run of thirteen #1 UK singles SAW would create for Minogue,

---

2   See, ladies? Even in pop songs, you apparently can't have it all.

I SHOULD BE SO LUCKY

179

their most successful act. And while Minogue later distanced herself from many of her early singles, 'I Should Be So Lucky' remained in her touring set for decades.

The SAW golden age began to tarnish in the 1990s, when their brand of upbeat pop seemed hokey and dated. The team's final UK #1 was courtesy of Kylie—her saccharine cover of 'Tears On My Pillow' in 1990—and Aitken quit the trio in 1991 when the pressure got too much for him. Waterman and Stock split in 1993, and although the three would periodically work together in various combinations, it wasn't until 2015 and the Christmas single 'Every Day's Like Christmas' (written by Coldplay's Chris Martin) that they would reunite with Minogue. Despite being touted as a possible Christmas #1, 'Every Day's Like Christmas' didn't even make the top 100.

By that stage Kylie had become a proper National Treasure in both the UK and Australia, having managed the rare feat of remaining relevant in the fickle world of pop for a solid four decades. Some years were more successful than others but she never had an out-an-out flop, and those albums that didn't do so well (such as 1997's cred-chasing *Impossible Princess*) were critically acclaimed cult successes.

The weird thing about Kylie Minogue: Pop Star, however, was that she never really stopped being the sexless ingenue of 'I Should Be So Lucky'—and that's rare in pop music, and particularly rare in pop music by female performers. Even when she was pumping out bedroom-based beats as per later singles like 'Confide in Me', there's never been anything tantalisingly carnal about her music—unlike, say, Madonna or Britney Spears or Katy Perry or Rihanna or Beyoncé or any number of other female pop icons whose sexuality was part and parcel of their music.[3] In that sense she provided a model for future Australian chart-toppers like Delta Goodrem, who similarly parlayed a TV career into a pleasant and entirely unerotic pop career.

Years later Kylie would attempt a hard reset on the public perception of her as an unthreatening pop starlet, but that's a story we'll get to in chapter 39. In the meantime, things were heating up in Australia's political songscape.

---

3   Back in 2010 I reviewed Minogue's album *Aphrodite* and wrote something along the lines of 'if Lady Gaga is the sound of unfettered emotional instability in pop music, Kylie Minogue is what happens when the meds work exactly as prescribed'. I always liked that description and, damn it, I'm reusing it here.

30

1987

Beds Are Burning

Midnight Oil

*In which Australia is reminded exactly
what its Bicentenary is built on*

Something very important happened to Midnight Oil between
1984's *Red Sails in the Sunset* and 1987's *Diesel and Dust*: they
found a cause to believe in.

See, Midnight Oil had not always been a political band.
When they started out they were a rock group that played surf
clubs and didn't allow their personal beliefs to influence their
music particularly—which is why, for example, their sincere
religious leanings were such a big surprise to a lot of fans.
Social issues didn't really appear in the lyrics until their third
album, 1981's *Place Without a Postcard*, which included songs
like the anti-war 'Armistice Day', the rejection of small town

development in 'Burnie' and the all-purpose rejection of pretty much everything in the barrelling 'Don't Wanna Be the One'.[1]

The album flopped outside of Australia but that didn't stop the band honing its growing social conscience on the breakthrough album, 1982's *10, 9, 8, 7, 6, 5, 4, 3, 2, 1*, which took swipes at the risks of constant international conflict in the high-stakes nuclear age ('Short Memory'), the media ('Read About It'), nuclear testing on Aboriginal land ('Maralinga') and the very particular flavour of Australian complacency in the mighty 'Power and the Passion'.

That song had made the sneering point that few Australians actually had any experience of the outback and the hard-touring band members were determined not to be hypocrites by snubbing the vast Australian inland. They'd been making an effort to get out of the rut of the city and suburban touring circuit, so when they met and signed Warumpi Band, who offered the Oils the chance to tour through Central Australian regions that would normally be all but impossible for a non-Aboriginal band to play, they rose to the challenge.[2] Thematically it seemed like a great fit too, since the band's staunch anti-nuclear stance dovetailed into its zeal for Aboriginal land rights,[3] as rapacious mining

---

1   It's one of a bunch of songs that reference colour television as a thing, along with Dire Straits' 'Money for Nothing'. Anyone looking for a cultural studies thesis topic should consider 'RGB Pixels as Harbinger of Consumerist Armageddon: Colour TV as symbol of western decadence in popular music, 1974–85'.

2   And you already read all about that in chapter 23. ARTFULLY CONSTRUCTED JIGSAW PUZZLE.

3   In the early eighties nuclear disarmament was the band's premier passion. It came up in multiple songs—notably 'When the Generals Talk' and 'Minutes to Midnight' on *Red Sails in the Sunset* (whose cover art by Tsunehisa Kimura of a Sydney Harbour devastated by a nuclear strike is still the stuff of nightmares), but also in that Peter Garrett ran as a NSW senate candidate for the Nuclear Disarmament Party in the 1984 federal election and only just missed out on winning a seat. It's interesting to consider the music upon which we'd have missed out had Garrett been successful.

companies had been profiting handsomely from both uranium mining and stalling progress on native title for decades.

In 1985 there had been talk of a gig at Uluru to mark the passing of Halley's Comet, on which a lot of Central Australian towns had been pinning their economic hopes as a massive tourist draw—Alice Springs in particular embarked on a flurry of hotel-building—but to no avail, for the crowds never arrived. However, when Halley Fever seemed set to make the red centre a tourism hotspot Midnight Oil was approached about playing the Uluru show as part of a proposed line-up that also included Dire Straits and Sting.[4] The idea of drawing attention to the contemporary disputes over the stewardship of Uluru seemed appealing, but the Oils' manager, Gary Morris, thought it sounded a little off and contacted Gary Foley, director of the Aboriginal Arts Board, to ask if this would be appropriate in such a sacred place. The answer was a resounding nope.

If the band wanted to draw attention to the issue of land rights, Morris was advised, they should speak to the Pitjantjatjara and Yankunytjatjara people of Mutitjulu about what might be an appropriate forum. As it happened, there was a documentary in the works to celebrate the return of Uluru to the traditional owners—*Uluru: An Anangu Story*—and the band was invited to contribute a song to the soundtrack.

The band worked on three songs for submission—'The Dead Heart', 'Beds Are Burning' and the unreleased '40,000 Years

---

4 Andrew McMillan's long-out-of-print book about this tour, *Strict Rules*, was reprinted in 2017 and is an astonishingly good document of this whole period. Just saying.

Come Home'. The first was chosen, and during the discussions the idea of doing some Central Australian shows was raised—and thus did the tour with Warumpi come together.

Although 'Beds Are Burning' didn't make the cut for the doco, Rob Hirst knew it was something special even in demo form. 'The song has become something of a theme for this tour,' Hirst said of the still-incomplete piece on the *Black Fella/White Fella* documentary covering the tour.[5] 'I've always had this dream that this band could write an Australian music which people overseas could get on to and understand which would enlarge their whole vision of Australia past Vegemite sandwiches and kangaroo hops.'[6]

The song appears in a nascent live form in the film: the chorus is there and sounds tremendous, but frontman Peter Garrett is clearly still toying with the verses. They sound extemporised and rambling, which might explain the reaction from the audience—tolerant bemusement—compared with the enthusiastic response Warumpi received.

By the time the band actually recorded the song, after three weeks of playing makeshift shows on red dirt stages, the lyrics had become lean and economical. Garrett had winnowed them down to a series of impressionistic vignettes, painting

---

5 .... which you absolutely need to see. Honestly, it's a goddamn blinder of a doco, and there's one bit where Warumpi are playing 'Blackfella/Whitefella' with members of the Oils joining in on the coda while members of Warumpi step off as the song morphs into 'The Dead Heart'. The moment where Gordon Butcher Tjapanangka seamlessly relinquishes the drum stool to Rob Hirst without missing a beat is especially brilliant.

6 See chapter 16.

BEDS ARE BURNING

the Western Desert as a living thing and name-checking settlements like Yuendumu and Kintore.[7]

And then things get absolutely unambiguous with the pre-chorus hook of 'the time has come to say fair's fair'. It's bold and clear, but had particular resonance to an Australian audience, evoking as it does the archetypically Straylian and much-politically-exploited notion of the Fair Go.

The music was just as strong thanks to Hirst's irresistible chorus, the rumbling bassline of Peter Gifford and the glorious three-note brass bursts that turn the song into a literal rallying cry (played live on the tour and on the subsequent recording by trombonist Glad Reed).

It's also important to note that the language changed subtly between the two songs; 'The Dead Heart' put Midnight Oil as the well-meaning spokespeople of the disenfranchised with the use of 'us' and 'our', while in 'Beds Are Burning' the band was no longer speaking as anything other than a member of the white mainstream, with the pronouns switched to 'them' and 'their'.

By the time *Diesel and Dust* was released Gifford had left the band, his health having taken a beating from the constant touring. His place was taken by Bones Hillman ahead of what was to be the band's most intense international touring schedule.[8] 'Beds Are Burning' was the second single from the album

---

7 Just to clarify a common misconception, the line is 'From Kintore, east to Yuendumu'. There's no such place as Kintore East, not least because the town only has a couple of dozen buildings and is therefore not a place where residents would need to clarify that they were living in the fancy side of the town, for example, with the better-quality crocodiles (see chapter 23 for more on Kintore's storied croc situation).

8 Hey, remember back in chapter 27 when he didn't get the gig with Crowded House? What a happy ending!

('The Dead Heart' had been released ahead of the album in 1986) and became Midnight Oil's most internationally successful track—although it's interesting that it failed to get to #1 in Australia while topping the charts in two other Commonwealth nations that have done a far better job of reconciling themselves to their colonial past: Canada and New Zealand. It was also voted the third-greatest Australian song of all time in that APRA seventy-fifth anniversary chart that has already been mentioned a dozen or so times, beaten by the songs in chapters 5 and 9, and was the sole Oils song to make the 2009 Triple J Hottest 100 of All Time in 2009, coming in at #97.

What made the song even more powerful was that it was released just as the nation began to embark on an orgy of self-congratulation ahead of the 1988 Bicentennial of European occupation of Australia. In that sense, it's a companion piece to the final song in this book, laying out in no uncertain terms that the building of Australia has come at a terrible and largely unacknowledged cost—although the tenor of the songs is very, *very* different.

The message proved timeless, too. When Midnight Oil were invited to perform at the closing ceremony of the Sydney Olympic Games in 2000, they took the opportunity to apologise to the stolen generations—something that the prime minister, John Howard, had refused to do. Before an audience of millions, they performed 'Beds Are Burning' in black outfits with 'sorry' printed thereon. See, John? It's that easy.

The love and respect meted out to the band in general and Garrett in particular was tarnished somewhat when the Oils split in 2002 ahead of the beginning of the frontman's political career as a Labor member of parliament. There was something deeply unsettling about watching Garrett the articulate idealist make pragmatic decisions as a government minister. A lot of that was the inevitable effect of Labor's caucus discipline—no sitting party member can vote against a party policy without resigning from the party—but many observers watching him announce his approval of the Four Mile uranium mine in South Australia in 2009 wondered why the hell he'd become environment minister if not to stop exactly this sort of thing.

Even so, the enthusiasm that followed the announcement that the Oils were re-forming for a world tour in 2017 showed both how much the band had been missed and how frustratingly relevant its songs remained. Listening to 'Beds Are Burning' again today reminds us that we should really have moved a lot further on these issues than we had in 1987. Yet here we still are.

31

1988

Under the Milky Way

The Church

*In which one of Australia's greatest bands
is forced to create a classic*

'Flat, lifeless and sterile.' That's Steve Kilbey's assessment of 'Under the Milky Way', the best known and most beloved song by the Church. That would seem like a particularly cruel assessment even if Kilbey wasn't a) the lead singer, bassist and sole constant member of the Church, and b) the man who co-wrote the song.

Kilbey would not be the first nor the last artist to resent the way his biggest song overshadows much of the rest of his vast and varied career. Plenty of groups refuse to play their biggest hits, or cynically save them for the encores purely to punish the percentage of the crowd who are poised to walk out the second they hear the only song they know. The problem is, he's wrong. 'Under the Milky Way' is beloved by millions because it's a genuinely beautiful song. It's as simple and as powerful as that.

Kilbey wrote 'Under the Milky Way' with Karin Jansson, the Swedish singer/songwriter and creative mainstay of the Sydney band Curious (Yellow). She and Kilbey were in a relationship in the mid-eighties, during which time they worked together on music—Kilbey produced Jansson's band's first EP—and also collaborated on twin daughters Elektra and Miranda Kilbey-Jansson, who comprise the excellent Swedish shoegaze/dreampop band Say Lou Lou.[1]

It might not sound like an especially Australian song, but here's an astronomical fact for you: thanks to a quirk of the earth's axial tilt, the southern hemisphere has the superior view of the edge-on view of our mighty galaxy. You can absolutely see it from the northern bit of the planet, but in Australia it spans the entire length of the night sky at certain times of the year—and, if you're out away from the light pollution of the cities, it can shine bright enough to cast a shadow.[2] If you do happen to find yourself under the Milky Way, you're probably standing on this half of earth.

And that's where the couple were when the song was written: specifically, on the north coast of New South Wales, visiting Kilbey's mother. The story goes that he popped outside to

---

1   Jansson had been guitarist in the feminist punk band Pink Champagne in Stockholm. The lead singer, Ann Carlberger, also moved to Australia and also partnered up with a Church member: she and Marty Willson-Piper have a daughter, Singe, who occasionally appears with her dad in the Swedish-based jam band Acres of Space.

2   As another bonus for local stargazers, we get to see two other galaxies the northern hemisphere never gets to see: the Small and Large Magellanic Clouds, which are nearby globular dwarf galaxies. Goddamn, we have good skies down here.

enjoy a sneaky joint and avoid doing the washing-up when the initial idea for the tune popped into his head. He was fiddling on the piano when Jansson wandered over, and the song came to life with remarkable speed: he told *Guardian Australia* that the lyrics were decided on 'in about three minutes' and: 'It's not about anything. Like all my songs, it's a portal into your own mind where I give you a guided meditation. It's a blank, abstract canvas for people to lose themselves in.'

Curious (Yellow) used to do its own version of 'Under the Milky Way', often with Kilbey, who was an occasional touring member. Perhaps unsurprisingly for a fairly insular band with no shortage of complex and ever-shifting internal politics, the other songwriters of the Church—guitarists Marty Willson-Piper and Peter Koppes—weren't super-enthusiastic about doing this tune Kilbey knocked up with his girlfriend.[3] Kilbey wasn't particularly fussed about it either, but the band's management smelled a hit and insisted that the band record it, thus guaranteeing from the outset that performing the song would be an exercise in succumbing to external pressure. The only member who *was* immediately enthusiastic was drummer Richard Ploog, who would end up being the only member of the band not to actually appear on it.

The creation of *Starfish*, the album which 'Under the Milky Way' was to make an international hit, was a nightmare for the band. At the insistence of their new US label Arista, they

---

3   Not that they had any particular problem with Jansson, to be clear. 'Under the Milky Way' wasn't the first Kilbey/Jansson song the band had done; they'd also recorded 'Youth Worshipper' on 1985's *Heyday*, and two other songs recorded in the Starfish sessions—'Anna Miranda' and 'Nose Dive'—were credited to Kilbey/Jansson/Koppes/Ploog/Willson-Piper.

were recording in LA for the first time and working with the production team of Waddy Wachtel and Greg Ladanyi, who did not care for this Australian band they'd been assigned to record and were reportedly not shy about expressing the fact that they felt this assignment was beneath them.[4]

The Church had made four albums in Australia by the time they entered the studio for *Starfish* and were confident that they knew what they were doing, but that assurance was about to get badly shaken. Ploog in particular was deemed not up to standard by the producers and was replaced on 'Under the Milky Way' by session drummer Russ Kunkel. The humiliating experience broke something in him and he eventually left the band during sessions for the next album, 1990's *Gold Afternoon Fix*—which was also produced by Wachtel, also involved a lot of heavy-handed micromanagement from Arista, and was also a fairly unpleasant experience for everyone involved.

But whatever the interference from management, record company and producer, the fact was they were right about 'Under the Milky Way'. The final recording was perfect: Willson-Piper's shimmering twelve-string guitar chords, Koppes's understated lead lines, Kilbey's laconic, intimate vocal and a solo which is . . . hold on, is that bagpipes *again*?

Actually, not quite—although the details are complicated.[5] If you want to make the sound yourself at home, be advised

---

4 The band got their own back in the cuttingly brilliant 'North, South, East and West', which was a savage expression of the band's disgust with the vacuity of LA. For my money that and the gorgeous 'Hotel Womb', which closes *Starfish*, are among the band's greatest songs.

5 When researching this, I discovered that the internet has no shortage of angry bagpipers taking to forums to furiously pipesplain that OBVIOUSLY it's not bagpipes on 'Under the Milky Way' and that bagpipes can't even play those notes. Just a warning in case you plan to ask a piper to rock you a version of the song.

that part of the effect derives from playing a Fender Jazzmaster guitar with an ebow,[6] and the other part from a Synclavier, an early sampling keyboard. However, Kilbey himself confirmed in an email that the break contains a recording of 'an African bagpipe, played backwards', and he ought to know. But, in any case this puts 'Under the Milky Way' in that rarefied company of those two other classic Australian songs about which you've already read.[7]

Arista's charismatic head Clive Davis immediately heard a hit-in-waiting and made the song the album's lead single. Bizarrely, for a song so beloved in Australia, it didn't even crack the top 20 here—it stalled at #22, two spots higher than it managed in the US—but despite the somewhat anaemic charting, it never left the public imagination.

The song was used in the soundtracks of several films and TV series, perhaps most significantly during a key scene in the cult film *Donnie Darko*. It's also been covered dozens of times, including two particularly great versions by artists from this book: Jimmy Little included it on *Messenger* in 1999, and Sia released her own version of it in 2010. *Starfish* went on to sell 600,000 copies in the US alone, giving the band an enviable US audience.

So perhaps the band's ambivalence about 'Under the Milky Way' has more to do with the circumstances of its creation than anything intrinsic to the song itself. In any case, over the

---

6 For non-guitarists: an ebow ('electronic bow') is a little handheld device that effectively does the same trick as angling a guitar into an amplifier: it sets up a standing vibration which gives a sustained note. They're really fun.

7 Incidentally, Willson-Piper was to unambiguously use actual bagpipes on his solo album *Rhyme* the following year, after recruiting a busker to play on 'Forever'.

years even Kilbey has come to accept the horrible burden of having written a beloved and timeless classic.

'It's not like, say, I was Joe Dolce and I had to keep doing "Shaddap You Face",' he told music writer Iain Shedden when 'Under The Milky Way' was voted *The Australian*'s best Australian song since 1988, 'like you had a song that was your song and it was a real stinker. I reckon "Down Under" would tire me out. But if I had to be saddled with one song that everyone wants me to do, I figure "Milky Way" is an OK one.'

32

1990

I Touch Myself

Divinyls

*In which Australia's most joyfully sexual performer
teaches a generation to get off*

Divinyls—or, more accurately, lead singer Chrissy Amphlett—
never shied away from the power of sexuality.[1] While a performer
like Kylie Minogue could be undeniably beautiful while
thoroughly unerotic, Amphlett was always immediately, deeply,
irresistibly sexy. More importantly, she entirely owned her sexual
power: she wasn't a fantasy minx cavorting before the male gaze
so much as a force of pure animal lust. Even the school uniform
seemed less about pandering to sleazy *Lolita*-style fantasies and

---

1 Several of my friends can trace their first acute awareness of their sexuality
to the moment they beheld David Bowie's tights in the movie *Labyrinth*; I had a
similar personal revelation when the 'Boys in Town' video screened on the ABC.

more about contrasting her power with an incongruous stage costume, more Angus Young than Britney Spears.

And there was much more to Amphlett than her looks—she was a great songwriter, a ferocious and unique vocalist, a compelling performer and a goddamn hilarious interviewee. It was this mix of qualities that made her delivery on her band's definitive song so uniquely powerful and enduring.

She'd followed her cousin Patricia (who you met in chapter 2) into the music industry at the age of fourteen and was an experienced professional singer with the band Batonrouge by the time she was twenty-one. That was in 1980, when she was also introduced by her bandmate Jeremy Paul—not long out of platinum-selling soft-rockers Air Supply—to a lanky blond guitarist named Mark McEntee.

The band the three of them formed enjoyed an early breakthrough when Divinyls provided music for Ken Cameron's film based on Helen Garner's novel *Monkey Grip*, in which Amphlett had a small role. Their debut EP consisted of songs recorded for the film, including their first single 'Boys in Town', which hit #8 on the charts in 1981. Amphlett and McEntee also began a romantic relationship, ending McEntee's marriage, and by 1988 the band officially consisted of the couple and whoever else they hired at the time.

Their Australian success had been considerable—'Science Fiction' and 'Good Die Young' were also high-charting hits, while their debut album *Desperate* reached #5—and they immediately determined that the US would be a fertile market. Rocking songs, a sexy lead singer, a shit-hot live band: how hard could it possibly be?

The answer: *weirdly* hard.

The recording process for album number two, 1985's exasperatingly titled *What a Life!*, stretched for two years and three producers until they finally hit semi-paydirt with 'Pleasure and Pain', which seemed perfectly tailored for Amphlett's heaving sensuousness. They didn't write the song, though: it was foisted upon them by their producer, Australian expat Mike Chapman,[2] who'd co-written it with fellow backroom songwriting superstar Holly Knight. And while it did well in Australia, getting to #11, it still didn't break the band in America and stalled at a disappointing #76.

The band stuck with Chapman for what their US label Chrysalis made very clear was the make-or-break release, *Temperamental*, which had a minor hit with 'Back to the Wall' but failed to reverse their commercial fortunes and left the band with a seven-figure debt to the record label who had unceremoniously dumped them.

With their career seeming all but over, McEntee and Amphlett cut a deal with Virgin and met with the hit songwriting team of Billy Steinberg and Tom Kelly in an eleventh-hour attempt to achieve that elusive stateside smash.[3] Steinberg had already started writing 'I Touch Myself' as a bit of a lark, but the quartet decided to turn it into a proper song when

---

2 Chapman was best known for his work with Nicky Chinn. Together they produced/wrote/basically created a host of huge teen acts in the 1970s, including Racey, the Sweet and Suzi Quatro.

3 Steinberg and Kelly certainly knew how to write for strong female voices: aside from 'I Touch Myself' they wrote Madonna's 'Like a Virgin' and Cyndi Lauper's 'True Colours', and co-wrote the Bangles' 'Eternal Flame' (with Susanna Hoffs) and the Pretenders' 'I'll Stand By You' (with Chrissie Hynde). One assumes they own very, very nice houses.

Amphlett rewrote the lyrics, turning it from a smutty joke to a celebration of love, desire and sexual gratification.

The song is explicitly about someone in a relationship missing their beloved, and yet it's impossible to make sense of just how controversial the song was at the time. You'd think that groups like the PMRC—the wowsers that started forcing record companies to put those parental warnings on records lest the young people find their ears corrupted with naughty words and sexy thoughts—would welcome a song rejoicing in the joyful fulfilment possible in a monogamous partnership, but that was comprehensively not the case.

'I Touch Myself' wasn't the first song about female masturbation to get mainstream airplay and chart success—Cyndi Lauper's 'She Bop' had done that in 1984, although her song was a little less blatant about it and therefore could slip under the censorious radar. US radio was leery about (ahem) touching it, and the band had the power cut on them midway through a performance of it at the 1991 Aqua Fest in Texas—presumably for fear that it would cause a horrifying outbreak of enthusiastic female masturbation. This avalanche of wowserism wasn't limited to the US either: the video—directed by future 'splosions'n'robots blockbuster filmmaker Michael Bay, bizarrely enough—was even banned in Australia.

Regardless, as with 'I Am Woman' back in chapter 8, a massive and predominantly female audience connected with the song: it rose to #4 on the US charts, #10 in the UK and was a platinum-selling #1 in Australia. Chrysalis must have been seething. Mind you, they might have at least taken some perverse pleasure in the fact that this album was also Divinyls' last. Amphlett and McEntee's relationship fell apart shortly after the band's final, self-titled album came out, and the band went with it. Amphlett married the band's last drummer, Charlie Drayton, a few years later and swapped music for musicals, winning rave reviews for her performance as Judy Garland in the first touring production of *The Boy From Oz*.

After a decade in which they barely spoke, Amphlett and McEntee resumed contact ahead of Divinyls' induction into the ARIA Hall of Fame in August 2006, which led to a reactivation of the band. They recorded a new double A-side single 'I Don't Wanna Do This'/'Asphyxiated' (which was made in two countries without the musicians physically working together: Amphlett and Drayton recorded their parts in Las Vegas, McEntee did his in Perth) and had plans for a new album. A new line-up of the band was convened for a tour, including a headline performance at the all-Australian Homebake Festival in December.

Lest there be hope of a comeback, however, there was some sobering news: in an interview with *A Current Affair* on the eve of Homebake, Amphlett revealed that she had multiple sclerosis. The band's subsequent performance was, unsurprisingly, an emotional one.

Despite hopes of more recording, in 2009 Amphlett confirmed that the mooted album was no more and that she and McEntee were no longer working together.[4] Instead she was concentrating on work with her and Drayton's new band in New York. And while Amphlett's MS was largely under control, there was another horror about to come galumphing over the

---

4   Said revelation occurred while she was in Australia to induct her cousin Patricia Amphlett, aka Little Pattie, into the ARIA Hall of Fame—in the same year in which Kev Carmody, who's in the following chapter, was inducted. See how this whole book fits together?

horizon: in 2010 she was diagnosed with breast cancer, a situation dangerously complicated by her MS,[5] and died on 21 April 2013. She was fifty-three years old.

In a touchingly appropriate tribute, 'I Touch Myself' was rerecorded by a coterie of Australian female artists as part of a public education campaign to combat breast cancer. Once it had been the most controversial song on the airwaves; now it was helping to save lives.

The song endured in numerous cover versions, although most of them deliberately poked fun at the explicitness of the song. One artist who embraced the message wholeheartedly and un-ironically, however, was US singer Pink, who performed it throughout her 2009 tour behind the multi-platinum *Funhouse*.

In 2017 it was announced that Divinyls were 're-forming' for a show celebrating Wheels & Dollbaby's thirtieth anniversary in Perth, with McEntee and former rhythm section of Rick Grossman and Richard Harvey augmented by the Preatures' creative axis of Izzi Manfredi and Jack Moffitt in what sounds like a well-intentioned idea that should have been quietly abandoned. After all, a Divinyls without Chrissy is no Divinyls at all.

---

5   Aside from the obvious point that someone struggling with the sheer exhaustion of MS is going to find the most often-used cancer treatments incredibly debilitating, there are other problems facing MS sufferers fighting cancer. Chemotherapy drugs are also used to treat MS, so while sometimes the drugs can complement one another, more often their treatment of one disease precludes using them to fight the other. Radiation therapy, meanwhile, seems to exacerbate MS symptoms. In Amphlett's case, both options were excluded because of her condition.

33

1990–91

Took the Children Away/ From Little Things Big Things Grow/Treaty

Archie Roach/Paul Kelly and Kev Carmody/Yothu Yindi

In which Aboriginal issues explode into mainstream consciousness, and Paul Kelly is revealed as the unexpected Zelig-figure of Indigenous music
(Aboriginal and Torres Strait Islander readers please note that this chapter contains the names of deceased persons.)

Let's be clear: the reason that these three songs are combined into a single chapter is no reflection on their importance—each could sustain an entire chapter without any trouble—but is designed to make clear just how powerful a movement for change there was at the beginning of the nineties and how, tragically, that momentum ebbed away within a few short years. When these songs came out Aboriginal history was almost entirely an afterthought; most formal history education at school consisted of Captain Cook/convicts/explorers/sheep/gold/Anzacs/Don Bradman/World War II/Menzies/America's Cup. The songs of this chapter did much to change that.

These three songs are linked for two broad reasons: one, because they show the power of protest music acting as an oral history of repressed knowledge at a pivotal moment in Aboriginal policy in Australia, and two: they all had an unexpected helper elf in the form of the singer/songwriter Paul Kelly. The dude, it has to be said, gets around.

———

Archie Roach was born in Mooroopna, a settlement which is now the bit of Shepparton west of the Goulburn River.[1] His family was moved to another settlement before the authorities thought twice and just took him and his siblings away. Roach went first to an orphanage and then to two unhappy foster placements before he was put with a family who encouraged his musical interests—but after the reality of what had happened to him became clear he took his guitar and left, ending up homeless and drinking on the streets of Adelaide at the age of sixteen.

It's a story that could have ended very differently, but Roach met another homeless sixteen-year-old who'd been removed from her family: a fellow musician named Ruby Hunter. They

---

1 As you've seen in chapter 3, and will see again in chapter 50, Shepparton has been so central to Australian music it should really be our Nashville. Yeah, that's right, Tamworth: you heard me.

encouraged each other's music, and started two major projects: a family and a band. The latter—called the Altogethers and featuring both Archie and Ruby out front—started to build up an audience thanks in part to the opportunity to do some touring opening for Paul Kelly and the Messengers after guitarist Steve Connolly saw them play.

'Took the Children Away' had appeared on *Koorie*,[2] the cassette that Roach and Hunter had been hawking at gigs, and at this stage Roach wasn't even considering a solo record until he did a live performance of 'Took the Children Away' on Melbourne community radio station 3CR and saw the switchboard light up with listeners wanting to know what they'd just heard and how they could hear it again.[3] Kelly and Connolly offered to produce, but Roach wasn't convinced about doing a record under his own name until Hunter talked him into it. (As he later recalled, 'She said, "It's not all about you, Archie Roach!"')

The result was Roach's debut solo album—the bare bones, no-budget masterpiece *Charcoal Lane*, which emerged in 1990. The effect of that record, and especially of 'Took the Children Away', was nothing short of seismic.

As songs of loss go, 'Took the Children Away' is heart-breakingly immediate. Over a slow-building song, rising from understated organ to guitars and tambourine, Roach's vocal is given space to tell his story of being removed from his family by

---

2   Koorie (or Koori) is a collective term for the Aboriginal groups of New South Wales and Victoria. There are about a dozen geographical terms for different areas of Australia. Yolngu represents a number of groups based around Arnhem Land in the Northern Territory, where Yothu Yindi formed.

3   Still pumping out the good stuff at 855 on the AM dial!

authorities who assured him it was for his own good. You can hear why the 3CR switchboard went crazy: for most of white Australia it would be the first time they'd heard of the stolen generations. The term didn't even exist in the mainstream, and the Australian Human Rights Commission's Bringing Them Home report would not be published until 1997. Then, as now, there was even widespread denial that such a practice existed, and that if it did it was nowhere near as disruptive as those affected were claiming. 'Took the Children Away' did much to win hearts and minds.

The album won Roach two of the four ARIAs he was nominated for the following year (Best New Talent and Best Indigenous Release) and kicked both Roach and Hunter's careers to the next level. They amassed a considerable body of work together and individually while raising their family and opening their own home as a de facto halfway house for homeless and neglected Aboriginal children suffering the pressures they had experienced.

This ended abruptly in 2010, when Hunter died suddenly from a heart attack and Roach suffered a stroke the same year. While recovering, he was diagnosed with lung cancer, which necessitated surgery. Since then, however, he's made two albums, including 2017's jubilant *Let Love Rule*, and continued his work with young people at risk because apparently he's immortal.

In 2015 *Charcoal Lane* was reissued with a bonus disc of covers of each track from the likes of Paul Kelly, Courtney Barnett, Urthboy, Dan Sultan and Leah Flanagan, while Briggs, Dr G Yunupingu and Dewayne Everettsmith provided a sequel to Roach's masterpiece in the form of 'The Children Came Back'.

And the song's redemptive power even works on its writer. 'Every time I sing that song, I let that much of it go,' he told *The Age*'s Kylie Northover in 2015. 'One day I'll be singing it, and that last bit of grief or sorrow will leave me, and I'll be free.'

———

In May 1991 Paul Kelly and the Messengers put out what was to be their final album before Kelly let his long-time sidemen go and went on alone. The sprawling double album *Comedy* suffered by comparison with his previous double, 1986's undisputed classic *Gossip*, though it contained some of Kelly's finest songs—'Stories of Me', 'Don't Start Me Talking', 'Sydney from a 747' and the underrated single 'Keep It to Yourself'—but the song at the end of side C was a landmine waiting to explode.

Earlier that year Kelly had been out on a camping trip with the singer/songwriter Kev Carmody. They were talking about what happened at the Wave Hill cattle station in August 1966, when Vincent Lingiari announced that the Gurindji people were going on strike and walked off the station. The station's management eventually offered a pay rise only to discover that the group wasn't interested in money: they wanted their land back.

After a nationwide campaign, the new Labor government of Gough Whitlam returned a portion of the land to the Gurindji people in a ceremony that took place on 16 August 1975 (that's what's happening in the song when the 'tall stranger' arrives, pouring sand from his hand to Lingiari's), and the Aboriginal Land Rights Act was made into law the following year.

That might seem a lot of detail to pack into a song—and there are eleven verses in the thing—but, as Carmody told the ABC, it all came very easily. 'We just kind of pulled it out around the campfire. Paul had a good chord progression and I thought it would be good to tell a little story over it. So, by about two o'clock in the morning, we had a six-minute song.'

Carmody and his brother had been among the stolen generations, removed from their family and taken to Toowoomba to be educated until the age of sixteen. Carmody had worked as a shearer and labourer for seventeen years before enrolling in university, at which point he also decided to take up the guitar. Because his education had left him only semi-literate, he asked if he could present his history tutorials orally, accompanied by guitar, until he got his writing up to standard.

While his educational career flourished—he was awarded a Bachelor of Arts and a Diploma of Education before embarking on a PhD—so did his musical one. His unique approach to oral history now formed the basis of two albums, 1988's *Pillars of Society* and 1990's *Eulogy (For a Black Person)*, both produced by Steve Connolly of the Messengers. That Carmody and Kelly would connect over a song exploring Australia's history seemed inevitable.

Carmody did his own version of 'From Little Things Big Things Grow' on his next album, 1993's *Bloodlines*, with Kelly performing alongside him, but the song had already taken on a cultural significance far beyond either artist's recordings. This was in part because it is so easy to play. It's a classic protest song in four chords (C major, A minor, E minor, G major, played with a capo on the fourth fret. Try it at home!) and was therefore a straightforward song to adopt for the protests and media coverage that the land rights movement was gaining as the high-profile Mabo case crawled to its eventual landmark 1992 High Court ruling.

In July 2007 Kelly and Carmody performed the song at the Live Earth concert in Sydney, along with John Butler and Missy Higgins, where its anthemic status was cemented by the massive crowd singalong. The following year an all-star version by the GetUp Mob went to #4 on the national charts—and in December 2014 Kelly and Carmody performed their ode to the Tall Stranger himself at Gough Whitlam's funeral.

In other words, 'From Little Things Big Things Grow' rapidly became part of the cultural fabric of Australia. But there was another little tune about land rights that was also about to grab the public consciousness.

———

When his band first formed, Mandawuy Djarrtjuntjun Yunupingu was working as a teacher in Arnhem Land,[4] where he was determined to overturn the notion that had prevailed during his own education: that it was only by embracing European-style culture that his charges could be part of mainstream Australia. On the contrary, he believed that Yolngu culture and that of mainstream Australia could complement each other in the classroom and in the wider society. The Yolngu had a term for this 'dynamic balance', as he described it, based

4 In life Mandawuy Yunupingu was known as Tom Djambayang Bakamana Yunupingu. After his 2013 death from renal failure, he was referred to only as Dr Yunupingu during the period of mourning. Due to the tragic passing of the second Dr Yunupingu in July 2017, I've used Mandawuy's name for clarity.

on the words for mother and child and meaning something similar to yin/yang: *yothu-yindi*.

As well as being a teacher, Mandawuy was also a musician, and when the all-white local band the Swamp Jockeys merged with the nameless folk band of which he was a part, he made the term the band's name and philosophy.

At first the band was limited by the members' other jobs and responsibilities—most notably that following the publication of a paper outlining his 'both ways' educational philosophy, Mandawuy was made the principal of Yirrkala Community School, the very school he had attended as a child. In addition, one member, Mandawuy's nephew, Dr G Yunupingu,[5] was blind—although he was an extraordinarily talented musician and would later go on to become the most successful Aboriginal artist of all time. Even so, Yothu Yindi was signed to Mushroom Records for its debut album, 1988's *Homeland Movement*, but as a Northern Territory band that could only tour during the school holidays, the label didn't expect huge things from them—although they did tour overseas with Midnight Oil in 1988.

That same year Prime Minister Bob Hawke attended the Barunga Festival as part of the Bicentennial celebrations. Mandawuy's older brother Galarrwuy Yunupingu and the artist Wenten Rubuntja presented him with a statement of political objectives which the people of the region wanted to see enacted. Hawke promised that a treaty with Indigenous

---

5   After his time in Yothu Yindi Dr G Yunupingu would form the Saltwater Band, and would subsequently make three solo albums: 2008's *Gurrumul* (which went triple platinum), 2011's *Rrakala*, and *The Gospel Album* in 2013. He died far, far too young on 25 July 2017 of kidney and liver disease, aged forty-six.

Australia, similar to the one struck in Canada, would be entered into by 1990.

This ambitious-sounding deadline was not met, not least because Hawke was distracted by the close-run 1990 election and the unravelling of his relationship with his treasurer and eventual replacement as leader, Paul Keating, and Mandawuy figured that a song might refocus attention back on the neglected matter. With the help of Midnight Oil's frontman Peter Garrett and some lyric sessions in Sydney with Paul Kelly, the band got to work.

The result was 'Treaty', which was released as a single in June 1991. It's a solid slice of four-on-the-floor eighties-inflected mainstream funk—as is a good slab of its parent album, *Tribal Voice*, which appeared in September 1991. And the single was a favourite on Indigenous channels, the ABC and SBS, but was utterly ignored by mainstream broadcasters; however, that was soon to change.

Robert Goodge had been a member of Melbourne post-punk experimentalists Essendon Airport in the late seventies and early eighties, before most of the final line-up dissolved and morphed into the wildly successful pop-soul concoction I'm Talking.[6] When that split in 1987 he went even further into dance music, forming a DJing partnership called Filthy Lucre with Gavin Campbell, who had started the dance label Razor Recordings under the Mushroom umbrella, and DJ Paul Main.

---

6 Goodge aside, I'm Talking turned out to be massively influential on the next couple of decades of music: not only did it introduce the world to the voice of Kate Ceberano, but its manager was a guy named Ken West, who would also handle Ceberano's solo career for a little while before leaving management to concentrate on a little touring festival he and fellow promoter Vivian Lees had concocted called the Big Day Out.

While in the Mushroom office Campbell saw a promo photo of an Aboriginal ceremony lying on a desk with a Mushroom Records logo thereon. Intrigued, he investigated and discovered the band and the song. In an interview for the National Film and Sound Archives, Campbell explained what happened next:

> I went into the other office where the head of A&R, Simon Baeyertz, was and I said, 'What about these guys? Who are they? Can we listen to something for a Razor remix?' and he said, 'Well, the thing is, two albums have been made, and not yet recouped on what it cost to produce them', and that Mushroom wouldn't want me to remix this band. And he was spot on: the walls went up. And so, I may as well say it now, I snuck the tapes out of the building.

Aside from upping the beats (and some samples from Hamilton Bohannon's 1978 hit 'Let's Start the Dance'), the remix brought the chant to the foreground and trimmed the verses back, putting them though a filter to sound as though they were being yelled through a megaphone at a rally. But then the Filthy Lucre trio started to second-guess themselves: after all, they'd done this remix without permission. What would the band and label make of it?

Campbell decided to try the track out in an environment where it would be too embarrassing to punish him: at a party held by Mushroom's legendary founder Michael Gudinski in his mansion in Toorak. Even then he was too scared to put it on the sound system himself and asked fellow guest Molly Meldrum to do it instead.[7]

---

7 Campbell claims that it was the Mushroom Christmas party, which was presumably held in 1990. If that's correct, Mushroom sat on the song for an implausibly long while if 'Treaty' was released in June 1991. Maybe they had one of those Christmas In July bashes.

Needless to say, it went down extremely well with the label, with the band and—most gratifyingly of all—with the public in general.

The remix almost cracked the top 10, stalling at #11, but proved a sensation. It filled dance floors and airwaves, won multiple ARIAs, put *Tribal Voice* in the charts for almost a year,[8] and turned Yothu Yindi into unlikely rock stars—even getting a berth on the very first Big Day Out in Sydney in 1992, performing *after* Nirvana.

But the biggest effect was that it made mainstream Australia aware of the need for a formal arrangement between the country's original inhabitants and the European settlers. It was a watershed moment, from the dance floor to the media to the parliament to the singles charts.

Pretty amazing stuff for a single song.

---

8 The album was reissued in 1992 with the remixes and a new version of 'Djapana', which had also appeared on their debut album.

34

1991

The Horses

Daryl Braithwaite

*In which a former pop star consolidates his second act,
and creates a beloved Australian classic
(by an American)*

Let's get this out of the way early: Daryl Braithwaite's signature number, beloved by audiences and practically etched into the cultural DNA of every Australian who had ears in the 1990s, isn't remotely an Australian song. And yet it has become one of our Alternative National Anthems, sung at sporting events and by drunk twenty-somethings, and is inevitably used as the background music for each and every television report involving matters equestrian. It has transcended its origins and entered the pantheon of classic Australian songs—and it's damn near impossible to work out why.

The lyrics, such as they are, are vague to the point of meaninglessness (not least because they've been edited, for reasons that will become clear). Furthermore, it's difficult to see why riding on the horses, yeah yeah, would be so deeply evocative to Australian audiences. Does it evoke a national memory of the wild bush brumbies that Banjo Paterson celebrated in *The Man from Snowy River*? Does it tap into our bizarre identification with Phar Lap? Does it bring up happy memories of Karen from Marketing organising the office Melbourne Cup sweep? Who can say?

What's certain is that the writers of the song were not seeking to draw upon any sense of Australian identity at all, since they were resolutely American. More specifically, they were the singer/songwriter and knitted-cap enthusiast Rickie Lee Jones, who was working on what was to become her 1989 album *Flying Colours*, and the album's producer Walter Becker (better known as one half of the creative axis of Steely Dan). While the song was deemed strong enough to be the album's opening track, it didn't make the cut for release as a single. The album itself was a moderate success but far from a chart-topping smash.

And there's a connection between the position Jones and Braithwaite found themselves in at the tail end of the eighties, with both increasingly struggling for relevance in the decade after their biggest success. Jones had been a breakout star in the late seventies, thanks to the mega-hit 'Chuck E's in Love' and some sexy-but-tasteful *Rolling Stone* covers, but by the late eighties she was out of commercial favour.

Braithwaite, similarly, had been a teen idol in Australia as the frontman of *Countdown*-bestriding hit makers Sherbert.[1] Sherbert were legitimate platinum-selling superstars in Australia: they had eleven top 10 singles, were the first Australian band to sell a million dollars' worth of records, pioneered merchandising as a promotional move (especially via their hideous logo-emblazoned satin bomber jackets) and—as mentioned back in chapter 10—even had a proper Beatles versus Stones-style rivalry with Skyhooks. Their #1 single, 'Howzat!', was also a top 5 hit in the UK: fitting, since it was pretty much the only other country on the planet where the use of a colloquial cricketing expression would seem like a perfectly reasonable metaphor for a relationship torn asunder by the lusts of a faithless partner.[2]

Despite this massive success, by the second half of the eighties Braithwaite, like Jones, was in something of a career slump. While still technically under contract, his label CBS (later Sony) wasn't interested in actually investing money in any recording, meaning that Daryl had to fund his sessions himself and then license the album back to his corporate masters. And since there was no debt to recoup via the labyrinthine accounting wizardry that labels employ when determining whether or not their artists get paid, that ended up working out exceedingly well for him with the massive

---

1 'Howzat!' was yet another song that only just missed out on making the cut for this book, by the way. Don't write in.

2 'Howzat', as everyone knows, is an abbreviation of 'housecat', and is a shouted warning that there is a cat on the pitch that must be humanely removed to the stands. It's excitingly common, happening five or six times a game, since cats regularly mistake the dry, gritty surface of cricket pitches for litter boxes. On a related point, I don't much care for sport.

success of *Edge* in 1988, buoyed by the upbeat single 'One Summer' and the anthemic 'As the Days Go By'.

He decided to repeat the model with the follow-up, *Rise*, and as the recording was nearing completion, Braithwaite heard 'The Horses' and decided it would be a good addition. The version he cut was very different from Jones's meandering original—in a feature on the song producer Simon Hussey told News.com that his plan was to 'make it like a Peter Gabriel track', which involved some slicing and dicing of the lyrics, among other things. 'My role as a producer and arranger was that I'd get the scissors out, make the songs more succinct,' he explained. 'I just cut it into verse/chorus/verse/chorus from the Rickie Lee Jones original.' The other inspired move was to make the song a semi-duet. After Braithwaite had recorded his bit and popped off to China on holiday, Hussey decided the song needed a female harmony, and enlisted New Zealand singer Margaret Urlich to do the all-important counterpoint vocal. Once that was in place, and the record company heard Hussey's work, the song went from side two space-filler to second single.

It was released as a single in February 1991 and turned out to be a slow burner, buoyed by a video of Braithwaite emoting shoelessly along the shoreline in response to a ghostly female singer who, um, clearly wasn't Urlich. Apparently she was in the middle of recording an album in London at the time and didn't fancy interrupting the sessions for a lightning visit back to Australia, even if it would have given her a chance to dance about on what seemed to be a really nice beach, and thus the role of Braithwaite's vocal foil and spectral love interest was performed by lip-synching model Gillian Bailey, who later claimed that she was teasingly called 'Gilly Vanilli' for pretending to sing someone else's vocals.[3]

In any case, the clip suited the song's laidback vibe and helped propel it to the top of the charts, eventually climbing to #1 in May.[4] That was impressive enough, but the slow burn didn't stop there. The song just never went away. It's been a staple on commercial daytime radio ever since, which typically is some sort of strange death-in-life for a song, yet somehow 'The Horses' endures. It crops up in ads, it crops up in unimaginative cover versions by reality TV hopeful Taylor Henderson, and—as mentioned above—it crops up in all news footage of horse-related events, such as horse racing and horse jumping and . . . horse poker? That's a thing, right?

Speaking of which, 'The Horses' has also enjoyed a second life in the world of sportsball. Twenty years after its release the song became the anthem for Hawthorn in the AFL and Melbourne Victory in A-League, sung every time the respective team squadrons collect a victory point,[5] giving Braithwaite a lucrative sideline in finals appearances.

In fact, despite its American origins, 'The Horses' is now part of Australia's musical heritage. And be honest: it's playing in your head even as you read this, little darling, because you're acutely aware of the fact that that's the way it's gonna be. Yeah, yeah.

---

3   . . . after Milli Vanilli, the late 80s pop duo of models Fab Morvan and Rob Pilatus, who lip synched to tracks recorded by studio musicians.
4   Fun fact: its tenure at the top was bookended by Ratcat, first with the *Tingles* EP (which had 'That Ain't Bad' as the focus track) and then with 'Don't Go Now', both of which were also on the long list for this book. Honestly, this was a brutal editing process.
5   Yeah, I *really* don't care for sport.

35

1993

Sweetness and Light

Itch-E and Scratch-E

In which Australia learns to feel it, not fight it

While rock was in the ascendant in Australia in the early 1990s, there was a parallel revolution taking place at the other end of the spectrum as the hitherto largely underground dance music scene reached its crossover point—and the song that tipped it over was a shimmering mix of beats and keys appropriately called 'Sweetness and Light'.

Dance music in Australia had a venerable history by this point, having literally changed the law around the importing of records from overseas,[1] but was still to some degree

---

1 The Melbourne record store turned national chain Central Station had been at the forefront of the decade-plus battle to overturn laws that effectively meant if a label with the local licence for a record decided not to press and release it in Australia, there was no legal way to get hold of it short of physically going to another country and buying it. For years Central Station (and other stores) would sell these 'illegal' records to customers they knew and trusted, periodically getting busted by record company plants for dealing in contraband funk.

siloed between cities. This had led to unique little ecosystems growing up around the country, where the development of the local scene was guided at least in part by the publications on the ground, the tastes of DJs on community radio and what the local stores brought in (and often sold under the counter).[2] In Brisbane Italo house was especially huge. In Adelaide the cool kids were into Detroit techno. In Melbourne it was soul and funk. And in Sydney it was a weird amalgam of just about everything, but from the outset was centred around the gay venues of Oxford Street.

Dance music had become something of a haven for Sydney's non-straight musicians who didn't fancy either staying in the closet or remaining vigilant about being awfully coy about the person with whom they were stepping out. Most LGBTIQ artists, like Savage Garden frontman Darren Hayes, would be proudly out a few years down the track, but at this point it was very much don't ask, don't tell.

Dance music was so central to gay culture in Sydney that it transformed the annual Gay and Lesbian Mardi Gras in the eighties, turning it from a largely political exercise into a massive citywide party. The Mardi Gras Sleaze Ball and other huge EDM events held by over-the-top party promoters such as Recreational Arts Team (RAT) and Sweatbox attracted a straight crowd as much as the gay one.[3] By mixing up young people from all sorts of backgrounds, classes, ethnicities and

---

2   It's also worth adding that Australian-pressed vinyl was of an inferior quality to that pressed overseas, especially in the US, and as DJing became more of an art form in the 1980s and 90s there was a growing demand for records that were more robust and had better sound quality.

3   You know the term EDM, right? It's electronic dance music.

sexualities and bringing them together on a dance floor, the Sydney dance scene did much to encourage a tolerant and diverse community. The ecstasy helped, admittedly.

Rave culture had been characterised by secret non-legal events held in bushland or warehouses, with the location a carefully guarded secret until the last minute. And while there had been a clear divide between the rock fans and the ravers, that was starting to be broken down by bands who either tried to weld both genres together, like Caligula and Def FX, or simply by punters gradually realising that they weren't obliged to choose one or the other. Again, the ecstasy helped.

One mighty leap in that direction occurred in 1994, when the second Big Day Out added the Boiler Room to their previously all-band line-up, creating a specific venue in which DJs and EDM artists were able to perform. One of the big acts on that year's bill was Itch-E and Scratch-E, a Sydney duo formed three years earlier, consisting of Andy Rantzen and Paul McDermott—better known as Paul Mac.[4]

Rantzen had played in the electro duo Pelican Daughters, while Mac had already made a name for himself in a plethora of endeavours. He was one-third of the Lab, the industrial-influenced synth pop band who had signed to rooArt and never quite did the business it was predicted to do,[5] and had worked with venerable Australian electronic music pioneers Severed Heads. He'd also been one of the closeted gay kids for whom dance music and Sydney's club scene had been a wonderful revelation in the late eighties.

---

4   Not to be confused with Paul McDermott, television personality and Doug Anthony All Star.

5   rooArt was an indie label about which you will learn more in the next chapter.

Both Mac and Rantzen wanted to do something a little more playful and techno-focused than their other, more artsy projects, and the name they chose to do it under made their intentions very clear. First, it was a reference to the Simpsons' hyper-violent animated cat-and-mouse duo Itchy and Scratchy, indicating that this project was definitely not going to be especially po-faced. The second was the spelling of the name with the prominent 'E' suffix, an unsubtle nod to MDMA. Their first album, *Itch-E Kitch-E Koo*, appeared in 1993 and contained a track that was to change the way that Australia's booty was shook. That track was called 'Sweetness and Light'.

Despite the changes in musical fashion over the years it still stands up remarkably well today, thanks in no small part to the sheer craftsmanship in the song's composition. The pair had collaborated with Rantzen's former Pelican Daughters bandmate Justin Brandis to create a gradually building masterpiece of hectic breakbeats, intertwining keyboard melodies and a sampled hook of . . . a breathy female voice? A manipulated industrial noise? An alien language? It was impossible to tell.

The power of 'Sweetness and Light' was not in the chart placing, which was a less-than-stellar #65; it was that it was all over the airwaves—on Triple J, on community radio, on the dance music stations that were starting to pop up around the country—and sounded like a message from the outer space of the future. Australian electronic music had never been this airy, not to mention this danceable, and the duo were rewarded by reaching #21 on that year's Triple J Hottest 100.

For an entire generation of radio listeners, 'Sweetness and Light' was their gateway into the world of EDM.

Triple J and the Big Day Out had made an impact, but another sign that dance music was crossing over came when ARIA added a new category to its annual awards, Best Dance Release, for which 'Sweetness and Light' was nominated. When Itch-E and Scratch-E unexpectedly won, Mac made history by doing something interesting—which was more or less unheard of at Australian music's night of nights. While most speeches were a dull litany of people's names, he declared on live television: 'We'd like to thank all of Sydney's ecstasy dealers, without whom this award would not be possible.' Predictably, there was massive outrage—not least with the National Drug Offensive, one of the sponsors of the ARIAs, which pulled its financial support as a result—but, to be fair, he had the facts very much on his side.

In 1996, as they started looking at overseas releases for their music, they were forced to abandon the Itch-E and Scratch-E moniker, since too many other acts had chosen confusingly similar names, and therefore settled on Boo Boo & Mace for 1998's *Sublimely Pointless*, but then reverted back to their original name for 2001's *It Is What It Isn't* before announcing their split. Rantzen settled down and started a family while Mac did the opposite, making three solo records, becoming an unofficial fourth member of Silverchair and forming I Can't Believe It's Not Rock with lead singer Daniel Johns (recording an EP of the same name in 2000), which then morphed into the Dissociatives in 2004. Mac and Rantzen reconnected in the late noughties and reactivated Itch-E and Scratch-E to record 2010's *Hooray For Everything!!!*[6]

'Sweetness and Light' had hit hard, but the golden age of dance music had petered out in Australia by the mid-nineties as police crackdowns on illegal raves and the widening war on recreational drugs took its toll on big events and bush doofs alike. By this stage, however, dance music was no longer a niche interest but an established part of the mainstream in Australia and around the world. These days, 'Sweetness and Light' is one of those songs that makes a broad, wistful grin pass over the face of people of a certain age, as they forget their children and professional responsibilities for a moment and recall a time when they could dance for an entire night before getting home at dawn with pupils like dinner plates. Oh, to have that stamina again . . .

---

6 And while I realise that there's something a bit pathetic about saying 'b-b-but my band used that Simpsons reference first!', the 1999 debut EP for my second band Career Girls was entitled *Hooray For Everything*. I'm just saying that we and I&S both have exquisite taste in record titles.

36

1994

Berlin Chair

You Am I

In which the Australian alterna-rock explosion begins

Let's clear something up before we get going: the word in the first line in the chorus is 'aches', not eggs.

That needs to be made clear because generations of You Am I lovers have been belting out the malapropism 'If you wait, I'll give all my eggs to you'—which is evocative and powerful, but also incorrect. Although given the stick insect frame of the band's singer/guitarist/songwriter Tim Rogers,[1] the idea of him laying eggs in someone isn't as outlandish as it might otherwise seem.

---

1 Tim Rogers' real name is Tim Rogers. Tim Rogers is also the real name of the Sydney singer/songwriter Jack Ladder, who is an entirely different person, and whose glorious 'Hurtsville' was also on the longlist for this book.

Rogers had seen the 'Berlin Chair' in question (a piece by the Dutch furniture designer Gerrit Rietveld) in a touring exhibition in Canberra when he was a student at the Australian National University. It inspired a single that is not just one of the greatest You Am I songs—which is a tough call, given the size and quality of their still-growing catalogue—but is also officially the actual greatest Australian song of the 1990s, according to a poll conducted by Double J in June 2017. That's just science, that is.

The melody goes right at the top of the young Rogers' range, giving his delivery a beautiful desperation that perfectly reflected the lyrics. Said lyrics, in turn, articulate a perspective few songwriters have successfully managed, and which Rogers has successfully done throughout his career: a sincere and passionate declaration of devotion, qualified by a comprehensive breakdown of the narrator's shortcomings. After all, even if you know it's a terrible idea, how could one not fall for a man who describes himself as 'the re-run that you always force yourself to sit through?'

By the early nineties three things had reshaped the Australian musical landscape: the worldwide popularity of grunge music, the ubiquity of the now-nationwide Triple J as the voice of Australian youth,[2] and the annual nationally touring Big Day Out festival.

Grunge brought the underground overground, mainly in that the massive, unprecedented success of Nirvana suddenly

---

2   Double J had been a Sydney-specific station, but in 1989 Triple J was expanded to become a national youth network across Australia. Suddenly those too far out of the major cities to hear community radio were being exposed to the current Australian and international music, and the effect was . . . actually, you'll see next chapter.

BERLIN CHAIR 227

made record companies aware that dollars could be minted off the bands that had hitherto existed exclusively in the indie charts and hip music press. In the US, artists like Sonic Youth and the Flaming Lips suddenly had charting singles, stadium tours and songs appearing on movie soundtracks, and in Australia all the inner-city bands that would have been lucky to fill the Annandale Hotel for a CD launch were abruptly considered reasonable bets for major record deals.

A local Nirvana-style breakthrough was predicted, and seemed to happen when Ratcat suddenly hit big with 'That Ain't Bad' from their *Tingles* EP in 1990 and 'Don't Go Now' in 1991, eclipsing contemporaries like the Hummingbirds and the Falling Joys.[3] And while that turned out to be a short-lived blip on the musical radar, it made major label Warner Brothers realise that the rooArt label it signed up to distribute in 1991 might have been an unexpectedly shrewd arrangement.

It was a free-for-all for the big labels at that time. Geelong sludge rockers Magic Dirt also signed to Warners, as did Brisbane funk-punkers Regurgitator. Melbourne art rockers Something for Kate and Perth trio Ammonia signed with Sony's faux-indie label Murmur. Mushroom signed Melbourne acoustic-poppers Frente!, Polydor picked up Finley-via-Melbourne weirdos Spiderbait, Mornington Peninsula experimentalists the Fauves and the grunge-looking,

---

3 Incidentally, Ratcat's Simon Day had based 'Don't Go Now' on a song that Hummingbirds' bassist Robyn St Clare had written for her previous band, Love Positions, called 'Don't Slow Down'. She got a co-writing credit and a far bigger hit than the Hummingbirds ever managed.

Neil Young-influenced Brisbanites Powderfinger (and, as distributors for Red Eye, scored big with the Cruel Sea and also scored much, much smaller with the Clouds).

But rooArt had a head start: first with Ratcat and the Hummingbirds, then by creating a dedicated indie-rock offshoot, rA, which snapped up Brisbane quirk-rockers Custard, Melbourne's elegantly literate Augie March, and Adelaide's mighty shoegaze heroes the Mandelbrot Set, who should have been globe-bestriding superstars on the basis of their song 'More Than Happy' but ended up doing two EPs and calling it quits because the world is a cruel and unfair place. Oh, and there was also a little Sydney combo named You Am I.

The band had formed in 1989 and after a few line-up hiccups had settled into the power trio of Rogers, bassist Andy Kent and drummer Mark Tunaley. They'd built up enough of a live reputation to get a gig with the Big Day Out festival in 1993, and Rogers decided that was reason enough to send some stuff to Sonic Youth's co-guitar-torturer Lee Ranaldo, as his band was also on the bill.[4] Ranaldo liked what he heard and while in Sydney he produced the band's *Coprolalia* EP, and later that year he and the eager young trio decamped to Minnesota, where Renaldo helmed You Am I's debut album, *Sound As Ever*. 'Berlin Chair' was the second single, emerging in February 1994, and charted at a disappointing #73 (although it was #23 on that year's Hottest 100, which is something).

4   Fun fact: at the Adelaide leg of the Big Day Out that year was a little local band called The Undecided, fronted by one Andrew P Street. We were on at the same time as Nick Cave and the Bad Seeds, so even if you were there, you definitely didn't see us.

Even the glorious one-shot video with a weird silver-suited dancing chap didn't help.[5]

However, the US label thought it had a hit on its hands and commissioned another cleaner, more straightforward clip and an alternative mix of the single for release stateside, because it had some wonderful news. As Rogers explained to Andrew Denton in a 2008 episode of *Enough Rope*, Warner Brothers welcomed the band to the US with a marvellous plan: they were about to use 'Berlin Chair' as the soundtrack of a national TV campaign for Budweiser Beer. This was a huge opportunity to get the song in front of millions and millions of people who, like the band, enjoyed a beer or many.[6] And the band said no.

'We were just thinking we just can't do that kind of thing: it's *selling out* and *commercialism* and there was a lot of to-ing and fro-ing and at a certain point they went, "Oh well, bugger you; we'll give it to this prettier band,"' a slightly chagrined Rogers explained to Denton. 'There were tears, and now it seems that giving a song to a company to advertise something is like, "Oh yeah, yeah, well it'll get us this and get us that," and there's no conjecture about it.'

One of the greatest questions about You Am I was why they never cracked the US market, and the answer might be

---

5   He's known only as PJ and was a former boxer turned regular gig goer in the early 1990s. Russell Hopkinson, who replaced Tunaley as drummer immediately after *Sound As Ever* was recorded, explained: 'We just got him along, paid him some cash, put him in a silver suit, and said, "Dance away, my son"—and he did it spectacularly.'

6   Years later the band was to launch its own lager, Brew Am I, which is the best beer in the world. Honestly, it's the atmosphere of a summer beer garden with all your friends distilled into glorious fizzy drunk-water. I could go one right now, actually.

as simple and as stupid as that 'Berlin Chair' was too precious a song to them, and that pissed off the wrong person at their US record label.

It might not have made them American millionaires, but the song proved immortal. It was a staple of the band's sets forever, although Rogers would go through periods of peevishly refusing to play it.[7] It was also covered by several different artists, including Something for Kate's frontman Paul Dempsey and emo-rock kids Kisschasy, although Holly Throsby's haunting waltz-time cover for Triple J's Like a Version in 2009 most perfectly captured the fragile beauty of the lyrics.

Irritatingly, one of the best 'Berlin Chair'-related stories turned out to be false. The Newcastle band Silverchair thought the actual story behind its name was insufficiently cool and so cooked up an alternative one that they correctly thought would curry favour with Triple J and their rockin' credentials. But that's another story—one which you'll read over the page . . .

---

7   See also chapter 31 for more artists going 'How DARE you ask me to play that song you love!'

37

1994

Tomorrow

Silverchair

*In which that long-awaited rock breakthrough
finally arrives*

As you read in chapter 36, by the early nineties the Australian music revolution was in full swing: You Am I and the rest of the inner-city indie rock explosion had propped the door open for a breakthrough act to become the definitive band of the moment, but none seemed especially capable of doing the job themselves. You Am I was too traditional, Something for Kate too smarty-pants and Powderfinger—at this point, at least—too lousy.[1]

---

1   They were to find their sound remarkably quickly—and there's loads more to come on this subject in chapter 40—but in 1994 no-one heard *Parables for Wooden Ears* and went 'Wow! This brilliantly titled album is a sonic smorgasbord of original songwriting and top-flight musicianship!'

What Australian rock needed was a group of ambitious outsiders to come in and shake things up with the modern sound that was changing the world—or, failing that, to be super marketable and sound enough like Nirvana to sell by the truckload. And three teenagers from the beachside quasi-city of Newcastle were ready to fulfil that promise.

Singer/guitarist Daniel Johns and drummer Ben Gillies were childhood friends who met bassist Chris Joannou at Newcastle High. In 1992 the trio formed a band named Death Rides a Sandwich, which morphed into Innocent Criminals by the time they were playing around the Hunter region and entering the YouthRock competition for school bands, which they handily won. Meanwhile the national broadcasters were working on a joint project that was to have massive consequences for a band that, despite clearly being very competent, were still a) teenagers and b) in Newcastle: a national competition for unsigned bands called Pick Me, run as a collaborative endeavour between Triple J and SBS's music and culture TV program *Nomad*.

There was one important change to come first, though: Innocent Criminals was an objectively terrible name to give to anything, and thankfully the band noticed this glaringly obvious fact and came up with a far superior one: Silverchair. What's more, they initially invented an origin story for the new name that played to the tastes of their contemporary audience, claiming that teenage music fans Johns and Gillies were writing down songs to call in to Triple J's Request Fest and happened to put Nirvana's 'Sliver' next to 'Berlin Chair', and thus was history made. It's a cool story, and a far better one than the truth—that the band had taken its name from the fourth of C.S. Lewis's Narnia Chronicles, *The Silver Chair*. Think about that: we could almost have gotten Dawntreader, or Princecaspian, or Thehorseandhisboy.[2]

In April 1994 the newly renamed band won the Pick Me competition. The prize included professional recording of the winning song and the shooting of a video clip, and thus did their entry—the infectiously chunky 'Tomorrow'—start a bidding war between every major label in the country before Sony's Murmur imprint signed them for a three-album deal. 'Tomorrow', obviously, would be the debut single.

Johns and Gillies were only fifteen when they wrote the song, supposedly inspired by a documentary Johns saw on SBS in which a rich person was freaking out about being forced to stay overnight in a slum hotel. Musically it was almost grunge-by-numbers: mid-paced, loud-quiet-loud dynamics, a big searing guitar solo after the second chorus, and gruff, almost unintelligible vocals. In other words, it was the perfect distillation of everything that was happening in music at the time.

It was a huge, huge hit, spending six weeks at #1, while the parent album, *Frogstomp*, went nine times platinum in Australia. It also got a release in the US, reaching #9 in the charts, though reviews were rather less kind—and there was something of a coals-to-Newcastle element in sending a band whose vocalist sounded as though he was doing his best

---

2 Coincidentally, US singer Ben Harper would later adopt Innocent Criminals as the name of his backing band. Maybe he felt 'Ben Harper's Lion, Witch and Wardrobe' sounded weird.

impersonation of the mumble-mouthed vocal inflections of Pearl Jam's frontman, Eddie Vedder.[3]

Silverchair also had the one thing all great bands need most: an enigmatic frontman-slash-creative force. While they initially seemed like a cute shaggy unit of fresh-faced adolescents, it didn't take long to establish that Daniel Johns was the real creative powerhouse in the band. He also had the hardest time of it, developing an anxiety-related eating disorder (which he dealt with publicly in 'Ana's Song', a message to his own anorexia) and suicidal depression, marrying and then divorcing the beautiful model turned soap actress turned pop star Natalie Imbruglia,[4] suffering bizarre health issues such as reactive arthritis, copping a drink-driving charge, and embarking on extracurricular activities such as the Dissociatives along with dance music maven Paul Mac,[5] while the other two got on with the business of, um, politely keeping out of the way and turning up to make records.

Silverchair would release three more extremely successful albums and became unquestionably the biggest band in the country. But their legacy was even greater than that, for their success was directly responsible for the discovery and the careers of a slew of new acts from Australia's regions.

Pick Me had only been a one-off, not least because *Nomad* vanished from the SBS schedule, but the success of

---

3   Um, that's the *other* Newcastle.

4   Ben Gillies also married a television star, although she lacks the credibility even of *Neighbours*. His wife Jackie—a 'professional psychic', which is a thing that adults can apparently be—is one of the stars of *The Real Housewives of Melbourne*. Is 'stars' the right word?

5   You met him a few chapters ago: again, marvel at how artfully constructed a jigsaw puzzle this artfully constructed jigsaw puzzle is!

Pick Me in general and of Silverchair in particular made Triple J realise that a competition in which it sought out the best unsigned talent outside of the capital cities could well turn up the next big thing. Thus, in 1995 the Unearthed competition began, and over the next few years would make varying degrees of stars out of bands from Bathurst (the Tenants), Dubbo (Drown, who would later become Thirsty Merc), Darwin (Sophie Koh), the Goulburn Valley (Killing Heidi), the ACT (Bumblebeez) and Lismore (Grinspoon), as well as Melbourne (Missy Higgins) and Sydney (Sick Puppies)—and Newcastle again, for that matter, with indie pop kids Muzzy Pep.

In 2006, as entries skyrocketed, the station turned Unearthed into a website where people could listen to, download and vote for tracks by new artists, with the most popular winning berths on festival line-ups and gaining regular Triple J airplay. Over the next decade this would act as a launch pad for an astonishing number of significant artists: among the hundreds of acts were such future stars as Megan Washington, the Jezabels, Snakadaktal, Lanie Lane, Oh Mercy, Ball Park Music, Dune Rats, Richard in Your Mind, the John Steel Singers, Young and Restless, Hockey Dad, Philadelphia Grand Jury, and an act you'll read about in chapter 49 named Flume. In 2011 Unearthed became its own digital radio station and now acts as a feeder system for new artists to get airplay on Triple J. And it's all a direct spinoff of Silverchair—that's a legacy of which to be mighty proud.

Silverchair would go on to make much better and more sophisticated music before in 2011 putting the band into an 'indefinite hibernation' that has shown no sign of thawing. But there's still something deeply appealing about the unself-conscious exuberance of 'Tomorrow'. Truly, it was a more innocent (criminal) time.

38

1995

(He'll Never Be An) Ol' Man River

TISM

In which a band that no-one took seriously—least of all themselves—find themselves going dangerously mainstream

There are few activities more futile than attempting to explain This Is Serious Mum to someone unfamiliar with their work. This is especially true when attempting to explain them to someone not from Australia, or unfamiliar with Melbourne landmarks and/or AFL personalities.

The notion of the pseudonymous band playing in disguise was not unique—the Residents had been making music in disguise and without revealing their true identities since 1969. Even the idea of a band with some sort of artistic manifesto wasn't exactly new: Devo had been presenting themselves as an art project for the best part of a decade by the time TISM appeared.

TISM shares some characteristics with both—the use of elaborate matching outfits, the use of often ridiculous choreography, staging that emphasises the idiocy of the entire enterprise—but the difference between them and the aforementioned artists is both obvious to the eye and difficult to parse. Like pornography, it's easier to identify than describe. They both were the joke and were in on the joke.

While bands like Devo and the Residents (and Oingo Boingo, and They Might Be Giants, and Ween, and Camper Van Beethoven . . .) have undeniable absurdist and satirical elements, they're rarely deliberately comedic. TISM were unashamedly comic—although they were never a comedy band per se. They could never have played comedy festival shows the way that an act like, say, Tripod could. They'd never fit all the dancers on stage, for one thing.

And if TISM were unambiguously an art statement, part of that art statement was about how stupid art statements were. Their manifesto, scratched into the run-out groove of their EP, *Form and Meaning Reach Ultimate Communion*, and later acting as the title of a song in its own right, neatly captured their ambiguous stance with regards to their own existence: 'It's novel, it's unique, it's shithouse.'

TISM had existed as a band for over a decade when they finally enjoyed actual success. Having formed briefly in 1982, they started taking things . . . well, 'seriously' seems a strong word for a band playing songs like 'The Fosters Car Park Boogie' in matching balaclavas with half-a-dozen ridiculous dancers in synchronised movement, but in any case from 1984 to 2004 they consistently existed, at least.[1]

They rapidly became darlings of community radio, particularly Melbourne's RRR, with their 1985 demo and 1986 debut single 'Defecate on my Face'—a merry tribute to the alleged coprophilia of Adolf Hitler—ahead of the release of their debut album, *Great Truckin' Songs of the Renaissance*.

Their songs were generally ridiculous rather than satirical—'40 Years—Then Death', 'If You're Creative, Get Stuffed', 'I'm Interested in Apathy', 'Martin Scorsese is Really Quite a Jovial Fellow'—with more than a few undergraduate references (T.S. Eliot, existentialist philosophy, eye-rhymes, World War II history) which suggested a very well-educated brand of silliness.[2] Their nom de plumes also gave a reasonable indication of their sense of humour, mixing highbrow references with the lamest puns imaginable: Humphrey B. Flaubert, Eugene de la Hot-Croix Bun, Les Miserables . . . you get the idea.

A second album, *Hot Dogma*, followed in 1990 and consolidated TISM as favourites of community radio and university Orientation Balls, and as a band who posed absolutely no threat to the mainstream. And then, thanks to the vicissitudes of fashion, within a few short years TISM were unexpectedly working within the zeitgeist.

---

1 Every show since their shambolic first gig—the 'Get Fucked' concert in December 1983, after which they broke up—was billed as a reunion gig.

2 For whatever it's worth, I contend that the apogee of the TISM art was *Hot Dogma*'s spirited opening track, 'The TISM Boat Hire Offer', which is the most upbeat song about fishing/politics/at-risk rock stars you are likely to hear. Why and how it exists has never been remotely clear to me, which is what makes it so impossibly perfect.

Their third proper album, *Machiavelli and the Four Seasons*, was their most electronic to date, for several reasons. One, they'd been touring with the very rock-heavy Big Day Out in 1994 and had decided they loathed rock and everything associated with it. Two, in 1992 they'd recorded a mini-album, *The Beasts of Suburban*, with Birthday Party producer Tony Cohen that contained their most guitar-heavy work to date, but struggled to follow it up (several sessions with a variety of producers went nowhere, although the band did put out the self-produced *Australia The Lucky Cunt* EP[3] in 1993, which for the most part pushed the band back into electronica). And three, they decided they were sick of producers and would do everything themselves—at which point they were rewarded for their decision by losing all their nearly completed demos to a computer virus.

Thus, the album didn't arrive until 1995, giving people a chance to miss them. By then the world was ready for a single like '(He'll Never Be An) Ol' Man River', a song mocking dead celebrity worship and taking its inspiration from the 1993 death by overdose of US actor River Phoenix.

In poor taste? Absolutely. A thin joke? One hundred per cent. The sort of feeble musical gag that would become a massive favourite on mid-1990s Triple J? Couldn't have been more perfect: its listeners voted it #9 on that year's Hottest 100, with the album's follow-up single, 'Greg! The Stop Sign!!', at #10.

---

3   Original copies of the EP are collectors items these days, since it was withdrawn thanks to a legal threat by the artist Ken Done, whose work they parodied on the cover. The replacement, with Sinead O'Connor tearing up a piece of paper reading 'TISM', was retitled *Censored Due to Legal Advice*.

Bizarrely for a song that mixed techno drum machines and loud guitars in a way that had sounded tired when Jesus Jones was charting half a decade earlier, the single even hit the mainstream Australian charts and reached a respectable #23—and would probably have done even better had it been titled by the most identifiable line: 'I'm on the drug that killed River Phoenix'.[4] Its parent album reached #8, which seemed as weird then as it does in hindsight.

It couldn't—and didn't—last. 'Greg! The Stop Sign!!' stalled outside the mainstream charts and the following album, 1998's *www.tism.wanker.com*, didn't do anywhere near as well—possibly since the first not-entirely-radio-friendly single was entitled 'I May Be a Cunt But I'm Not a Fucking Cunt'.

There were two more albums before TISM finally ground to a halt—*De RigueurMortis* in 2001 and the DVD/CD pack *The White Albun* in 2004[5]—and by that stage the band's shock value had diminished back to their original cult status. There was no announcement of the band's demise, but their Earthcore performance in 2004 turned out to be their last. And without them, Australian music got a lot more dull.

The weirdest thing about 'Ol' Man River' was that it inadvertently unmasked TISM seven years after its release, thanks to SBS's unfortunate, if admirable, adherence to copyright law.

The network screened the acclaimed music documentary series *John Safran's Music Jamboree* in 2002, and each episode

---

4 Wisely, Shock Records put that quote at the very top of the single's cover with the actual title at the bottom in a much smaller font.

5 The misspelling is deliberate; as frontman Ron Hitler-Barassi put it in the accompanying documentary, 'What we're doing here is basically what Jet are doing, which is taking the Beatles' ideas and changing them a little bit at the end. If it's worked for Jet, it's going to work for us, that's what we're hoping.'

finished with a band performing one of their best-known songs on unfamiliar instruments. TISM performed their sole hit on traditional Greek instruments in a performance that was, to be charitable, spirited—but evidently no-one in the legal department thought there'd be a problem with dutifully putting the songwriter information in the credits. And thus everyone who had woven elaborate theories as to the true identity of TISM (were they secretly Hunters & Collectors? Painters & Dockers? The Wiggles?) would find their theories depressingly deflated to discover the song was written by 'Damian Cowell/Peter Minack/Jack Holt/James Paull/ Eugene Cester'—a bunch of people who were, well, just a bunch of people.[6]

Hopes for the band's return faded with the appearance of the comedy country band Root!, whose lead singer DC Root was revealed to be one Damian Cowell, who sounded awfully like M. Flaubert—and then rather gave the game away with his next band, the DC3, and their debut single 'I Was the Guy in TISM'. And that basically killed any chance of a comeback. After all, as Kiss proved to the world, no costumed band is worth a damn once it has been unmasked—and in any case guitarist Paull, aka Tokin' Blackman, was tragically felled by cancer in 2008.

There was a brief tongue-in-cheek campaign to have TISM represent Australia at the 2015 Eurovision Song Contest, as

---

6 Eugene Cester is also the uncle of Nick Cester, frontman of Jet. As the previous footnote may have indicated, Jet were a particular target of TISM during their heyday, with Flaubert asking *Age* journalist Michael Dwyer: 'When you go and interview the boys from Jet, are you sitting there and going, "Well, they're nice guys, they're not that smart, I can't really get out the rapier wit here, so I'll just peddle the usual record company line"?'

an enduring testament to just how beloved they remain. But a word of advice: if you've ever loved TISM (and you should) then don't do *too* much research on them. Their power as costumed superheroes and national treasures is somewhat diminished when you know they're ex-punk rockers-turned-lawyers and school teachers with real names and families and so on.[7] Far better to imagine them dancing off into the ether in matching balaclavas filled with helium balloons, with an arc-welder building a sculpture as they go.

---

7 The ex-punk rockers thing? The core musical axis of TISM was in a punk band called I Can Run, which is a pretty great name.

39

1995

Where the Wild Roses Grow

Nick Cave and the Bad Seeds featuring Kylie Minogue

In which an unlikely duet becomes the game changer for two international Australian stars

Nick Cave is in many ways the epitome of what Australia looks for in its national treasures: someone who was largely ignored until the rest of the world loved him, and then immediately hailed as a local-born genius.

That's slightly unfair, but only slightly. After all, Cave's Australian musical career effectively ended when the Boys Next Door got on a plane to Heathrow in 1980. Since then he's lived in Germany, Brazil, England, and other nations that are united in not being Australia.

There's been a recurring theme in this book regarding how our artists have attempted, with varying degrees of success, to take their career outside of Australia. And the reasons for that are largely economic: a successful artist in the US or the UK can potentially make a decent living playing in their own country, but the Australian population—and therefore the market for any music, regardless of how mainstream it is—is just too small. This is why you never see US artists basing themselves out here in a desperate attempt to 'break' Australia; what the hell would they stand to gain?

Even chart-topping pop masters Savage Garden, who were hitting big with songs like 'To the Moon And Back' in 1996, didn't hesitate for a second to get themselves to the US, because even a platinum Australian album isn't exactly something upon which lifetime fortunes are made. So Cave's career is especially illuminating in that he shows what success looks like for an Australian artist who is working far off the mainstream—and this was the greatest success he would ever have.[1]

It's possible (and illustrative) to categorise Cave's musical career into eras defined by whoever was his prime musical collaborator at the time. Mick Harvey had been Cave's (red) right hand since they were at high school together until finally resigning from the Bad Seeds in January 2009, following the Bad Seeds-curated All Tomorrows Parties festivals in Australia, having racked up a total of thirty-six years at Cave's side.[2]

---

1   Well, to date, at least. You never know with Nick Cave.
2   For the rest of the 2009 dates his place was taken by Ed Kuepper—you know, from chapter 12. JIGSAW.

WHERE THE WILD ROSES GROW 247

But if Harvey was Cave's long-suffering musical wife, then the Black Crow King also flaunted his affections with a series of creative mistresses. First, as you discovered in chapter 14, there was Rowland S. Howard, who transformed the perfectly decent Boys Next Door into the wiry, inflammatory Birthday Party. But Cave and Howard's relationship became strained and eventually snapped after Cave became creatively enamoured of Blixa Bargeld, guitarist and noise-demon of German industrial experimentalists Einstürzende Neubauten. The Cave/Bargeld partnership became the creative axis of the Bad Seeds for thirteen years, until a new and exciting and beardy force appeared in the form of violinist Warren Ellis.

Ellis was one-third of the instrumental trio the Dirty Three, who had drifted into the Bad Seeds' circle a few years earlier. The mixing and final overdubs to the previous album, 1994's *Let Love In*, had been done at Metropolis Studios in Melbourne—the first time in decades that a Cave record had been made on Australian soil. As a result, a bunch of locals sashayed along to lend their talents, including Howard, Tex Perkins and David McComb[3]—and Ellis, making his first Bad Seeds appearance on two tracks. From this low-key beginning he and Cave connected, and by the time the band started work on what was to be *Murder Ballads* in 1996, Ellis was officially a Bad Seed.

While that dynamic was starting to alter the band's internal structure, there was another important thing happening: Cave seemed determined to lose all the commercial momentum he'd built up. *Let Love In* had been critically praised and,

---

3   You know, from chapter 26.

surprisingly for the Bad Seeds, also sold by the shedful thanks to its haunting, freakish, largely-invented-on-the-day single 'Red Right Hand', which had been used to great effect in the wildly successful *Scream* series of horror films and on TV hit *The X-Files*. Rather than capitalise on this, Cave felt the need for a concept record. He'd started listening to American gangster rap and had fallen in love with the format's precise descriptions of extreme violence, which took him back to the blues records he'd been obsessed with as a younger man. He'd also been half joking about making an album of murder ballads, and had even stockpiled a few songs such as 'O'Malley's Bar', which was written circa 'Henry's Dream' but had been deemed unsuitable for that and the following record. Cave wanted to create an album to put these songs on.

In addition to this, the domestic harmony that had infused *Let Love In*, with Cave happily married to Brazilian journalist Viviane Carneiro and raising their son Luke, had ended badly by the time *Murder Ballads* came about, and the last thing a wounded Cave wanted to do was write a batch of introspective and personal songs about a very painful set of circumstances.[4]

So, with the brief that this was a 'comedy' record designed to piss away all the goodwill built up over the last two albums, the Seeds re-reconvened in Melbourne with producer Tony Cohen to do an album all about lurid brutality. And it became their biggest-selling record to date. That was mainly down to one thing: Nick Cave's genuine—if slightly creepy—obsession with one Ms K. Minogue.

---

4   That he'd leave to the heartbreaking catharsis of the next album, *The Boatman's Call*.

He'd been talking with varying degrees of seriousness about his desire to record with her for six years, and decided that he'd found the right track when he finished work on a song that was, according to Cave, in the episode of SBS's *Great Australian Albums* dedicated to *Murder Ballads*, 'a dialogue between a killer and his victim', loosely based on the Appalachian-via-Ireland folk ballad 'Down in the Willow Garden'. He also had a convenient way of contacting her: she was seeing INXS lead singer Michael Hutchence at the time, and Harvey had his number. A call was made, contact was established,[5] and Minogue nailed her vocal in a handful of takes.[6]

As befits a professional actor, Minogue took direction well: at first she belted it out, but Cave advised her to approach it as a character piece. 'Make it smaller, smaller, smaller,' she later recalled him directing her. 'Make it like you're telling the story, you're speaking it.'

Cave had never exactly had a 'hit' before, but 'Where the Wild Roses Grow' was a genuine smash upon its release in September 1995. It went top 5 in Australia (where it also went gold), Sweden, Norway, Finland, Austria and Belgium, and rose to #11 in the UK—though the album got to #3 (as it also did in Australia)—and while it didn't chart well initially, it ended up selling a quarter of a million copies in Germany thanks to its appearance in the soap opera *Gegen den Wind*.

---

5   Hilariously, since both Cave and Minogue lived outside Australia and mobile phones weren't yet a thing, they were forced to leave messages for one another via their Melbourne-based mothers.

6   She had a demo of the song against which to practice, with her part sung by Bargeld in a performance Cave called 'seriously creepy, with a capital K'. It later turned up on the *B-Sides and Rarities* compilation, and Cave is correct. Sorry: korrect.

It put Cave in an interesting predicament, in that his biggest hit was a song he couldn't really perform live, although Minogue got around it by adding the chorus to a medley she performed in her late-nineties tours and she guested with the Bad Seeds on several gigs when they were in the same town—including the Sydney Big Day Out in 1996. But the impact of the song on both artists' careers was considerable.

For Cave, it opened him up to the pop audience—who bought *Murder Ballads* in droves, and were largely horrified by the non-Minogue songs thereon.[7]

For Minogue the reverse was true: it made her a credible artist and led her to make the album that is most often cited as her best, and inarguably was her lowest-selling: 1997's *Impossible Princess*,[8] which featured collaborations with Brothers in Rhythm, Rob Dougan and members of the Manic Street Preachers.

For his part, Cave is certain that Minogue's team never forgave him for the career blip. 'I think her management wasn't that happy about it,' Cave told Jessamy Calkin at the *Daily Telegraph* in 2014. 'I mean, we were just a bunch of junkies sitting in the studio and she walked in full of life and love and goodwill.'

---

7   Chart-wise it was the band's largest success until *Push the Sky Away* in 2013, although the chart rules had changed so much by then it's hard to do a direct comparison on which was the more successful.

8   In her defence, the album was her first and only for deConstruction, a dance label that was going through massive managerial and distribution crises at the time of *Impossible Princess*—and the album also had a name change in Europe following the death of Princess Diana, which delayed it in a number of key regions. A similar thing happened a few years later, when Sydney trio Gerling released their master-piece *When Young Terrorists Chase the Sun* in early September 2001, just before . . . well, you probably remember what happened on the eleventh of that month.

WHERE THE WILD ROSES GROW

Still, a hit's a hit, and the lesson for non-mainstream Australian artists was clear. You could absolutely be successful—all you had to do was ride the commercial coattails of a mainstream pop star whose audience didn't listen to albums too closely before buying them. It's just that easy!

40

1998

These Days

Powderfinger

*In which Australia reaches its peak in
local stadium rock*

In the late 90s Powderfinger was well on the way to becoming the biggest band in the country. Sure, their first album, 1994's *Parables for Wooden Ears*, was as lousy as its title[1]—but they'd done that rare and wonderful thing of getting orders of magnitude better with each album: 1996's *Double Allergic* was a massive step forward in songwriting, performance and production —and the band was rewarded with triple platinum sales locally, buoyed by the singles 'Pick You Up' and 'DAF'. Things got even better with 1998's *Internationalist*, which

---

1 I know, I've mentioned it before. Honestly, it's a stinker of a record.

went five-time platinum, with 'The Day You Come' their first true crossover hit.

The third single from the album was a rockin' number called 'Passenger', which just brushed the top 30 of the ARIA charts in 1999. It's B-side, however, was a song the band had been invited to write by director/screenwriter Gregor Jordan for his Australian indie film *Two Hands*. That film was Jordan's directorial debut and a breakout hit with great reviews and strong box office. *Two Hands* didn't make its director a star—he suffered a big budget flop with *Ned Kelly* in 2003 and went on to concentrate on documentaries—but it launched the careers of its young leads, Heath Ledger and Rose Byrne, and gave a little Brisbane band the song of their career.

Powderfinger's frontman Bernard Fanning was starting to draw more and more on his past for inspiration in the lead up to what was to be the band's masterpiece, 2002's *Odyssey Number Five*. The success the band had enjoyed made him think back to the period when it had all felt like an enormous risk, giving up his journalism studies to concentrate full time on music. He told Christie Eliezer that 'It was when I left home, joined a band, with all the risks involved. Few bands become successful and make a living out of music. That period was a big change for me. I left university, and broke out of the sheltered private schoolboy life. I was ambitious, it was never an intention to muck around with music for the laughs and the beer. I took it seriously, we all did.'

The mix of uncertainty and anxious hope was in his head when he and the band were shown scenes from *Two Hands* for which Jordan needed a song. The fact that it was effectively a work-for-hire gave the band a little emotional distance from it. 'It was the first time there was an outside reason to write a song, rather than my own emotional response to something.'

'These Days' might have been designed for the film, but the central theme—not getting the life you hoped for—was a remarkably universal one, speaking to everyone's inner disapproving twenty-two-year-old self.

The song was given one of the most generic titles ever, which hid the fact that the band had written its greatest song to date and, arguably, its best song ever. Far from being a half-arsed soundtrack contribution, 'These Days' showed Powderfinger discovering just how surprisingly good they were at that most despised of genres: the power ballad.

And yes, 'These Days' is a power ballad—the slow build, the emotional delivery, the layers on layers adding as the song moves on, the big focus guitar solo—it's all there. And the band clearly didn't realise what they had at the time or they wouldn't have just dumped it on the flipside of 'Passenger'.

Two Hands was released the following year with 'These Days' the focus track, and that's when the song became a monster. With no video clip and no record to buy without forking out for the soundtrack album, the song should really have just vanished into the ether.

But that's not what happened.

If anything, the lack of a physical copy made it *more* precious, and thus 'These Days' became the first ever B-side to top the 1999 Triple J Hottest 100. It ended up being remade and included on *Odyssey Number Five* in 2000 where it informed another song with a similar tempo, a similar sense of hopeful melancholy that topped the Hottest 100 the following year, 'My Happiness'.

For well over a year the band was omnipresent as it entered its Imperial Period, when the album not only sold by the truckload—eventually going eight-times platinum—but was blaring from every car in Australia. It's impossible not to sound snide when saying this, but it's meant with sincerity: 'These Days' was the song with which Powderfinger also found its cultural niche, which was making music for straight men to hug to.

That isn't even remotely a joke either. In the hyper-masculine world of Australian rock anything that even remotely suggested sensitivity or empathy was historically at best feminine and at worst probably gay. So when a band came along with unimpeachably masculine credentials and yet also somehow made it okay for drunk dudes to embrace one another and scream 'I fucken love you, mate' into one other's faces, it had a powerful effect. Prior to Powderfinger, only Cold Chisel had anything approaching this power

And like Chisel, this period of Australian superstardom was assumed to lead naturally to international success, which wasn't to be. Maybe it was timing. Had *Odyssey Number Five* come out in 2004 rather than 2000 maybe Powderfinger could have been Snow Patrol, blasting emotional big-gesture music off American stadium walls. Extensive US touring and big promotional pushes on 'My Kind of Scene' (which got a berth on the *Mission Impossible 2* soundtrack) failed to translate to Coldplay-sized audiences—who, to be fair, were probably seeing Coldplay.

It seemed that the fire went out of the band a little at that point. The rock-heavy 2003 album *Vulture Street* was the first album not to represent a step forward, and then the band went on a break during which its members released largely-ignored side projects—with the exception of frontman Bernard Fanning whose debut solo album *Tea and Sympathy* went to number one and made very, very clear just who was the band's key member in the eyes of the public.

Two more albums followed: 2007's troubled *Dream Days at the Hotel Existence*, recorded in the US with mainstream rock producer Rob Schnapf (and accurately described by *Sydney Morning Herald* reviewer Bernard Zuel as 'Powderfinger's first dull album') and finally the solid-but-unexceptional *Golden Rule* in 2009. Made back in Australia with regular producer Nick DiDia, it sounded like a full stop to the band's career, confirmed by the announcement not long after the album's release that the band was splitting up, since 'we feel that we have said all that we want to say as a musical group'.

A massive national tour followed and that was that. Fanning's solo career continued, guitarist Ian Haug joined the Church after the band had one fight too many with Marty Willson-Piper, drummer John Coghill became a Gold Coast-based journalist with the ABC, guitarist Darren Middleton recorded as Drag and opened the Red Door studio in Melbourne, and bassist John Collins opened a music venue in Fortitude Valley called the Triffid.

The strangest thing about the end of Powderfinger was that it left the way open for a new popular mainstream Australian stadium rock act, and absolutely no-one stepped up. For a while it looked as though Perth trio Eskimo Joe were set to become the drunk-bro-hugging band of choice, but ultimately they fizzled out rather than leaping to the next level. That role ultimately went to hardcore bands like Parkway Drive.

In fact, Powderfinger represented the last real Australian rock band that could, for example, headline a major festival. Other mainstream crossover acts would emerge, but none would be guitar bands—and actually, if you're looking for a cultural studies thesis topic you could do worse than 'Which died first: festival headliners, or festivals to headline?'

Still, 'These Days' has an enduring power and, as the last encore at Powderfinger's final ever show, on the Brisbane Riverstage on 13 November 2010, it has the distinction of being the final song the band ever played.[2] It turns out that it—and Powderfinger itself—was too hard an act to follow.

---

2   Fanning hosted a Powderfinger almost-reunion in July 2017 during his Splendour in the Grass set when he welcomed Haug, Middleton and Collins on stage for three songs. Coghill didn't even get an invite, finding out about the performance only after his phone started lighting up with congratulatory texts. That must have stung.

41

2000

Frontier Psychiatrist

The Avalanches

*In which some Melburnians with time on their
hands decide to create the best album of 2000
using only records from the past*

The notion of the DJ as an artist in their own right had
been percolating ever since Grandmaster Flash first worked
out how to create an endless loop by swapping between two
copies of the same record on two simultaneous turntables
during the legendary New York block parties that created
rap and hip hop, but the idea of using other people's records
to create new pieces of artwork was, at best, a controversial
one—at least, until technology and copyright law caught up
with it and made it both physically possible and a bureaucratic
nightmare.

But for a few shining years there, the rudimentary technology for what became known as sampling existed in a world unfettered by lawsuits over what constituted a sample, meaning that artists who had the patience to take a magpie approach to their record collections could cut and paste bits of their favourite songs together to create something entirely new.

Early sampling technology was both expensive to acquire and cumbersome to use, but hip hop and dance music rapidly realised the potential—and while sampling a song's drumbeat or hook became common, a few artists took the next step and began to build songs out of multiple cut-up pieces of source material.

Among the pioneering early adopters in the late 1980s were UK grebo band Pop Will Eat Itself, who wrote conventional songs based around samples of their favourite records and films;[1] studio project S'Express (whose biggest hit, 'Theme from S'Express' was achieved by layering Rose Royce's 'Is It Love You're After' beneath the vocal from TZ's 'I Got the Hots For You');[2] London pranksters the KLF, whose first #1, 'Doctorin' the Tardis' (released under the name the Timelords), answered the question: 'What if we just played a bit of a Gary Glitter song, then the *Doctor Who* theme, and then did that a few more times?';[3] and the Dust Brothers (Michael

---

1 For example: 1987 single 'Def.Con.One' marries the grinding intro of the Stooges' 'I Wanna Be Your Dog' with the riff from Lipps Inc.'s 'Funkytown', plus the opening theme of *The Twilight Zone*. Genius.

2 Fun fact: the 'hi-hat' sound that was to basically become the standard sound of acid house? That was Mark Moore on an aerosol can.

3 'Doctorin' the Tardis' was a number one hit, but the KLF regretted not just calling it by its hook of 'Doctor Who' and selling boatloads more, as they explained in their manifesto *The Manual (How to Have a Number One the Easy Way)* in 1988.

'E.Z. Mike' Simpson and John 'King Gizmo' King), a Hollywood production team who were creating intricate, layered songs made entirely of samples which became the basis of the Beastie Boys' groundbreaking 1989 album, *Paul's Boutique*. But even though these artists leaned heavily on samples, they didn't rely on them exclusively. There were still other elements added in the studio, like vocals or keyboards. Even as samplers started getting better memory capacity and became easier to use, no-one would have the patience to try to build an entire record from scratch using nothing but samples, unless they were insane studio rats.

Melbourne's premier insane studio rats Robbie Chater and Darren Seltmann discovered the power of the early floppy disc-driven Akai samplers available in 1995 and abandoned their previous musical exercises to form the Avalanches.[4]

While recordings were being pieced together in their home studios, the band slowly grew with the addition of turntablists Dexter Fabay and James de la Cruz, and keyboard players Tony di Blasi and Gordon McQuilten. The resultant album, *Since I Left You*, was world-shaking for a lot of reasons. One: it was created by building songs out of literally thousands of samples (Chater claimed it was around 3500 in interviews at the time, although estimates of 900 seem closer to the mark), becoming the touchstone in the emerging art of what was dubbed 'plunderphonics'. Two: it was the first time Madonna

---

4   Seltmann was the drummer for Ripe when they made 1993's *The Plastic Hassle*, possibly the most underrated Australian album of all time, goddamn it. He's also the husband of singer/songwriter Sally Seltmann, she of Seeker Lover Keeper and co-writer of Feist's '1234', and formerly known as New Buffalo. The couple have become a very successful soundtrack team in recent years.

had given permission to be sampled ('Holiday' is used for 'Stay Another Season'). Three: legend has it that the band actually lost money on the album, since the percentage of each song negotiated to each of the sampled artists often added up to more than 100 per cent.[5] And four: it was like nothing anyone had ever heard. And while much of the album was instrumental and gorgeous, there was one obvious killer single that in less accomplished hands would have been a pure novelty record: the irresistibly playful 'Frontier Psychiatrist'.

With this song, more than any other track on the album, the Avalanches tapped into the roots of hip hop. Specifically, an element that is too often overlooked when the roots of rap are discussed: old comedy records. Hip hop historians still argue this point, but many American scholars have concluded that the first recorded instance of someone doing what we'd now recognise as rapping—reciting rhymes in time with a beat—was not on an ultra-cool Gil Scott-Heron or Last Poets album, but in a popular 1960s routine by vaudeville circuit comic Pigmeat Markham called 'Here Come the Judge'. It's hardly high art, but that particular routine became Pigmeat's calling card and also ensured that humour and cartoonish braggadocio would be part and parcel of rap music.

The Avalanches continued this proud tradition by drawing their vocal track from comedy records—specifically, those of Canadian duo Wayne and Shuster. This venerable and deeply uncool mainstream comedy team were weirdly well known among Australian kids of a certain age thanks to

---

5 Obsessive fans should note that the Australian, European and US versions of the album are all slightly different due to licensing constraints on the tracks they used.

their self-titled TV show being part of the peculiar bundle of Canadian-made entertainment the ABC broadcast in the post-school-pre-news time slot in the 1980s.[6] Their show was made well after their prime and consisted of sketches they'd filmed in the sixties repackaged with new introductions by the now-elderly comic duo. One such sketch was an Old West parody entitled 'Frontier Psychiatrist', in which a Freudian psychoanalyst attempts to cure gunslingers of their tendency to violence—a genuinely funny premise killed by the overlong execution.[7]

The other big source of vocal samples for the song came from John Waters' 1981 film *Polyester*, whose major antagonist, Dexter Fishpaw, conveniently shared his first name with a member of the band. How could they *not* sample it?

The song barely cracked the Australian top 50, but was a top 20 hit in the UK and sent the album into the top 10. *Since I Left You* peaked in Australia at #15, but the album proved an enduring success and was acknowledged as a classic worldwide (even getting 9.5 out of 10 from notoriously sniffy online magazine *Pitchfork*).

The success of the album left the band with several challenges. For a start, the album was nearly impossible to re-create live, so they went for enthusiasm over sonic fidelity—which

---

6 We also got *You Can't Do That on Television*, which starred a very young Alanis Morissette, and *Degrassi Junior High*, for which my teenage self was enormously grateful. Many years later, as the show was bundled onto DVD sets by Shock, I got to interview my teenage televisual crush Stacie Mistysyn, aka Caitlin Ryan, and you know what? She was just *lovely*.

7 You know how *Saturday Night Live* is notorious for spending an excruciating eight minutes on a solid ninety-second premise? Wayne and Shuster all but invented the format.

meant a full band tour saw Seltmann break his ankle on stage and di Blasi suffer a concussion, which left Chater to finish the tour doing DJ sets.

Then there was the question of how the band could create a follow-up given the nightmarish ordeal of licensing increasingly pricy samples from artists now confident that an Avalanches album would be a sweet payday.

More urgent, though, was the fact that the members of the band were dropping like flies. In 2001 three members vanished in acrimonious circumstances, including Dexter, and by February 2014 even Seltmann was gone. The only members left standing were Robbie Chater and Tony di Blasi—and Chater had spent much of the previous three years sidelined with an autoimmune disease that made him unable to work.

Since I Left You seemed destined to be a one-off, but in 2016 the second Avalanches album, *Wildflower*, appeared—a decade and a half after their debut. It was received rapturously, although no-one so much as pretended that it matched *Since I Left You*, or that the single 'Frankie Sinatra' was a patch on 'Frontier Psychiatrist'.

You'd assume that now, with technology cheap and accessible and the entire world's recorded music library at the fingertips of anyone with an internet connection, records like *Since I Left You* would be all over the place. Then again, the copyright hurdles and licensing challenges would give any new artist pause. This means that the Avalanches occupy a unique space in Australian music as a vision of what music might have done. And if nothing else, for one glorious moment they made Wayne and Schuster relevant again.

42

2002

Get Free

The Vines

*In which Australia becomes the epicentre
of the dead cat bounce of rock'n'roll*

For ten years Australian music had been largely—although by
no means exclusively—the purview of lanky, moody-looking
men with guitars. Sure, there were dance hits and the beginning of a head-shaking dismissal of Australian accents in the
emerging local hip hop scene, and even a bit of a country
resurgence thanks to the massive crossover success of Kasey
Chambers. But these were all outliers, obviously, as a wave
of retro-sounding bands with big guitars and fuck-you attitudes broke big in Australia. They were unassailable proof
that the grunge-inspired early nineties explosion of indieness
would last forever, and the only skirmishes that remained

were for guitars to be finally reclaimed from nu-metal and the airwaves purged of that hippity-hop music and its drug-snorting pop-EDM compatriots.[1]

Instead, it turned out to be the last bright hurrah of guitar rock.

Australia wasn't alone in interpreting this blinding sunset as a second dawn. If the last thing you saw before slipping into a fifteen-year coma had been a copy of *Rolling Stone* from 2002 you'd have very reasonably expected that the bands of the day would still be venerated by generations of new artists as having so comprehensively blazed the trail that no under-growth would ever grow there again.

There was a confident assumption that bands like US duo the White Stripes, suit-wearing Swedish rock machine the Hives and New York trust fund slackers the Strokes had fundamentally changed the very essence of modern rock'n'roll, along with a bunch of artists with similar backgrounds—essentially a mix of upper-middle-class kids with good drugs and expensive haircuts, including the Yeah Yeah Yeahs, Interpol, the Von Bondies, Electric Six, Black Rebel Motorcycle Club and the Black Keys. Later the trend spread to the UK and launched the likes of the Arctic Monkeys, Kaiser Chiefs and the Libertines, but in Australia there were two leading lights of this New Rock Renaissance.

---

1 Nu-metal was another big trend at the time that has proved rather more enduring. It was basically heavy metal but with hip hop-style phrasing and drop-tuning to make everything sound super-heavy, and in Australia was led by acts like the Butterfly Effect, Karnivool and Cog. Fans of all these bands will angrily tell you that they definitely were not nu-metal and throw around terms like 'progressive metal' and 'melodic hardcore' and so on. Those people are lying to you.

In Sydney there was a more-heard-of-than-heard band based around the photogenically stoned Craig Nicholls, son of a Sony accountant, who had apparently discovered the perfect synthesis of nineties grunge and Oasis-style classic rock with his band, the Vines.[2] Eighteen months later a wildly hyped buzz band named after Paul McCartney's single 'Jet' would draw breathless notice in inner-city Melbourne, even as editorials straightfacedly compared them to the Beatles and the Easybeats.

Not long after a third key band would appear, led by a mighty shock of fuzzy hair attached to a singer-guitarist named Andrew Stockdale, whose band Wolfmother was perfectly poised in the middle of the early noughties Bands with Wolf in the Name zeitgeist,[3] presumably because they thought calling themselves We Enjoy Sabbath and Zepplin, Us would give the whole game away.

All three inspired record company bidding wars, all three harkened back to a simpler, rockinger time when guitars were loud and bands exuded outright contempt for their audience, and all three would be hailed as the future of rock'n'roll in the international music press. And, to be fair, they were—in the sense that rock'n'roll itself was also doomed to fracture and collapse into utter irrelevance within a few short years.

---

2 Named after The Vynes, the sixties psych band in which Nicholls' dad failed to become a rock star.

3 Between about 1998 and 2004 there were approximately a billion bands with Wolf in the name: Wolf Parade, Wolf Gang, Wolf & Cub, Wolf Eyes, We Are Wolves, Wolves in the Throne Room, Turbowolf, Superwolf, Seasons of the Wolf, Tiger Bear Wolf, AIDS Wolf and the metal band Wolf, among many, many, many others. Some speculated that there were more wolf bands in the wild than actual wolves.

The Vines had started life doing Nirvana and You Am I covers at parties under the godawful name of Rishikesh, but soon streamlined their sound and their name. When their indie single 'Factory' was made Single of the Week in the *NME*, Capitol (the US arm of EMI) presumably forgot what happened the last time it had hastily signed an Australian band on the strength of a single British review and promptly snatched them up.[4]

The band's garage sound was perfectly attuned to the trends of the time, especially in the US, so it made sense for it to record its debut album in LA with ultra-cool Rob Schnapf, who'd co-produced most of Elliot Smith's records and was to go on to make *Dream Days at the Hotel Existence* with Powderfinger.[5]

The album's second single, 'Get Free', was the break-through. It got to #7 on *Billboard*'s Modern Rock chart and #24 in the UK singles chart, with Australia playing catch up over a band that had been a cult deal in its hometown and basically unknown everywhere else before the overseas cover stories began. The album sold 1.5 million copies world-wide and saw the band hailed as 'Saviours of Rock' in *Rolling Stone*'s October 2002 cover story.

And while the bands that were to follow the Vines consciously wore their record collections on their sleeves, 'Get Free' was pure roaring male id. The lyrics are repetitive to the point of a mantra, delivered in Nicholls' furious monotone. It was the distillation of everything that a seventeen-year-old

---

4 Remember the story of the Saints back in chapter 12? Oh, we were so much younger then . . .
5 Which, you might recall, was their 'first dull album'.

plugging a crappy pawn shop guitar into their first overdriven practice amp wants to sound like: bold, unhinged and, most of all, loud. It's a youthful 'fuck you' in musical form.

And if you want to draw out that Saints comparison even further, it's similarly economical: the song barely cracks two minutes (which still makes it 25 per cent longer than previous single, 'Highly Evolved', which clocked in at a furious ninety seconds). It's still a thrilling listen and deserved every plaudit it received.

But even when the Vines were at their height, things seemed dangerously volatile. Drummer David Olliffe was discarded soon after the album was complete, eventually replaced by Hamish Rosser, and second guitarist Ryan Griffiths was flown in from Sydney ostensibly to flesh out the band's sound live, but also to cover for Nicholls, who was becoming more and more unreliable. TV appearances and live shows were inevitably ending with Nicholls smashing up his bandmates' gear and, later, occasionally smashing up his bandmates too.

In May 2004 things came to a head when the band played a gig for Triple M at the Annandale Hotel in Sydney. It wasn't a proper Vines gig—most of the crowd were competition winners, the rest were radio biz sorts—and Nicholls didn't care for feeling like he was a performing monkey at the behest of commercial radio. First he kicked a photographer, breaking a camera. Exasperated bassist Patrick Matthews walked off stage. Nicholls then took umbrage at someone laughing while he was playing the intro to a slower song. 'Why the fuck are you laughing?' he demanded, before mocking the crowd for being there. 'You're all a bunch of sheep. Can you go *baa*?'

Matthews never came back; he got in a cab, went home and quit the band. Triple M announced it'd never play a Vines song again. Eventually Nicholls would announce that he had Asperger's syndrome and that his behaviour was a combination of confusion, high stress and the heroic amount of marijuana he was smoking at the time, and the band effectively stopped playing live lest his fragile mental health be further damaged.

That year's patchy *Winning Days* had been the first hint that maybe the band weren't garage rock savants after all, and by the time of album number three, 2006's perfectly decent *Vision Valley*, the world had moved on.

Jet, meanwhile, were getting a similarly lacklustre response to second album *Shine On*, which had left them looking like yesterday's men,[6] but by 2008 the wheels had really fallen off the Australian rocknaissance. The non-Andrew Stockdale members of Wolfmother quit in frustration, leaving him to pursue what amounted to a solo career; Jet was working on what was to be its final album, the fine-but-whatever *Shaka Rock*; and the now solo-project-in-all-but-name Vines was putting out *Melodia* on Sydney indie label Ivy League to a much-reduced listenership.

The Vines, Jet and Wolfmother would continue for several more records, with only Jet taking the hint and bowing out of its own accord, while the other two bands chased diminishing returns through a number of line-ups and record labels. But this

---

6   *Shine On* received one of the least fair and most genuinely hilarious reviews of all time from *Pitchfork*, which contained no words at all. Instead it was an animated GIF of a chimpanzee pissing in its own mouth. Now, this is not actual criticism—*Pitchfork*, for its faults, does excellent analysis of music and culture, and that was a cruel joke. But it's also an incredibly funny one.

was where the indie rock dream of taking over the world finally petered out.

There would still be boys with guitars, but from here on they were in the minority. A new avenue for young artists had opened, and it was about to change everything—though, arguably, not necessarily for the better . . .

43

2003

Angels Brought Me Here

Guy Sebastian

*In which reality television gives Australia one of
its biggest, worstest singles of all time*

In 2003 an exciting new vector to stardom opened up for young, talented, photogenic Australians with a very specific skill set who also hungered for the chance to perform gladiatorial karaoke in front of the entire nation in the hopes of possibly winning a horribly one-sided record contract.

That vector was called *Australian Idol.*

The idea of the televised talent competition was not a new one for Australians. After all, *Young Talent Time* had established a template for photogenic youth singing saccharine versions of modern pop hits on television, and had even created one legitimate star in the form of Tina Arena. More recently, the *Popstars* program had led to the brief heyday of Bardot in 1999.[1] Their single 'Poison' was a #1 hit on the back of the show, which immediately afterwards vanished from public consciousness before elevating absolutely no-one else to stardom and eventually limping to a halt in 2004 after four seasons. The winners of the subsequent seasons were Scandal'Us, Scott Cain and Kayne Taylor, all of whom you might recognise as being artists of whom you have never heard.

However, the first season of *Australian Idol* was a roaring success, aping the show's cultural impact in the US and UK, and created stars of both the winner, Guy Sebastian, and the runner-up, Shannon Noll, plus several of the middle-placers, including future musical stage star Rob Mills and disco divas Paulini and Ricki-Lee Coulter.

It's interesting to note that while *Australian Idol* made some honest-to-God stars, they tended not to be the people who actually won the show. In fact, it was generally better to come second: Sebastian aside, the biggest *Idol*-forged stars were Noll, Anthony Callea (runner-up in 2004), Jessica Mauboy (runner-up in 2006) and Matt Corby (runner-up in 2007), all of whom comprehensively outshone the winners of their respective years—Casey Donovan, Damien Leith and Natalie Gauci. You didn't even have to place that high, it turned out: Lisa Mitchell was signed to Warner and became a proper star despite coming sixth in 2006—even, like Corby, enjoying

---

1   Weirdly enough, *Popstars* was where all the singing talent show things began. It was invented in New Zealand and the Australian version 'inspired' Simon Fuller to create *Pop Idol* in the UK. That became the format of all the international *Idol* programs, with the US version the most successful, outlasting all the other programs before fizzling out in 2016 after fifteen seasons.

plenty of coverage on the traditionally *Idol*-averse Triple J. On the other hand, singer/songwriter Wes Carr won the 2008 competition and spent the next few years trying to escape the shadow of the show, eventually making the surprisingly excellent alt-country record *Roadtrip Confessions* (which was bought by no-one) under the nom du rock Buffalo Tales.

Then again, the idea that winning the competition was more of a curse than a blessing makes more sense when you consider that the winner of each season of *Australian Idol* had to knock out an album that would be available for purchase by a still-giddy fan base immediately after the credits rolled on the grand finale, and that the material on said album was generally dreck. The songs were written by hack writers-for-hire knowing they had to be applicable to whoever happened to win the competition, and thus meaningful works of great art they comprehensively were not.

The winner got the rawest end of the deal. They would be under contract and have to bang out a record that was all but guaranteed to suck, while the runner-up was often put under contract too but had a significant advantage in that they had more than a week to work on their album. Losing *Australian Idol*, in other words, was inarguably a better deal than victory.

The final of each season would involve the two remaining singers performing what would become the debut single for the winner. 'Angels Brought Me Here', therefore, was significant in being the first commercial single for Guy Sebastian and the re-establishment of televised talent shows as a legitimate path for young artists. Which is amazing, because it's also an absolute turd of a song.

It was written by jobbing songwriters Jörgen Elofsson (a Swedish songsmith who'd written for Britney Spears and *American Idol* winner Kelly Clarkson) and British DJ John Reid as an all-purpose triumphant power ballad for the eventual winner, whoever it ended up being, containing as it does a story about a journey full of trials and tribulations—you know, *just like what they did in the show!*—and vague metaphors about strength and overcoming and love and prayers and whatever else Reid and Elofsson could think of in the twelve minutes they presumably spent labouring over the lyrics. Bad scansion? Check! Rhyming 'feel' with 'feel'? Bingo! A chorus made up entirely of non sequiturs? Perfect!

Musically it had every cliché you'd want in a shitty ballad: tinkly synth piano, flourishes of classical guitar, the inspirational key change into the chorus and a melody line build to the big held note ripped straight out of the Bangles' 'Eternal Flame'. On paper, it looks more like a delicious satire of a modern R&B ballad than an actual sincere artwork made by humans with genuine emotions and a concern for professional standards.

And yet, thanks to the power of television and the level to which viewers were invested in the journey of the finalists, the song was still a monster hit. It topped the charts in both Australia and New Zealand, going three times platinum and becoming the biggest-selling Australian single of 2003, thereby guaranteeing that it will be forever immortalised in our national chart statistics instead of being buried deep in the centre of the earth and forgotten, as it so richly deserves.

What's perhaps even more amazing, given the unspeakable awfulness of the song, is that it ended up launching the legitimate pop career of Sebastian. Despite his debut single, he turned out to be far more capable a performer and artist than the show had suggested—although success did involve him getting as far away from the saccharine balladry as he could. Once he moved into the funk, soul and R&B that he loved, and to which his voice was far better suited, he transformed into a sleek, international lover man star far removed from the fuzzy-haired Pentecostal Christian from Adelaide that the nation met on *Idol*. He has enjoyed a record-breaking six #1 singles to date, making him the most successful male solo artist in Australia's history, and 2012's 'Battle Scars' (a sort-of duet with US rapper Lupe Fiasco) broke him worldwide.

Noll also did a version of 'Angels Brought Me Here' on the show, although being more of a meat-and-potatoes rock'n'roll belter he had a lot more difficulty with it than the melisma-adept Sebastian—going so far as to tell journalist Christie Eliezer in an unguarded moment at the 2003 ARIA chart awards that it was 'too hard' for him to sing.

Not having to release 'Angels Brought Me Here' was just the first in a lot of things going remarkably right for Noll. His debut single was instead a cover of Moving Pictures' mawkish tribute to self-interest, 'What About Me', and became the biggest-selling single of 2004. While Noll has never quite matched the sales of Sebastian, he's had more chart success— ten consecutive top 10 singles, three of them reaching #1—and his ocker, Southern Cross-tatt-sporting, she'll-be-right attitude was so beloved by the public that it was seriously suggested his arrest for assaulting a bouncer outside Adelaide's venerable Crazy Horse strip club in January 2017 might have just been a viral marketing stunt.

And while *Australian Idol* burned out in 2009, reality television singing competitions still exist, sort of. *The Voice* was still hanging in there in 2017, with judges Delta Goodrem, Seal, Boy George and Kelly 'the third most important member of Destiny's Child' Rowland all putting their careers on hold to get some much-needed face time with the people who still bought music. It was also the last of the singing shows standing, with *X Factor* gasping its way to cancellation in 2016.

Then again, the end of reality television has been confidently predicted for the best part of a decade and yet the format seems to cling tenaciously on. As long as there are hopeful young people, indifferent Scandinavian songwriters and a music industry unwilling to risk spending development money on any artist without a solid media profile, angels will no doubt bring it here.

44

2003

The Nosebleed Section

Hilltop Hoods

In which Australia finally gets over its weird aversion to the biggest musical genre in the western world

First up, let's address the elephant in the room: despite the jubilant party-at-the-gig message of Hilltop Hoods' breakthrough single, the nosebleed section *isn't* the area at the front of the stage.

You'd think that it would be, especially at Australian gigs: down the front is where the action is generally the most physical, where one could presumably get slammed in the face by an overenthusiastic fellow punter—and since that's where the biggest fans go, it makes sense to assume that being slammed in the face would be part and parcel of the experience for the true believers who put themselves in physical peril for their love of hip hop.[1]

However, it's actually the opposite; it was coined as a derogatory term for the cheapest seats at the top of US sports stadia, the furthest distance from (and therefore with the lousiest view of) the activity on the field. The joke was that punters in said section were so far away and in air so rarefied they'd get nosebleeds.

In the US hip hop was—initially, at least—the music of the black underclass. In Australia it was the music of choice for middle-class white kids, and thus it's no surprise that the group that took Australian hip hop into the charts was from Adelaide, perhaps the middlest-classest place of all. The members of Hilltop Hoods all attended Blackwood High in the thoroughly pleasant Adelaide foothills (hence the band's name) to the south of the city. Blackwood is a nice suburb,[2] about twenty minutes from the city, inhabited by professional families in good-sized houses. And the Hoods experienced no end of criticism for delivering their rhymes in recognisably Australian accents: specifically, the accents of middle-class Adelaideans.[3]

---

1   In Adelaide, where Hilltop Hoods are from, the area in front of the stage is more often known as the Semi Circle of Death, into which no sane person would dare travel. For a long time touring bands would gauge their level of popularity by marking the point at which their A-town gigs were no longer distinguished by the presence of a large empty area in front of them, ringed by punters with their arms crossed.

2   Full disclosure: my family lived in the neighbouring suburb of Eden Hills and for a long time Matt Lambert's brother Nick, who is a genius guitarist and an amazing musician generally, was m'bandmate in the Undecided. Hi, Nick!

3   Despite having lived in Sydney for over a decade now and losing many of my long South Australian vowels, whenever I get overtired or drunk they come creeping out. 'Another Ceeoopers Pale,' I'll slur to the bartender, as though I'm back at uni and making bad decisions about tomorrow's tutorial.

The Hoods formed when Matt Lambert met Daniel Smith at school. In 1991 they teamed up with Ben Hare, who called himself DJ Next, and adopted their stage names of Suffa and Pressure to form Hilltop Hoods, based on the topographically accurate point that Blackwood was—and, for that matter, still is—on top of a hill.[4] Their first release was a seven-track EP called *Back Once Again*, which was engineered by Barry Francis, aka DJ Debris. When Next left the band after the release of 1999's *A Matter of Time*, Debris joined in his place—and this, to all intents and purposes, marked the beginning of Hilltop Hoods proper.[5]

Left Foot, Right Foot in 2001 was (ahem) a step in the right direction, but it was the 2003 release of *The Calling* that finally fulfilled the band's potential. It was also their first release for Obese Records, the Melbourne-based record store and hip hop label, whose marketing muscle and distribution helped make it the first Australian hip hop record to go gold, and then platinum.[6] This was epoch-changing stuff, although it wasn't obvious at the time. The Hoods preceded the release of the album with 'Testimonial Year', a triumphant track declaring the success of the band and its crews after ten years of performing,[7] and, um, nothing happened and the single sank without trace.

---

4 DJ Flak from Cross Bred Mongrels supposedly bequeathed them the name.
5 They clearly concur: all of the Hoods' catalogue is readily available bar those two long-out-of-print early releases.
6 Obese not only broke the Hoods but also Bliss n Eso, Spit Syndicate and Illy. The Hoods left in 2008 to set up their own label (Golden Era Records) and Obese attempted to expand their retail and management arms while also maintaining the label. The entire operation shut down for good in May 2016 after twenty-one years.
7 Although Suffa does declare in the third verse that it near broke his heart when Next left the group. Awww.

Fortunately they had a little something in their pocket: a cutesy tune about people who go to hip hop shows, featuring an irritatingly catchy flute riff lifted from a very unlikely source.

'The Nosebleed Section' is based around a sample from 'People in the Front Row', a typically tremulous 1972 song by US folk singer Melanie Safka (best known for 'Brand New Key') that provides the flute hook, the chords and the chorus about falling in love with the people in the front row. And thematically it's on message too: her song's all about how The Biz doesn't get what she's doing, but that's fine because her real people are the true fans who know what's *really* going on—which turned out to be even more true than the band realised at the time. Not only did this salute to the audience connect in a way that the bragging, in-joke-heavy 'Testimonial Year' did not, it accurately summed up the way popular music was changing at a wider level. It was the perfect song to emerge just as hip hop moved from niche passion to mainstream popular music.

The fact that hip hop was replacing rock as the music of the young people was given a nod, perhaps inadvertently, in a line sorta kinda taken from (and sung to the tune of) Powderfinger's 'These Days'.[8] As a sign of things to come with hip hop's Australian audience, it was remarkably prescient.

See, for all of the criticism levelled at the Hoods and other early Australian adopters (like Sydney's the Herd) for rapping in noticeably Australian accents, it turned out to be the secret weapon for spreading hip hop through suburban Australia. To a generation of teenage boys, these voices sounded just like them and their mates, and 'The Nosebleed Section' also

---

8 Which you learned about in chapter 40. Puzzles, jigsaws, artful constructions.

mixed up distinctly Australian messages, referencing Friday night footy and the necessity of grabbing beers for one's mates.[9] This was the moment when hip hop became the voice of suburban male Australia.

That year's Triple J Hottest 100 reflected the new reality: while Jet's 'Are You Gonna Be My Girl' was #1, the fact that Outkast were at #2 was a sign that the guitar-slinging dinosaurs were about to get out-competed by these more nimble hip hop mammals. 'Dumb Enough', also from *The Calling*, came in at #44, but 'The Nosebleed Section' broke the top 10, coming in at #9.

It didn't chart, however, because despite being the band's commercial breakthrough in 2004, it was done off the back of radio airplay—specifically, on Triple J—and was never released as a single. Let's just emphasise this point: the song that established Australian hip hop as a viable musical genre was an album track, and the Hoods' first actual hit single didn't arrive until 2006 with 'The Clown Prince'. And the upshot was that by the time someone thought, 'Oh, we should shoot a video for this,' the song was already a firm live favourite—meaning that footage from their many festival appearances, including a performance at the Adelaide leg of the 2004 Big Day Out showing hundreds of people screaming the lines back to the trio, could be included.[10]

---

9   It also has a shout-out to their hard-disc recording system, which was relatively new at the time, by dismissing analogue recording formats and praising their digital toys—which is much funnier if you know that most of *The Calling* was recorded on the computer belonging to Suffa's mum.

10   They were on the touring line-up the following year; the 2004 performance in the Atrium Stage was an Adelaide exclusive, with people literally climbing up and dangling off trees in an attempt to see the band. I couldn't get anywhere near the stage and went to see someone else.

The song remained popular, too: it came in at #17 on Triple J's Hottest 100 of All Time in 2009 and #4 in their Hottest 100 of the Past 20 Years in 2013. And as that enduring appeal would presumably indicate, it has remained in their live set lists ever since, even getting a new life with an arrangement for the *Restrung* recordings and tour on which the Hoods performed with a full symphony orchestra. And according to Suffa, having 'The Nosebleed Section' as a perennial set inclusion is entirely okay with him.

'We were at rehearsals the other day, and we were putting together a set list,' he told Triple J in 2013, 'and Dan said to me, *You gotta put "Nosebleed" on the set list—you realise you're gonna be playing that song for the rest of your life, don't you?'* We love playing it. If it was a track that was lame to perform I'd be bummed out, but it's such a fun track to perform, it's fine.'

45

2004

Breathe Me

Sia

*In which the new musical economy creates
a synching superstar*

By the early 00s the music industry was starting to realise that its entire business model had collapsed about a decade earlier and the old system of making money by selling records to people had been somewhat undermined by essentially training an entire generation to expect their music to be free. And while this led to a bloodbath of cuts at record companies, the people most affected were artists. Record sales had once been a means for them to survive financially during the gaps between the more-profitable tours—the gaps being the times when new records were written and recorded—but any artist relying entirely on sales was about to find rent increasingly difficult to cover. And this was when reliance on the less-sexy but far more lucrative bit of most artists' deals turned from 'nice little earner' to 'economic lifeline'.

Publishing deals mean people are given money for the rights to the songs they have written, with the idea being that the publisher will do boring admin stuff like ensure that their royalties are collected from all the different territories in which it is played,[1] but also do things like pitch songs to other artists, suggest collaborations between writers, and nut out deals to have their artists' songs used in advertisements, movies and—importantly for this chapter—TV.

Sia Furler had grown up in Adelaide, where she'd come to notice as the singer with local funk band Crisp. When they split in 1997 she made her first solo album, *OnlySee*, which remains out of print for the same reason as the Hilltop Hoods' early material: it's a bit embarrassing and not really indicative of what was to come.

She then made plans to move to London and further her career, not least because her estranged partner Dan Pontifex was already living over there and they intended to reunite and do some travelling together. On her way to the UK she stopped in Thailand, and while there she got a call from her mother with the tragic news that Dan had been killed in a traffic accident. After his funeral in Adelaide, in what was either the best or worst decision of her life, she accepted

---

1   Most countries have their own not-for-profit organisation doing this on the behalf of songwriters. In Australia it's the Australasian Performing Right Association, or APRA, which, as you might remember also promoted that chart of the greatest songs of all time that so many of these chapters celebrate. It does excellent work and is a tireless advocate for songwriters and their rights. Salut, APRA!

the invitation of his London-based housemates to come stay with them.

On the plus side, this gave her a support network as her career began to take off. She was doing vocals for electronic outfit Zero 7 and writing what was to be her first proper Sia album, 2001's *Healing Is Difficult*. On the minus side, she also embarked on what she later described as a six-year bender that did little to help her growing insecurities and fragile mental health.

Healing Is Difficult was all about grieving and trying to numb herself to the terrible things she was feeling, a theme that carried over to 2004's *Colour the Small One*, in which she was finally starting to find some degree of peace and acceptance while also making the best music of her career. Her British label didn't seem to know what to do with it—everyone agreed it was a masterpiece, but no-one knew how to market that fact to the record buying public.

This was demonstrated with the haunting 'Breathe Me', a painfully intimate song in which the narrator confesses to needing someone to rescue her from her self-destructive behaviour. What's especially beautiful about the song, however, is that it's something more subtle than a desperate plea to be saved; it is a cry for human connection.

Given the events that preceded the album, it's impossible not to see it as autobiographical, but the economical verses and melodic chorus made it universal, while the chiming piano provided a memorable hook over the sleek rhythm track. The largely animated video clip, involving more than 2500 Polaroids, was similarly simple and effective, and you'd naturally assume that this would be a slam-dunk hit in the making. Not so: the single cracked the top 20 in Denmark but stalled at #71 in the UK and didn't even chart at all in Australia.

Deciding that enough was enough, she moved to the US in 2005 and signed a new record deal, deciding to focus more on writing for other artists. And then suddenly she was hot, and it was all because of 'Breathe Me': the single that had flopped a year earlier. What broke Sia was not airplay in the conventional sense. It was that this heartbreaking song begging to be comforted was surprisingly perfect for big emotional moments when characters in films and television reach a cliffhanger end-of-series crisis point and need to look wordlessly off into the middle distance for a bit.[2]

Sia's publisher had scored one hell of a coup when 'Breathe Me' was selected to score the final scene of the final episode of the final season of hit HBO series *Six Feet Under*. It was a must-see television moment for any fan of the show, and suddenly everyone wanted to know what that gut-wrenchingly beautiful song was. Importantly, for the first time she had management and a label with the ability to exploit the momentum, and her career started to ramp up significantly.

In the years since, she's become a millionaire as writer for artists such as Christina Aguilera, Rihanna, Kylie Minogue, Beyoncé and more, while maintaining her own career through another four albums to date, including huge hits as a featured vocalist with Flo Rida ('Wild Ones') and fellow Adelaideans Hilltop Hoods ('I Love It'). Since then, 'Breathe Me' has

---

2   These days that role often falls to Coldplay's 'Fix You', which is approximately a dozen times less subtle and a million times more lousy a song.

turned up in literally dozens of shows—including *Luther, The Secret Diary of a Call Girl, The Hills,* and *Orange is the New Black*—and inspired numerous sound-alikes in which breathy female vocals emote pure vulnerability over tinkling piano.

What sent Sia's career into the stratosphere, though, was taking her mental and physical health seriously and deciding in 2009 neither to tour nor especially promote her records unless she felt up to it. By the time of her smash hit 'Chandelier' she wasn't even appearing in public much anymore; appearances were made on her behalf by Maddie Ziegler, a child adorned with a face-covering half-black, half-platinum blonde wig styled in Sia's signature bob. When performing live, Sia herself adopts the same face-obscuring look.

And that impersonal quality has moved into her work, too. One of the most frequent criticisms of 2016's *This Is Acting* was that the songs sounded as though they could have been written for anyone. It was even suggested that these were leftovers she'd been unable to shift. What made this criticism sting was that it was entirely correct: 'Bird Set Free' had been rejected for *Pitch Perfect 2* and as a single for Rihanna, 'Move Your Body' was originally intended for Shakira, while lead single 'Alive' had been co-written with Adele for her last album before being cut from the running order. In fact, Sia later confirmed that only one song on the album—'One Million Bullets'—hadn't been pitched to and rejected by at least one other artist. Far from dredging her psyche for deeply personal work, even she was now effectively covering her own material.

And while that's probably for the best for Sia's own peace of mind, it means losing the insight and intimacy of her earlier records. 'Breathe Me' might have ended up as a master-class in How To Make It In The Post-Internet Music Biz, but it was also the sound of an exceptional songwriter crawling from the wreckage of genuine tragedy and finding something exquisitely beautiful there.

46

2005

Shark Fin Blues

The Drones

*In which the notion of bold Australian masculinity
is given a much-needed kicking*

There's been a recurring story about Australian male identity popping up in the last few chapters of this book, with regards to the notion that men could only ever touch one another in a non-sporting context when they were listening to music—and a very specific subset of music, too. Shows by Cold Chisel, Powderfinger and Hilltop Hoods had all been opportunities for men to get drunk, hug one another and bellow along with their mates without it being seen as weak or, worse still, gay.[1]

One performer whose masculinity has never been in question is Gareth Liddiard, the rake-thin singer, guitarist, songwriter

---

1 Oh, how this would change by the time of chapter 48 . . .

291

and sole eternal member of the Drones. His performances are the stuff of legend: passionate, unhinged, aggressive, raw. So if anyone was going to write the definitive Australian song about the male experience of depression, it was going to be him.

Australia's attitude to mental illness has historically been similar to that of the United States, Britain and other western capitalist democracies: it doesn't exist, and if it does it's because someone's too weak to handle this greatest of all possible eras in the greatest of all possible nations. Australia, also like America, has at its heart the image of the self-sufficient frontiersman (and always frontiersman—women don't factor into this vision) bravely carving out their own lives unencumbered by the shackles of government and the effeminate influence of modern society. Which would be fair enough if it was even remotely true, which it most assuredly is not in our overwhelmingly metropolitan country. This notion of the stoic and self-sufficient Aussie just getting on with the job permeates all our national myths about manhood, from Ned Kelly to Don Bradman to the Anzacs, and thus has guaranteed that suffering from a mental illness like, for example, depression has not only been considered unmanly but also suspiciously un-Australian.

It wasn't a theme unheard of in Australian music, mind. As we learned in chapters 13 and 20, both Cold Chisel's 'Khe Sanh' and Redgum's 'I Was Only Nineteen' elegantly depicted post-traumatic stress disorder and other mental illnesses as being something that could—and did—happen to men whose masculinity could not be called into question. Similarly, Models got to #2 on the national charts in 1985 with 'Barbados', a perky and summery ode to crippling depression and chronic alcoholism. The song's mournful lyrics were written and sung by bassist James Freud, a man who was writing from horrible personal experience—and who was to eventually end his own life as a result of both in November 2010.[2]

The Drones had formed in Perth in 1997 before relocating to Melbourne in 2000, and in 2003 Liddiard was attempting to write the follow-up to the previous year's well-received *Here Come the Lies*. However, the songs wouldn't come: the death of his mother had left him numb, furious and grief-stricken. There were snatches of ideas buzzing in his head but he couldn't find a tune for them—so he started putting words down over a Karen Dalton song, 'Same Old Man' (itself a version of the traditional bluegrass song, 'Old Man at the Mill'). There was one lyric that remained from Dalton's version, though: 'floating away on a barrel of pain.' And that's where the song began.

'I'd always wanted to write a sea shanty,' Liddiard told *Mess+Noise* in 2006. 'I guess that's a silly thing to want to do. I can't remember if the intention was to make it a silly sea shanty, or what it wound up as.'

And so the story was developed: the narrator is on a ship sinking into dark water—his thoughts interrupted by the night terrors of the captain, elsewhere on the ship—watching the fins of circling sharks break the surface as they await the inevitable.

The music beautifully matches the lyric: the guitars slightly out of tune, particularly when they yowl into the double solo of

---

2 Again, Models deserve so much more space than this book has given them. Goddamn, what a band. Vale, Colin McGlinchey.

Liddiard and co-writer Rui Pereira, anchored by the rhythm section (particularly the rock-solid bass of Fiona Kitschin; it's thematically appropriate that the song is held together by the lowest frequencies). The unusual phrasing of the song—the first three lines of each verse are a beat shorter than the fourth—complements the lyric perfectly, much as the bizarre time signature of the Go-Betweens' 'Cattle and Cane' did in chapter 19, but giving it a rolling, off-balance, seasick gait, as though the ship is listing as the song rolls on.

But the greatest power of 'Shark Fin Blues' is that this is a distinctly masculine take on grief and hopelessness, using aggressive imagery of sharks and ships and lightless depths, and delivered with manic conviction by a man who only a very brave or very foolhardy listener would accuse of being a coward. This is Hemingway grief, Indiana Jones depression: the entire song is of men of action facing oblivion with no means of escape.

The other thing the song articulates, and which should be familiar to anyone who has battled depression, is the feeling of inevitability about it. There's no resolution in the song, and no rescue from the sinking vessel—just the sharks approaching like slicks of ink, coming fin by fin by fin.

It was the opening track on *Wait Long by the River and the Bodies of Your Enemies Will Float By* on the album's eventual release in 2005,[3] and while it didn't chart the album did get nominated for the inaugural J Award (which it didn't win)

---

3 The album had been ready for almost a year but legal problems delayed the release. This is one of the reasons why the band's next album, *Gala Mill*, seemed to arrive so quickly: they'd already started work on it by the time *Wait Long By the River* was released.

and the inaugural Australian Music Prize (which it did win). What's more, a 2009 poll of seventy Australian songwriters concluded that 'Shark Fin Blues' was the greatest Australian song of all time. In this same year the band performed the album in its entirety in New York for the Don't Look Back concert series curated by the All Tomorrow's Parties festival.

It was also covered by Missy Higgins on her *Oz* album and was released as the lead single, at which point it finally charted . . . at #71, for one week, before vanishing again. A smash hit it was not.

And that seems entirely appropriate, really. After all, there ain't no sunshine way, way down.

47

2007

My People

The Presets

In which the torture of desperate people becomes the longest-charting Australian single of all time

In 1989 Australia passed the Migration Legislation Amendment Act, a tiny little piece of law that was to have mighty consequences. For this, gentle reader, was the beginning of Australia's modern obsession with locking people up for asking for help.

Australia had swung wildly between being deeply xenophobic and exceptionally welcoming to those who came across the seas over the course of the twentieth century. On the one hand, there was the whole White Australia policy (which existed, in increasingly watered-down form, from the establishment of the Immigration Restriction Act of 1901 until the Whitlam government brought in the Racial Discrimination Act in 1975); on the other there was Australia's generosity in resettling refugees after World War II and welcoming the influx of refugees from the Vietnam War. We liked to keep the world guessing by sending mixed messages about our local level of racism, basically.

In any case, by the late 1980s delight at the many benefits of multiculturalism was being replaced by xenophobic concerns over the number of Asian immigrants. Many of the refugees fleeing from Vietnam and Cambodia had arrived by boat, at which point they'd be housed in a detention centre for processing before being released into the community to start their new life. The 1989 law was the first time it had been suggested that people coming to Australia might not be 'legitimate', a term that was to be used with increasing vigour in the coming years to suggest that 'real' Australians were being taken advantage of by suspicious foreigners.[1]

In 1992 the Labor government of Paul Keating ramped things up with the Migration Reform Act, which was the first piece of Australian legislation to require the mandatory detention of anyone who showed up in Australia without a visa. This law—originally intended as a temporary measure—meant that people turning up in Australia without paperwork were deemed 'illegal', and it removed time limits on how long someone could be held, marking Australia's exciting entrance into the world of indefinite detention.

Once Keating was out of power and the Coalition government of John Howard began its epic run, the transformation of

---

1 As you can see there was also a sharp increase in 'scare quotes'.

asylum seekers into criminals really hit its stride. Howard had already spoken of the need to curb Asian immigration back in 1988, and the perception that he was bringing racist rhetoric into Australian politics cost him the leadership of the Liberal Party. But now, emboldened by the outspoken anti-Asian rhetoric of Queensland Liberal candidate turned independent Pauline Hanson, he started to see political mileage in the double whammy of restricting immigrants and—after the horror of September 11 in 2001—framing it as a national security measure.

The attack on New York's Twin Towers occurred a few months after the Howard government refused to accept Afghan asylum seekers who had been rescued from a sinking fishing ship by the MV *Tampa*, beginning the new rhetoric of sovereignty and border protection, as well as the hasty construction of detention centres on the broke and dysfunctional island republic of Nauru and a former US World War II air force base on Manus Island, part of Papua New Guinea—both of which sites, conveniently, were not part of Australia and therefore offered a level of official responsibility-dodging in what the Howard government barefacedly called 'the Pacific Solution'.

Both Labor and the Coalition were determined to use the treatment of desperate people fleeing persecution, war and sectarian murder for political gain through the early 2000s, but the Coalition did a better job of it, winning the 2001 and 2004 elections and building a shiny new detention centre on Christmas Island. Keeping people in detention in these far-flung places was far more difficult and orders of magnitude more expensive than detaining them in Australia, but it was the principle of the thing: this was intended as a deterrent to prevent other people coming to Australia by boat. However, by 2007 the Howard government was running out of steam, and public anger about offshore detention was on the rise—and being exploited by Labor under the leadership of Kevin Rudd, who promised to end offshore detention for good.

And against this backdrop a couple of guys in Sydney were working on their new record.

With their second album, *Apocalypto*, electro duo the Presets—with Justin Hamilton on voice and keys, and Kris Moyes on drums—had the challenge of bettering the success of their 2005 debut, *Beams*. On the one hand, it had done really well in achieving gold status on the back of singles 'The Girl and the Sea' and 'Are You the One?', along with some lucrative television syncs (including a spot on hit US show *The OC*) and ad placements.

However, *Beams* had been a sleeper—it hadn't charted at all well, and neither had its singles, but they hung around for ages—and the band's explosive live performances at the Big Day Out and other festivals had built up its audience to include rock fans who were gradually getting into dance music. Thus album number two had to be the career-making one, and most of all it needed one hell of a hit single.

And they delivered with 'My People', a stomping club banger whose chorus declarations about calling for their people to 'scream if you're with me' was a perfect summation of the insular feeling of clubgoers united in one glorious adrenalin-filled moment of unity. Or that's how it sounded on the surface.

MY PEOPLE

In actuality, Moyes and Hamilton had just got on the airwaves and dance floors with a subversive song decrying Australia's offshore detention system. It turned out that when Hamilton was singing about being locked up with all his people, he wasn't speaking metaphorically; this was a furious song sung from the perspective of someone held in detention. Which would probably explain why there are soldiers on the waterfront waiting to ship him away—something which, typically, wasn't true of Sydney clubs.[2] And it was significant that the band identified refugees as being not just people but *their* people after decades of very successful us-and-them politics.

By the time the Presets released 'My People' things were actually on the improve for the people they were singing about. Buoyed by a landslide win over the Howard government, the newly minted Rudd government declared it planned to completely shut down the detention camps. And it wasn't just talk, either: inside of three months the last detainees had been removed from Nauru and were being processed in Australia, and Manus Island and Christmas Island were not far behind.

'My People' also entered the Australian top 20 for the first time on its release in December 2007 (when it got to #19), but what made it a record breaker was that it stuck around for almost a year, until the band swept the 2007 ARIA Awards in October 2008, at which point it jumped from #52 to #14. Fittingly for a song about indefinite detention, it also broke the record for the longest Australian-released song to chart, staying

---

2 Well, in 2007 at least. Go back 170-odd years and passing out in a Sydney pub would often result in one waking up as a member of Her Majesty's Navy, press-ganged into service after being transported to the docks. The Hero of Waterloo in the Rocks still has a working trapdoor to the cellar with a smugglers' tunnel.

in the top 100 for a staggering seventy-six weeks.[3] Sadly, by the time the song finally left the charts in July 2009, Australia's brief experiment with treating asylum seekers as a humanitarian issue rather than a national security one had already ended. By that point the Rudd government was struggling against an increase in boat arrivals and, tragically, overloaded boats sinking in the treacherous seas between Indonesia (from which most of the asylum seekers were setting off) and Australia. This allowed the Liberal opposition under Tony Abbott to insist that its zeal for reopening the detention centres was all about 'saving lives at sea'. Labor was losing its nerve, too, and Rudd eventually resigned in June 2010 after a leadership challenge by his deputy, Julia Gillard. Under her leadership, Labor reopened Manus and Nauru and reactivated Christmas Island as well as many onshore camps, and from that point on there was little hope of a saner, kinder policy. Abbott would become PM in 2013, and . . . well, that's another story.[4]

In fact, in 2017, as the disorganised closure of the detention centre on Manus Island became another dark chapter in Australia's shameful history, 'My People' seems even more horribly appropriate. Scream if you're with me.

---

3   On the minus side, it was supposedly the song that inspired will.I.am to reconvene the Black Eyed Peas to make *The E.N.D.* The world is not the richer for that album's existence.

4   Street, A.P., *The Short and Excruciatingly Embarrassing Reign of Captain Abbott*, Allen & Unwin, Sydney, 2015.

48

2015–16

Blue Neighbourhood trilogy

Troye Sivan

*In which a child of the internet elegantly uses it to
send a powerful message of representation*

In 2014 the Australian government and a good slab of the conservative media decided that there was a national problem they needed to address: LGBTIQ people generally, and young ones especially, weren't being adequately demonised.[1]

They didn't phrase it in quite this way, to be fair, but that certainly seemed to be the intent. While the battle over whether same-sex marriage would somehow affect society in a way that it had failed to do in dozens of other countries continued to be debated, an attack was launched on the Safe Schools

---

1 For those not down with the abbreviation: lesbian, gay, bisexual, transgender, intersex, queer (or questioning).

program, which had been developed to combat bullying—and particularly bullying over sexuality and gender identity—in Australian high schools. Claims that the program was everything from a paedophile-grooming manual to encouraging reverse-homophobia against straight people would have been hilarious had they not been so poisonous (and successful: the federal government announced that it would not be expanding the program) and if they didn't completely ignore the fact that Australia's rates of suicide and self-harm among young people were strongly correlated with being bullied in the schoolyard, in public and in their own homes for reasons of sexuality.[2] So it was profoundly important that an artist appeared who was young and had an exclusively young audience, who had powerful friends and allies, and who was unambiguously, comfortably out.

It seems unfair to reduce Troye Sivan to one element, because the young Perth-via-South Africa star was also blessed with otherworldly good looks, a stunning voice and an annoyingly catchy way with a pop hook, but the fact that he spoke to so many people who were, at the time, being openly hung out to dry by their government and a good slab of the media turned what he did with his music from a strong artistic statement to a potentially life-saving initiative for social change.

And Sivan was the perfect ambassador, too. He was a massive YouTube star—so huge, in fact, that he was named

---

2 This remains an obsession with the conservative press. In July 2017 Sydney newspaper the *Daily Telegraph* (part of the Rupert Murdoch-owned News Corp) ran a piece on how unhealthy the Millennials are and interpreted the high rates of suicide and self-harm among young gay people as being evidence that gayness was a health hazard. In 2017. In a piece written by professional adults. Words fail me.

one of the twenty-five most influential teens on the planet by *Time* magazine in 2014, before he'd broken through as a musician—meaning that he was simultaneously an enormous celebrity among young people and utterly invisible to everyone else, having started his channel when he was fourteen and singing covers to what he hoped would be a receptive audience that could elevate him to the level of mega-celebrity enjoyed by earlier YouTube breakthrough Justin Bieber.

Sivan was born in 1995 in South Africa (his full name is Troye Sivan Mellet) but lived in the moneyed Perth suburb of Dianella from the age of two. Like another Perth-based immigrant you met back in chapter 6,[3] he soon started making local television appearances, including singing on telethons—one performance of which led to him being cast as the young Wolverine in 2009's fairly-terrible *X-Men Origins: Wolverine*.

But it was online that he became a phenomenon, with his regular YouTube updates generally garnering 500,000-plus views apiece. After four years spent amassing a worldwide audience, he sat before his computer in 2013 and officially came out.

'When I was born, I always knew there was something a little bit different about me,' he told the internet. 'I'm doing this today because I hope people like fourteen-year-old Troye are going to find this video because I watched pretty much every coming-out video on YouTube that has ever been posted.'

In other words, Sivan understood at a very personal level the power of seeing one's own experience reflected in the media. For kids coming to terms with their sexuality while

---

3   Can you remember who it was? No peeking back.

being exclusively bombarded with stories of straight romance, messages like these were a lifeline. The response was positive: #weareproudofyoutroye started trending on Twitter when the video was released. And this was significant, because as mentioned in chapter 35, the default assumption for every Australian artist was that they were heterosexual. There were gay and lesbian artists out there, obviously, but they tended to be either closeted or coy (with some notable exceptions, such as the gloriously provocative political drag artist Pauline Pantsdown, performed by Simon Hunt).

That started to change in the 00s, mind. Former Savage Garden frontman Darren Hayes confirmed that his partner was male. Expat Australian Sam Sparro became one of the planet's biggest stars with 'Black and Gold'. Unself-consciously out female performers like Monique Brumby, Holly Throsby and Jen Cloher found audiences without any stigma, and Cloher's guitarist and partner, Courtney Barnett, became a surprise global superstar with her laconic wit and killer choruses, looking downright subversive bashing out 'Pedestrian at Best' on US late-night television. In 2017 the actor and musician Brendan Maclean made a video featuring explicit gay sex for his single 'House of Air' and was rewarded with literally millions of views and a significant boost for his career.[4]

However, all these people were grown adults with a good deal of personal autonomy. When someone has a home and a job and a social circle it's not hard to be oneself; it's far, far harder to do when coming out could be at best awkward and

---

4   2.3 million as of July 2017.

BLUE NEIGHBOURHOOD TRILOGY

at worst an invitation to violence and potential homelessness. Thus, the coming-out of Sivan, a mainstream pop artist and teenager who lived with his mum, had far greater resonance to young audiences than even a performer like Barnett.[5]

Sivan followed up the success of his first two singles with 'Youth', a jubilant song about the fantasy of finding The One in one's teens and realising that you've experienced everything together,[6] as well as reflecting on Sivan's oddly public life. The song was a massive hit worldwide, going platinum in Australia and racing to #1 on the US dance charts. The lyrics to the song are typical pop stuff—love and fireworks and souls and whatnot—but the video was notable for featuring heterosexual and same-sex couples at a house party while Silvan wanders about singing. The inclusion of a variety of sexualities was very nice and all, but a much bolder project was to come.

Following 'Youth' Sivan made what was called the 'Blue Neighbourhood' trilogy of three videos for the songs 'Wild' and 'Fools' from the *Wild* EP and the single 'Talk Me Down',[7] showing the tentative development of a same-sex relationship between two childhood friends in the face of familial violence, societal disapproval and internalised self-hatred, and ending on an ambiguously chilling note. It's genuinely

---

5 Barnett was another last minute dis-inclusion for this book, despite being probably the most fascinating and exciting artist I've heard in years. In fact, let's all stop reading for a moment and watch the 'Pedestrian at Best' video together, huh?
6 Just a note for any teenagers reading this: honestly, the chances of this happening are vanishingly low and it's a dangerously silly fantasy that more often ends in resentment than jubilant party-going. Just saying.
7 Just parenthetically: kudos for including that 'u' in 'neighbourhood', Troye. Australia is nothing without its extraneous vowels.

heart-punching stuff,[8] and if the songs—melancholy tracks filled with yearning and downbeat electronica—were more like a soundtrack to the visuals, that's mainly because those visuals were so strong.

This wasn't just same-sex couples being included in videos by straight artists: this was a gay relationship being put front and centre, with all the dramas and joys and heartache of any relationship. In other words, this was what meaningful representation looks like.

Despite the contemporaneous hullabaloo over Safe Schools, the world didn't end when the trilogy went up on YouTube during September and October 2015, or when Taylor Swift tweeted it out to her millions of followers. In fact, the subsequent album, also called *Blue Neighbourhood*, went top 10 in the US, Sweden, Taiwan, Australia and the UK digital chart, and #3 in New Zealand. And they acted as something of a Trojan horse[9] for the fuller experience of the video clips; the object of his desires is referenced in the second person in all three of the songs, meaning radio stations that might be a little leery of promoting a clearly gendered love song wouldn't find anything to which they might object.

Troye Sivan wasn't the first Australian artist to promote LGBTIQ issues, but he was the first to be so clear and unselfconscious about representing the experience of being young and gay in Australia. That he was rewarded with international

---

8   Look, I cried my eyes out. There's a strong theme through the three videos of a boy denying his true self while trying desperately to win the approval of his violent, homophobic, alcoholic father, part of which I watched while nursing my then-seven-month-old son. So admittedly I was pretty susceptible to stories involving fraught parent–child dynamics.

9   I fought the urge to put 'Troyejan Horse' here, because I am a serious writer.

success rather than turned into another front in the culture wars was a significant moment in our music and our culture— as was the way that a child who grew up on YouTube was perfectly poised to use his internet presence to help Australia take an important step forward.

49

2016

Never Be Like You

Flume featuring Kai

*In which we look at the foreseeable future of
Australian music: low-key, beat-driven and twitchy[1]*

According to the fascinating *How Music Works*, the book written by former Talking Heads leader David Byrne, the story of music in any given epoch is to a large degree the story of the architecture and technology of that epoch's society.

The way Byrne tells it, the pounding rhythms of African drummers came about because percussion travels well outdoors—as anyone who has heard the approaching doof of

---

1 A lot of the ideas in this chapter were also laid out in an article I wrote for the real estate site Domain under the heading 'How inner-city apartment developments have killed Australian rock'n'roll', because I think it's important to send the message to the nation's investing classes that the decline in our creative industries is basically all their goddamn fault.

a car subwoofer can attest. The long, sustained notes of plainsong played to the cavernous and resonant spaces of medieval cathedrals, where the echoes and reverberations would turn complex polyphony into a discordant mess. Symphony orchestras evolved to overcome the noise of a carousing public in European playhouses that doubled as community meeting spaces, while the punchy guitars of rock'n'roll and country music played to the strengths of the low ceilings and bare walls of the taverns and bars in which they were born. Meanwhile, rap music couldn't exist in any meaningful form until technology made it possible. As chapter 41 pointed out, precursors to hip hop existed since at least the sixties, but until turntables, speakers and mixing consoles were cheap and plentiful, the art form couldn't develop much beyond beat poetry.

So, with this in mind, it's worth looking at what the situation was in Australia by the second decade of the 2000s.

Australia's biggest cities were no longer places where groups of artsy young people could afford to live on the dole. Freezes on unemployment benefits by successive governments had got to the point where payments were far below the poverty line, while the previously cheap and neglected inner-city suburbs were rapidly being gentrified. The old band districts of Melbourne and Sydney saw bungalows that were once crappy share houses torn down and replaced by million-dollar townhouses and apartment complexes.

This also had the effect of limiting the amount of noise local venues could make; instead of having neighbours who spent their days drinking and playing within their walls, now they were overseen by pricey developments inhabited by young accountants who had to get up early because those assets weren't going to strip themselves. Historically artsy areas like Darlinghurst, Newtown, Fitzroy and St Kilda were starting to lose their artists and their venues—and with those creative communities being dispersed as they moved further out, those venues were not being replaced.

If Byrne's thesis is correct, there are a few things you could predict about the way this was going to change the music coming out of Australia. For one thing, it was going to be a hell of a lot quieter; after all, you can't form a garage band if you can no longer afford a place with a garage. In fact, you could also predict fewer bands full stop. The greatest threat to being in a band is the pressure of a day job, and with stagnating wages and rising costs the chances of a group of people having the collective freedom to concentrate on a band diminished with every citywide rental increase.

You'd also assume that the music would be less—for want of a better word—live, and that it would not rely on being honed in the dwindling number of sweaty band rooms. Nor would it be reliant on expensive things like guitars and drums and amplifiers that took up a lot of space in more crowded living quarters, and would be instead knocked up on things that most twenty-somethings would already have to hand. Their laptops, for example.

In short, you could make two broad guesses about the coming trends in Australian music: one, that the loudest music wouldn't come from the big cities; and two, that the music from the cities would no longer be rock.

The emergence of emo-inflected hardcore as the guitar music of the age bore this out: Parkway Drive, the biggest metal band in the country, hailed from the bucolic coastal spaces of Byron Bay. The metal bands from Sydney, like Thy Art is Murder and Northlane, came from the outer western suburbs, where they were forced to put on their own shows in youth centres and community halls rather than in pubs, since there were few live venues in the area. Even the Rubens, the only Australian band to top the Triple J Hottest 100 in the last five years, didn't form in a city. They formed in Menangle, a mainly sheep-farming community in the Macarthur region of NSW—a place where a guitar-slinging five-piece could safely make a lot of racket.

The other Australian artists that hit the top spot in the Hottest 100 were from big metropolitan centres and were, well, less rocking.

In 2013 it was the year of Melburnian Vance Joy,[2] whose ukulele-strumming 'Riptide' was a jaunty acoustic number that sounded like the ultimate distillation of a million insurance jingles.

In 2014 it was the turn of Chet Faker—who now performs under his actual non-fake name of Nick Murphy—with 'Talk is Cheap', a twitchy, beats'n'samples number. Two other Chet Faker songs also landed in the top 10—'Gold' at #7 and '1998' at #8—which is another indication of just how much he was the zeitgeist.

The Rubens won 2015 with 'Hoops', a conventional rock song by a rock band, but 2016 was the year of the most widely predicted #1 in an age: 'Never Be Like You' by Flume featuring Kai.

---

2 Known to his mum as James Keogh. Actually, she probably doesn't use his surname; that'd be weird.

Flume—Northern Beaches boy Harley Streten—had already hit the Hottest 100 top 10 twice: first in 2012, with 'Holdin' On' reaching #4,[3] and then in 2013, with 'Drop the Game', a collaboration with the aforementioned Mr Faker, reaching #5. But 'Never Be Like You' was his international breakthrough and biggest Australian hit.

The song was co-written with the Canadian vocalist Kai—born with the rather less economical name of Alessia De Gasperis-Brigante—and reached #1 in the Australian charts and #20 in the *Billboard* Hot 100 in the US, eventually selling a million copies in the US alone. The lyrics are pretty straight-forward heart-versus-head, I-messed-up-please-forgive-me fare, notable for being a mainstream hit despite clearly featuring a repeated chorus line that contained the words 'fucked up'. But it's Flume's musical contributions—the stuttering beats, the cut-up washes of synths—that make this such an intoxicating listen.

The sonic landscape of the song is especially remarkable for something made with sounds that exist only on a computer. Even as electronica became the default music of young Austra-lian artists, Flume proved himself especially adept at making his sound organic and emotional, which is part of his appeal in a genre influenced so heavily by the icy detachment of EDM. As he told Adam Lewis at Junkee, he aims to 'make music that sounds like a computer, but feels human, or alive, or like it's got a heartbeat'.

But if you want to know what the sound of Australia is in this epoch then the music—twitching drum loops, synths

---

3 That year he also had three other songs in the countdown: 'Sleepless' (#12), 'On Top' (#67), and his remix of Hermitude's 'HyperParadise' (#18).

grated and layered like sedimentary rock, sparse percussion acting as musical punctuation—shows exactly where we are. Even the top-heavy mastering is ideally designed to punch through on the tinny headphones and computer speakers where it's most frequently going to be heard.

And it's a deserving #1 too. It's catchy as all get out and immediately sends an exaggerated sway to the hips. And hopefully it's a genre of music you especially enjoy, because it's almost certainly what things are going to sound like around here for a good while to come.

50

2016

January 26

A.B. Original featuring Dan Sultan

*In which Indigenous hip hop says,
'Fuck asking, now we're telling'*

You might recall that back in the nineties Indigenous artists were educating and enlightening primarily white audiences about a whole lot of history they had been denied, including the stolen generations and land rights.[1] So you'd think by 2017 these things would no longer be issues and we'd definitely not have a bunch of bigots angrily defending the already-arbitrary date of the national day against claims that maybe—just maybe—celebrating the day that marked the beginning of a system of dispossession and genocide might be a lousy idea.

---

1 At least, you would if you read this book in order. If you're just flipping through randomly then you're really destroying all the artful and nuanced plotting that I sweated blood over. Hope you're satisfied, random chapter-skipper.

And you'd be so, so wrong.

It appeared that serious change was on the horizon in the mid-nineties, when the Keating government seemed determined to address and make amends for Australia's shameful history with regards to its original inhabitants. But a couple of things happened to ensure that progress would be stalled and then actively reversed. The first was the 1996 election of John Winston Howard, a man who had lost the 1987 election while proudly advocating the winding back of the meagre lands rights provisions. Second, 1996 also saw the emergence of Pauline Hanson.

Hanson's explosion onto the political scene began with a letter to the *Brisbane Times* about how programs to support Aboriginal people were 'causing racism', which ended up costing her Liberal preselection but also won her a seat in parliament as an independent. She later formed the first iteration of the right-wing protectionist party One Nation, which proceeded to collapse under its own internal discord within five years before returning from the political wilderness with a refurbished brand name to win four senate seats in the 2016 double disillusion election that barely returned the government of Malcolm Turnbull.[2]

By 2017 the rate of Aboriginal deaths in custody was higher than ever, and yet the biggest issue was whether or not odious cartoonist Bill Leak should have been charged under

---

2   At the time of writing (mid-2017) Pauline Hanson's One Nation looked set to follow the proud example of its earlier incarnation, thanks to questions over the donation of a plane, a series of horrendously ill-equipped candidates, questions over the eligibility of its senators, and clashes between Hanson and her chief adviser James Ashby. Fingers crossed!

Section 18C of the Racial Discrimination Act for a cartoon in *The Australian* showing a beer-guzzling Aboriginal father unable to remember the name of his criminal son. That this was now the height of the debate over free speech was an indication of just how much overt racism had become mainstream.

And this is the background against which two Aboriginal artists—Yorta Yorta man Adam Briggs (best known professionally by his surname), who was yet another son of Shepparton,[3] and Ngarrindjeri man Daniel Rankine, aka Trials, from Adelaide's Hilltop Hoods-affiliated trio Funkoars—decided the time was right to turn their occasional collaborations into something more concrete. The pair had been friends for over a decade, guesting on each other's tracks and performing together occasionally, but it took an invitation from Triple J's fortieth-anniversary gig Beat the Drum to give them the impetus to create a new project together. As A.B. Original they took the opportunity to record some of the tracks they'd been working on, and this became the basis of their debut album, *Reclaim Australia*.

That this was a work of protest was made clear from the title: Reclaim Australia is the name of one of the dumber 'patriot' groups in the country, best known for getting around in Australian flag masks and being wildly outnumbered at rallies.[4]

---

3 Honestly, it's AUSTRALIA'S NASHVILLE. Let's get this campaign started!

4 I interviewed A.B. Original for *The Guardian* and Briggs explained that the title came from a charming misunderstanding by Michael Hohnen, the late Dr G Yunupingu's long-time friend, manager and collaborator. 'He rang me up and said, "I've seen the Reclaim Australia people—I thought they were going to be Indigenous guys, because who else could reclaim it?" [laughs] Oh, poor, endearing, naive Michael.'

And the album was preceded by one of the most outspoken protest songs ever written in Australia: 'January 26'.

The song's message is simple: Australia Day is a celebration of dispossession and genocide, so let's not do that. Musically it's catchy as hell, based around a bouncy bassline and a hook sung by Dan Sultan emphasising that flag-waving doesn't change the facts of history, while Briggs and Trials suggest that maybe mainstream Australia would be less supportive of a big national celebration held 'on your nan's grave'. What was most notable about 'January 26', therefore, was the change in tone compared with many of the other most influential tracks by Indigenous artists. If 'Blackfella/Whitefella' made a case for sanity and mutual respect between First Australians and those of European descent, and 'Treaty' was a call for government to move towards recognition and justice, then 'January 26' made clear that A.B. Original was not paying the slightest of lip service to anything that smacked of assimilation, much less implied deference to white Australia.

Back in chapter 30—oh, it was a more innocent time!— 'Beds Are Burning' drew mainstream attention to the fact that Australia was built on concentrated colonial theft. The difference in tone between that song and this is significant, though: Midnight Oil earnestly laid matters out and trusted that the listener would then do the right thing; A.B. Original know full well that the people they're criticising could not give less of a shit. They're not here to change your mind: they're pretty sure most of the people defending Australia Day aren't going to have their opinions swayed by nuanced discussions of history and appeals to common decency at this point.

Needless to say, the response was not universally positive.[5] Even the suggestion that Triple J should move the Hottest 100 countdown to a less divisive day has resulted in furious screeds about Political Correctness Gone Mad—although it's worth noting that the first Hottest 100 was in 1989 and Australia Day only became a public holiday in all Australian states and territories in 1994, so technically the countdown is a more venerable tradition than the holiday itself.

The album reached #10 in the ARIA charts, and considering that it all but dared Triple J listeners to change the date of the Hottest 100 it's remarkable that 'January 26' got to #16.

The future of A.B. Original has something of a question mark over it—Trials still has his own career and his work with Funkoars, while Briggs's star has been on the rise as a writer and performer with *Black Comedy*, *Cleverman* and *The Weekly with Charlie Pickering*, before being hired as a writer for Matt *'The Simpsons'* Groening's new animated Netflix series, *Disenchantment*. But if *Reclaim Australia* ends up being the only full-length statement by the band, it was a hell of a powerful one.

That said, it looks unlikely that they've said all they plan to on the matter of Australia Day either. When A.B. Original and Dan Sultan covered Paul Kelly's 'Dumb Things'

---

5 From the same interview: 'The second that you challenge the perceived Australian way, the detractors lose their fucking minds. The second you tell a white dude he can't do something—like, "Hey, man, maybe don't climb Uluru", it's immediately, "Fuck that, it's my right, I can climb it if I want!"'

for Triple J's Like a Version in 2017—with Kelly himself[6]—
Briggs made a point of adding a line in one of his new verses,
where the music stopped and he intoned to camera: 'The date
is changing.'

Australia, you've been told.

---

6   Seriously, the man's everywhere.

Fade out

.... And that bring us up to now.[1] Fifty-odd songs, telling a story of Australia. And as promised, there wasn't nearly enough EDM, or country music, or Models singles.[2] Again, best of intentions.

You've probably got a sense of the many, many, many byways this story could have taken. What of Australia's soul divas, from Renee Geyer to Tina Arena to Jessica Mauboy? What of films and television music, or the slogans-turned-singles like 'It's Time' and 'Up There Cazaly'? How come 'Redback on the Toilet Seat' didn't get a look in? How about more on the nineties punk explosion, or the dominance of hardcore in the noughties? And, perhaps most importantly, whither Kevin

---

1 Or then, depending how far in the future you're reading this.
2 Damn it. Still my favourite Australian band.

Bloody Wilson? This shouldn't be the end of the conversation, but rather a jumping-off point for many, many, many more conversations about Australian music. Which you can have among yourselves, thanks—I waste enough time on Facebook as it is.[3]

The main thing to remember, though, is that music only exists with an audience. And when you're in the audience, you've got to be responsive. So: go see a band. Subscribe to your local community station. Buy some records and play them loud to cover your squelchy sex noises or let your parents know they don't understand you. Help keep our nation's music alive, because it's pretty damn special stuff.[4]

---

3 Nah, you're welcome to let me know your own fifty-ish songs if you like, at andrewpstreet.com, @andrewpstreet on Twitter, or www.facebook.com/the andrewpstreet/. Or just accost me on a bus or something.

4 Except for 'Angels Brought Me Here', obviously, which is irredeemable. FACT. And did you find the other two lousy songs? Send me your answers.

Acknowledgements

This was a labour of love,[1] and like most labours of love was one of those things that seemed pretty straightforward at the beginning with the sheer scale of the endeavour only revealed when it was already far too late.

Thanks as ever to my excellent and long-suffering editors Richard Walsh and Rebecca Kaiser for going through several false starts and threading the needle between being warm and supportive and bashing me over the head with deadlines. Thanks also to Ali Lavau for copyediting like a typo-spotting, repeated-phrase identifying machine.

Much of this has been drawn from interviews conducted over the last twenty-odd years for *dB Magazine*, *Drum Media*,

---

1 Not to be confused with Frente!'s 'Labour of Love', which also should totally have had a chapter, damn it.

Time Out, *The Guardian*, the *Sydney Morning Herald*, *Mess+Noise*, *FasterLouder*, *The Vine*, *Australian Guitar* and *Rolling Stone*, and other publications both extant and much-missed. Thanks to everyone who's ever paid me to write about music for them, or at least convincingly assured me that my invoice was with accounts.

Thanks to everyone who suggested songs, contributed to the longlist and critiqued on chapters or on whose wisdom I drew for this book. Maddest of mad props to Ian Bell, Lani Wulff, Adam Lewis, Celeste Liddle, Lachlan Marks, Rina Ferris, Bernard Zuel, Barry Divola, Andrew McMillan, Kathy McCabe, Craig Mathieson, Clinton Walker, Stuart Coupe, Katie Dixon, Andrew Stafford, Marcus Teague, David Nichols and the entire Australian music writing community. Goddamn but there's no shortage of amazing work out there.

Special thanks to Lindy Morrison for giving the definitive word on *that* drumbeat and to Steve Kilbey for confirming that there *are* bagpipes hidden in 'Under the Milky Way'.

This was largely written in the joy-and-sleep-deprivation rollercoaster that is first-time fatherhood and so grateful, desperate thanks are due to Dee Street for being wildly supportive and amazing, and to James P Street for responding so enthusiastically to much of the music that got blasted around the house during his first eight months. Bless your tiny socks, you adorable sleep-vampire.